The Vulgaria of
John Stanbridge
and
The Vulgaria of
Robert Whittinton.

Early English Text Society.
Original Series, No. 187.
1932.
(for 1931)

Scene in a Schoolroom. Title-page of John of Garlandia's Vocabulary
Richard Pynson, 1503
Reproduced by permission of the Huntington Library

The Vulgaria of John Stanbridge
and the
Vulgaria of Robert Whittinton.

EDITED WITH AN INTRODUCTION AND NOTES

BY

BEATRICE WHITE, M.A.

LONDON:
PUBLISHED FOR THE EARLY ENGLISH TEXT SOCIETY,
BY KEGAN PAUL, TRENCH, TRUBNER & CO., Ltd.,
68–74 CARTER LANE, E.C.,
AND BY HUMPHREY MILFORD, OXFORD UNIVERSITY PRESS,
AMEN HOUSE, E.C.
1932.

Unaltered Reprint produced under joint sponsorship

EARLY ENGLISH TEXT   KRAUS REPRINT CO.
SOCIETY, Oxford   New York
1971

OXFORD

UNIVERSITY PRESS

Great Clarendon Street, Oxford OX2 6DP
United Kingdom

Oxford University Press is a department of the University of Oxford.
It furthers the University's objective of excellence in research, scholarship,
and education by publishing worldwide. Oxford is a registered trade mark of
Oxford University Press in the UK and in certain other countries

© The Early English Text Society 1932

The moral rights of the authors have been asserted

Database right Oxford University Press (maker)

First Edition published in 1932

All rights reserved. No part of this publication may be reproduced,
stored in a retrieval system, or transmitted, in any form or by any means,
without the prior permission in writing of Oxford University Press,
or as expressly permitted by law, or under terms agreed with the appropriate
reprographics rights organization. Enquiries concerning reproduction
outside the scope of the above should be sent to the Rights Department,
Oxford University Press, at the address above

You must not circulate this book in any other form
and you must impose this same condition on any acquirer

Published in the United States of America by Oxford University Press
198 Madison Avenue, New York, NY 10016, United States of America

British Library Cataloguing in Publication Data
Data available

Library of Congress Cataloging in Publication Data
Data available

Original Series, 187

ISBN 978-0-85-991689-9

E. L. B.

'Atque inter sylvas Academi quaerere verum.'

CONTENTS

INTRODUCTION
    I. Early Tudor Grammarians xi
    II. Vulgaria and Latin Teaching . . . xxxvii

VULGARIA STANBRIGIANA 1
VULGARIA ROBERTI WHITINTONI LICHFELDIENSIS 31
NOTES TO VULGARIA STANBRIGIANA . . . 129
NOTES TO VULGARIA ROBERTI WHITINTONI LICHFELDIENSIS 134
APPENDIX 145

INTRODUCTION

I. EARLY TUDOR GRAMMARIANS.

1. THE SCHOOLS.

The business of the Tudor Grammar School was the teaching of Latin, not only as a written, but as a spoken language. All subjects at the Universities were presented in Latin and a thorough grounding in the subject was essential for the student who aspired to grapple with the Trivium and Quadrivium. Entering the Grammar School at seven years of age the schoolboy would have some eight or nine years in which to become a good Latinist before proceeding to the University. At this time the study of Grammar still retained something of the dignity and scope bestowed upon it by Quintilian. It was so much more than 'the art of speaking correctly and the illustration of the poets'. It was combined with 'the art of writing and correct reading joined with the exercise of judgement'. 'Nor is it sufficient to have read the poets only; every class of writers must be studied, not simply for matter, but for words, which often receive their authority from writers. Nor can grammar be complete without a knowledge of music, since the grammarian has to speak of metre and rhythm.' 'A science necessary to the young, pleasing to the old, an agreeable companion in retirement, alone, of all departments of learning', it had 'in it more service than show'. After 1150 Grammar had quailed before the advance of dialectic and its true limits were lost to sight. It became a mere function of logic and was overlaid with gloss and comment. Such men as Valla and Erasmus freed it from dialectic speculation and restored it to its true order as 'formulation of inflection and construction determined by right choice of authorities'.[1]

The early sixteenth-century schoolmaster had a vast subject to tackle. His pupils belonged to the middle class. Grammar Schools, of ecclesiastical origin, were not for the scions of the nobility. Indeed, the attitude of the gentry towards

[1] W. H. Woodward, *Erasmus concerning Education*, p. 103.

learning was apparently hostile, for in his translation of Sallust's *Jugurthine War* Alexander Barclay remarks that 'at this tyme (*c.* 1519) the understandyng of latyn was almost contemned of gentylmen'. And Pace, in his *De Fructu*, relates how at a feast he met a gentleman who said, 'I swear by God's body I'd rather that my son should hang than study letters. For it becomes the sons of gentlemen to blow the horn nicely, to hunt skilfully, and elegantly carry and train a hawk. But the study of letters should be left to the sons of rustics.' So the gentry sent their sons as wards to the houses of wealthy patrons, there to be instructed in an elaborate code of manners and taught by private tutors those things requisite to their rank, while the lesser fry frequented the Grammar Schools, which, before the foundation of Winchester, were free from the intrusion of the nobility.

A study of the early sixteenth-century Latin text-books known as 'Vulgaria', which, fortunately, are rich in allusions to contemporary school life, convinces one very forcibly of the prevailing harshness of discipline in schools in Tudor times. The first requirement of the early sixteenth-century Grammar School master seems to have been a strong right arm. Actually, the symbol of his office was a birch, and when a school book bears a woodcut on the title page, he is usually shown holding it.[1] Nowadays we have grown squeamish and look on the rod as anything but an aid to learning. Your sixteenth-century schoolmaster was made of sterner stuff, and brandished the birch with a will. He was a man of terror, and Shakespeare's allusions to 'breeching scholars' and 'heavy looks' have all too loud an echo in other writers. There is a plaintive poem from the fifteenth century so indicative of the mood aroused in schoolboys by excessive beating that I quote it here.

> hay! hay! by this day!
> what avayleth it me thowgh I say nay?
>
> I wold ffayñ be a clarke;
> but yet hit is a strange werke;
> the byrchyñ twigg*is* be so sharpe,

---

[1] At Oxford the Grammar Masters entered on office by whipping a boy, who received a groat for his 'labour'. 'Palmer' and 'birch' were their symbols of Inception. See Rashdall, *Universities of Europe in the Middle Ages*, ii, p. 514 et seq.

hit makith me haue a faynt harte.
what avaylith it me thowgh I say nay?

On monday i*n th*e mornyng whañ I shall rise
at vj. of the clok, hyt is the gise
to go to skole w*ith*out a-vise
I had lever go xx^{ti} myle twyse!
what avaylith it me thowgh I say nay?

My master lokith as he were madde:
'wher hast *th*ou be, thow sory ladde?'
'Milked dukk*is*, my moder badde:'
hit was no m*er*vayle thow I were sadde.
what vaylith it me thowgh I say nay?

. . . .

I wold my mast*er* were an hare,
& all his bok*is* hownd*is* were,
& I my self a Ioly hontere:
to blowe my horñ I wold not spare!
ffor if he were dede I wold not care.
what vaylith me thowgh I say nay?¹

It is well-known how Tusser complains of the fifty-three stripes given to him by Udall at Eton when he was a new boy 'for fault but small, or none at all.'

Nash, in *Summer's Last Will and Testament*, has some trenchant remarks:

'Here, before all this company, I profess myself an open enemy to ink and paper. I'll make it good upon the accidence, body of me! that in speech is the devil's paternoster. Nouns and pronouns, I pronounce you as traitors to a boy's buttocks; syntaxis and prosodia you are tormentors of wit, and good for nothing, but to get a schoolmaster twopence a week!'

And Withals, in his *Dictionary for Young Beginners*, written 'to induce children to the latine tonge', might conceivably frighten them off school for ever by insisting on the dreadful insignia of learning:

'The schole with that belongeth therto, as here foloweth.
A rodde to do correction with, virga, gae.
 Verbero, ras, to beate.
 Vapulo, las, to be beaten.
 Flagello, las, Batuo, tuis, to beate.

¹ E.E.T.S., *Early English Meals and Manners*, p. 385.

A Palmer to beate or strike Scholars in the hande, Ferula.
A rebuke, contumelia.
A Stripe, Plaga, ge, vel ictus, tus.
  Percusio, onis, est actus percutiendi.
  Cedo, dis, cidi, cesum, & percutio, tis, ssi, ssum, to beate or strike.
A blowe or clappe with the open hand, alapa, pe.
A buffette with the fiste, colaphus, phi.
  Colaphizo, zas, to buffette.
Vibex, bicis, est vestigium verberis in corpore apparens, the marke or printe of a hurte in the bodie.'

The brutality continued, but here and there a rational mind would condemn it. Whittinton and Horman, rivals though they were, combined to deprecate wholesale beating. Erasmus and Vives deplored it. Brinsley, Mulcaster, and Hoole have reasonable attitudes, and the fine minds of Comenius and Locke speak out strongly against it. However, such a state of affairs was only to be checked by force of public opinion, and, as W. H. Hazlitt points out, in 1669 and again in 1698 petitions were presented to Parliament.[1] And yet, in fairness to the master, it must be remembered that the youth of the time were, in the mass, untamed and violent, and if they really needed such coaching in good manners as 'Stans Puer' and the rest imply, they must have been 'dirty and ill-mannered young gawks' indeed. Moreover, it is true that in spite of the asceticism of the medieval ideal, general independence and high spirits were rife, and so the reflection comes that perhaps, after all, the schoolmaster may have had no alternative but the rod to enforce discipline on an unruly school.

School Statutes,[2] detailed and specific, recreate a vivid picture of school life in the early endowed Grammar Schools which may serve to illustrate life in the still earlier Tudor school. The impression they leave is one of long hours, hard work, and little or no play. The aim of the Founder was invariably a pious one. He generally and emphatically declares that he would rather have the children 'nurtured and disciplined in good manners than

---

[1] *Schools, schoolbooks and schoolmasters*, 1888.
[2] *A Concise Description of the endowed Grammar Schools in England and Wales*, Nicholas Carlisle, 2 vols., 1818.

instructed in good arts.' There is always the ideal of *pietas literata*. Take, for example, the Statutes of Chigwell School, founded by that prop of the Church, Samuel Harsnet, Archbishop of York. He is most definitive in his ideas. The 'quality of the Latin Schoolmaster' and usher are very gravely stated:

'Item, I constitute and appoint that the Latin schoolmaster be a Graduate of one of the Universities, not under Seven-and-twenty Years of Age, a Man skilful in the Greek and Latin Tongues, a good Poet, of a sound Religion, neither *Papist* nor *Puritan*, of a grave Behaviour, of a sober and honest Conversation, no Tipler nor Haunter of Alehouses, no *Puffer* of *Tobacco*; and above all, that he be apt to teach and severe in his Government. And all Election or Elections otherwise made I declare them to be void *ipso facto*; and that as soon as the Schoolmaster do enter into HOLY ORDERS, either Deacon or Priest, his place to become void *ipso facto*, as if he were dead.

'Item, I ordain that the Second Schoolmaster, touching his Years and Conversation, be in all Points endowed and qualified as is above expressed touching the Latin Schoolmaster; that he write fair Secretary and Roman Hands; that he be skilful in Cyphering and Casting of Accounts, and teach his Scholars the same Faculty. . . .'

School hours are heavy. In summer 6–11, and 1–6, and in winter 7–11, and 1–5. There are to be no 'otiums' or Play Days, but a certain limited amount of what has happily been called 'ecclesiastical dissipation'. The 'Manner of the Schoolmasters' corrections' is clearly described and restricted to three stripes with the rod. Scholars are to be chastised severely for three vices, LYING, SWEARING, and FILTHY SPEAKING, 'that men seeing the Buds of Virtue in their Youth may be stirred up to bless them, and to praise God for their pious Education'.

At St. Albans parents of children attending the Grammar School had to submit themselves entirely to the discretion of the Schoolmaster, had to provide their children with those things requisite for the maintenance of study, and had to supply, for the exercise of shooting, arrows, bowstrings, shooting gloves, and bracers. At Manchester the Schoolmaster and Usher are expressly forbidden to accept money from scholars, 'such as Cock-penny, Victor-penny, Potation-penny'. It is significant that boys are forbidden to wear 'dagger, hanger, or other weapon invasive' in school, and that they could, apparently, make an affray on the master twice without serious penalty, though for the third affray they were suspended. Boys at Merchant Taylors' were forbidden to use 'cock-fighting, tennys-play, riding about of victoring, and disputing abroade, which is but foolish babling, and losse of tyme'.

2. THE MAGDALEN SCHOOL TRADITION.

As regards tuition, the century 1373–1473 saw the foundation of three great schools, Winchester, Eton, and Magdalen, each the 'expression of one idea developing historically', the Wykehamical idea, linking School to College, College to University. William of Waynflete founded his college of Magdalen in 1448, and later, in close connexion with it, a Grammar School, with an 'Informator' and 'Hostiarius', free to all comers.[1] 'The boys frequenting it were for a while taught in a low chamber on the south side of the ancient chapel of St. John the Baptist, but in 1480 a separate schoolhouse, 72 feet in length, was begun on the north side of the great gateway of the College.' Waynflete's 'Schola Grammaticalis' is taken by Bloxam to mean School in the sense of Faculty of the University. If this is to be credited, then the action of the College in absorbing the school subsequent to the visit of Dr. Cox's Commission to Oxford in 1549 is a justifiable though regrettable one.

It was at Magdalen School that a humble, indigenous movement towards improved methods of teaching Latin began. The method actually employed at Magdalen School of teaching Latin by way of English argues a healthy interest and pride in the vernacular that anticipates Ascham and Cheke. Waynflete's school produced a generous harvest of grammarians, beginning with its first Informator, Anwykyll, and proceeding to his successor Stanbridge, to Whittinton and Holt, and including no less a figure than Cardinal Wolsey, who was, for some six months, Informator in 1498.

Anwykyll.

A grammar more suited to the capacity of boys than the *Ars Minor* of the teacher of St. Jerome was clearly needed. John Anwykyll attempted to supply the need. He was Informator of

---

[1] See C. E. Mallett, *History of the University of Oxford*, vol. i, p. 391. This point is debatable—'Quoscumque ad scholam grammaticalem . . . accedentes.' Actually entrance seems to have been restricted to members, including choristers, of Colleges and Halls. Bloxam (*Reg. Univ. Oxf.* iii. 3-6) insists that the school was intended for academical persons only.

Magdalen School c. 1481-7 and his grammar was called *Compendium totius grammatice*, issued by T. Rood and T. Hunt at Oxford in 1483. Appended to this was the *Vulgaria quedam abs Terentio in Anglicam linguam traducta*, which was also sold separately. This is a collection of useful phrases from Terence. The palm for endeavouring to adapt classical Latin to the exigencies of contemporary English should, then, go to Anwykyll, who thus anticipated Udall's *Floures for Latine Spekynge*.

Anwykyll was succeeded as Informator of Magdalen School by his usher, John Stanbridge, in 1488. Of him Wood says:[1]

Stanbridge.

'This John Stanbridge was a right worthy Lover of his faculty, and an indefatigable Man in teaching and writing, as it may appear by those things that he hath published, very grateful to the Muses and publick concerns. The last of which he consulted more than his own private interest, and when in his old Age, he should have withdrawn himself from his profession (which is esteem'd by the generality a drudgery) and have lived upon what he had gotten in his younger Years, he refused it, lived poor and bare to his last, yet with a juvenile and cheerful Spirit.'

A gracious picture. Stanbridge was a Northamptonshire man and was born in Heyford in 1463. In 1475 he went to Wykeham's school at Winchester, and proceeded in the regular way to New College, Oxford, of which he was admitted Fellow in 1481. Thence he went to Magdalen School as usher under Anwykyll, to succeed him in his office of Informator in 1488 and to hold it till 1494. In April 1501 he was collated to the mastership of the Hospital of St. John at Banbury by Bishop Smith of Lincoln. This Hospital, which existed in the reign of King John, maintained a Prior and brothers and was situated 'just outside the town wall on the east side of the South Bar where the Oxford Road enters the town. . . . The establishment came under the Chantries Act and had a school.'[2] At the same time that John Stanbridge was Master of the Hospital at Banbury, Thomas Stanbridge, his brother (according to Bliss), or at any rate his near relative, who was B.A. in 1511 and M.A. in 1518, was Master of the Grammar School there.[3] He was the tutor of Sir Thomas

[1] *Athenæ Oxonienses*, ed. Bliss, i, p. 40.
[2] A. E. Shaw, *The Earliest Latin Grammars* (*Bib. Soc. Trans.*, v. p. 39).
[3] There is some doubt about this. A. F. Leach, *English Schools at the*

Pope, Founder of Trinity College, Oxford, and made the school where he introduced John's grammars so famous for his teaching that in two school statutes, Manchester and Cuckfield, special reference is made to the method of grammar teaching employed at Banbury school, 'wiche is called Stanbrige Gramyer'.

On 8 February 1507 John Stanbridge was appointed vicar of Winwick, near Gainsborough, and on 3 August 1509 he was collated to the prebend of St. Botolph's in the cathedral of Lincoln. He must have died before 8 September 1510, when he was succeeded by one Oliver Coren. There has been confusion between John, the grammarian, and Thomas, the schoolmaster, which may account for Wood's statement that John flourished *c.* 1522. Stanbridge's grammatical work was expanded and revised in the seventeenth century by Thomas Newton and by John Brinsley, the indefatigable schoolmaster of Ashby-de-la-Zouch. The *Vulgaria*, which is here reprinted,[1] was not a reassembling of Terentian phrases, but an attempt to supply schoolboys with the vocabulary of everyday life, and apart from phrases, contains lists of words arranged in convenient hexameters for easy committal to memory. 'Vulgars', which came to mean sentences in English to be translated into Latin as a school exercise, seem to have meant, at this early time, phrases of common occurrence in the vulgar tongue, and these early 'Vulgaria' were to the scholar much what the French and German phrase-books are to students to-day. They were an extremely useful acquisition, and it is small wonder that they were popular at Oxford, according to the evidence of John Dorne's *Daybook*.[2]

Stanbridge realized a fact that was grasped by all his successors, from Whittinton and Horman to Erasmus, Corderius, and Vives, that a text-book should have some topical interest to appeal to

Reformation, says that John was Master of the Hospital and Thomas of the Hospital School. I am inclined to agree with A. E. Shaw, *The Earliest Latin Grammars (Bibliogr. Soc. Transactions*, v, p. 39), that Thomas Stanbridge was Master of the rival establishment at Banbury and was not working in conjunction with John at the Hospital.

[1] These phrases may have been Stanbridge's work, but were probably introduced by a reviser. In this case 'vulgare' would mean not phrases but words of common occurrence for repetition.

[2] Dorne records eight sales of books by Stanbridge and his pupil Whittinton on the first folio.

Early Tudor Grammarians

schoolboys, and in this way the *Vulgaria* attributed to him is so much more than a mere collection of sentences, it is a social document.

After a pretty complete vocabulary, arranged, as I have said, in the form of hexameters, with the English above in smaller type, the 'auctour' expresses himself thus:

> All lytell chyldren besely your style ye dresse.
> Unto this treatyse with goodly aduertence
> These latyn wordes in your herte to impresse
> To hende that ye may with all your intelligence
> Serue god your maker holy vnto his reuerence
> And yf ye do not / the rodde must not spare
> You for to lerne with his sharpe morall sence
> Take now good hede / and herken your vulgare.

Pietas literata by way of the birch—a goodly sentiment!

Then, in the edition which I have used, printed by Wynkyn de Worde in 1519 and probably worked over by Whittinton or another, follows the 'Vulgaria quedam cum suis vernaculis compilata iuxta consuetudinem ludi litterarij diui pauli'—'according to the use of St. Paul's school'—so that at this time (1519) Stanbridge's method had been adopted by Lily at Colet's school.

There is a curious ingenuity about these sentences that must have been a source of fun to the boys who used them. 'How fares thou. I fare well thanked be god'. He tells us, 'I was set to scole whan I was seuen yere olde. From ẙ daye hiderwarde I was neuere kepte fro scole', and states that 'Scolars must lyue hardely at Oxforde', perhaps a reminiscence of student days at New College. There are frequent allusions to beatings—'I was beten this morning. The mayster hath bete me. The mayster gaue me a blowe on the cheke. I fere the mayster'— and the atmosphere of the schoolroom is eloquently suggested by such phrases as 'Syt awaye or I shall gyue the a blowe. He hath taken my boke fro me. Thou stynkest. Lende me the copy of thy latyn and I shall gyue it the agayne by and by. The latyn is full of fautes. I haue blotted my boke. The chyldren be sterynge about in the maistres absence (delightful touch!). Let me alone or I shall complayne on the. It is euyll with us whan the mayster apposeth us. I am fallen in the maysters conceyte. I haue gete the maysters fauoure', together with the heartfelt cry, 'Wolde god we myght go to playe', and the prudent resolve, 'I hadde leuer go to my boke than be bete', not to speak of the bold assertions, 'I am the worst of all my felowes', and 'My gowne is the worste in all the scole'.

Stanbridge's grammatical mantle fell on his pupil Robert Whittinton, but Magdalen College produced three other grammarians of note, John Holt, Thomas Wolsey, and William Lily. Holt, who had Thomas More for pupil, carried on Stanbridge's work of teaching Latin in a simplified way by means of the vernacular in his quaintly named grammar *Lac Puerorum or Mylke for Children*, 1497. He deserves great credit for his idea of arranging the cases and declensions on woodcuts in the shape of outstretched hands and other convenient forms, a hitherto undreamt-of condescension to the capacity of children's minds.

Wolsey. Wolsey's exploits in the field of grammar are so little known and so able that I propose to mention them briefly here. His *Rudimenta Grammatices & docendi Methodus*, intended for his school at Ipswich, undoubtedly shows the influence of Magdalen College School where for six months he had been Informator. After a preface, dated 1528, he proceeds to define quite clearly 'Quo ordine pueri in nostrum gymnasium admissi docendi sint, quique authores ijsdem praelegendi'.

Primae Classis Methodus.

'Principio scholam hanc nostram in Classes octo partiendam esse non incongrue placuit, quarum prima pueros rudiores in octo orationis partibus diligenter exercendos contineat, quorum os tenerum formare praecipua cura vobis sit, vtpote qui & apertissima, & elegantissima vocis pronuntiatione, tradita elementa proferant, siquidem rudem materiam licet ad quiduis effingere, & Horatio monente: Quo semel est imbuta recens seruabit odorem testa diu. Quamobrem hanc aetatem iusta vestra cura defraudare minime par est.' For the Second Class, 'Si authorem aliquem praeter rudimenta, adhibendum tenellae pubi censueritis, id erit vel Lilij carmen monitorium, vel praecepta Catonis, nimirum formandi oris gratia.' The Third Class had to read the Latin Aesop and Terence and tackle the *De Nominum Generibus* in Lily, while the Fourth Class read Vergil and grappled with *Verborum praeterita & supina*. The Fifth Class read Cicero (Select

Letters), 'quibus sane nullę alię uidentur nobis ad diuitem sermonis copiam parandam, neque faciliores, neque vberiores'. For the Sixth Class Wolsey proposed Sallust or Caesar and more of Lily's Syntax. The Seventh Class could read either Horace's *Epistles* or Ovid's *Metamorphoses* or *Fasti*. 'Audita ne effluant, aut apud vos, aut cum alijs puer retractet. sub somnum exquisiti quippiam, ac dignum memoria meditetur, quod proxima aurora praeceptori reddat. Interdum laxandus est animus, intermiscendus lusus, at liberalis tamen, & literis dignus. In ipsis studijs sic voluptas est intermiscenda, vt puer ludum potius discendi, quam laborem existimet. Cauendum erit ne immodica contentione ingenia discentium obruantur, aut lectione praelonga defatigentur: vtraque enim iuxta offenditur.' The Eighth Class studied Donatus and the *Elegantiae* of Valla, with the comedies of Terence, 'veluti comoediam Terentianam enarraturi, in primis authoris fortunam, ingenium, sermonis elegantiam paucis disseratis'. His insistence on classical authors in contradistinction to Colet bespeaks the true Renaissance spirit, and in this he is akin to Erasmus rather than to Vives. Wolsey concludes, 'Praeterea in ludo dabitis operam, vt grex, quam emendatissime loquatur, loquentem aliquoties collaudetis, si quid dictum erit aptius, aut emendetis, cum errabit. Interdum epistolae breuis argumentum, sed argutum lingua vulgari proponi debet. Postremo si libet, ostendatis formulas aliquot, quibus traditum thema, commode tractari poterit. His rudimentis pueri in nostra schola imbuti, facile declarabunt, quantopere referat ab optimis auspicatum fuisse, vos modo pergite, ac patriam bene merentem honestissimis studijs illustrare.' These *Rudimenta* prefaced Colet's *Aeditio* and were published by Treveris in 1529.

From the magnificent Cardinal to the by no means humble pedant is a far cry. Robert Whittinton, who acquired a not undeserved contemporary reputation for tremendous arrogance, was one of Stanbridge's pupils, and though, like his master's, his life is shrouded in obscurity, he emerges from the nebulous past a lively figure, connected somehow or other with most of the prominent people of the day, and engaged tooth and nail in a fierce grammatical controversy with Lily and Horman, the head masters respectively of St. Paul's and Eton.

Whittinton was a native son of Lichfield, and received his early education at the school of St. John's Hospital there. Proceeding

Whittinton.

to Magdalen College School he studied under John Stanbridge, for whom he had a healthy admiration, and who doubtless infected him with a love of grammar. According to Wood,[1] he 'afterwards made a considerable progress in logicals and philosophicals, but in what college or hall it appears not. However, his delight being much in the teaching of youth, he became so excellent in that way, that it was thought, especially by those that favoured him, that he surpassed W. Lilye.' In 1513 he appears in the Register of the University of Oxford[2] as supplicating the venerable congregation of regents for laureation in grammar. He represents himself in his *supplicat* as having spent fourteen years in the study of rhetoric and twelve in the informing of boys. '13 April 1513. Wyhttyndon or Wyntynton (Robert), cappellanus et scolaris artis rethorice sup. quatenus studium 14 annorum in eadem arte et informatione puerorum 12 annis sufficiat ut possit hic laureari. Hec est concessa sic quod componat C carmina et sumat gradum in proximo actu'; disp. 3 July 'ut utatur serico vel tartaro [sic] in suo capicio'; 4 July 'insignitus est laurea', and at the same time he was admitted B.A.[3]

He must, then, have been born about 1480, and was, according to Bale, in his prime in 1530. Like many schoolmasters, Whittinton seems to have been deeply imbued with a sense of his own importance and the dignity of a degree, and after his laureation, to have become outrageously conceited. He assumed the gratuitous title of 'Protovates Angliae', which was, to quote Wood, 'much stomached by William Horman and William Lilye, and scorned by others of his profession, who knew him to be conceited, and to set an high value upon himself, more than he should have done. He was then notwithstanding esteemed by many for his great skill he had in the Greek and Latin tongues, for his lepid and jocular discourse also, but much blamed by scholars for the biting and sharp reflections used in it, and in his books against several noted persons of his age.' I doubt

---

[1] *Athenæ Oxonienses*, ed. Bliss, i, p. 55.
[2] Boase, *Register of the University of Oxford*, i, p. 299.
[3] For Degrees in Grammar see *Register of the University of Oxford*, A. Clarke, ii, p. 8. They were inferior degrees in Arts and did not require residence. They conferred no Academical standing but some sort of status in popular estimation. The last record of their being granted is in 1568, but they are mentioned in lists of degree fees as late as 1602.

Whittinton's reputation as a Greek scholar. He must have been completely eclipsed by such men as Linacre, Erasmus, and his own grammatical opponent, William Lily. His unenviable reputation for vainglorious boasting impressed Fuller,[1] who inveighs against him in his quaint English :

'Robert Whittinton was no mean grammarian. Indeed, he might have been greater, if he would have been less ; pride prompting him to cope with his conquerors, whom he mistook for his match. The first of these was W. Lillie, though there was as great difference betwixt these two grammarians as betwixt a verb defective and one perfect in all the requisites thereof. The two other were William Horman and Alderedge, both eminent in the Latin tongue : but some will carp at the best, who cannot mend the worst line in a picture,—the humour of our Whittinton, who flourished 1530.'

His industry is evident from his enormous output.[2] He was a prolific and diligent worker, and, though his work was necessarily derivative, he possessed the power of reassembling and simplifying his material to such good effect that his books were in great demand among students.[3]

Whittinton's critics.

He sheds a certain amount of light on himself in his Latin prefaces. From the first he seems to have attracted, perhaps wantonly, bitter opposition, which he very strongly resented and to which he loses no opportunity to refer in sarcastic terms. His work began to issue from the press of Wynkyn de Worde in 1512, and from that date onwards there are allusions to harsh and envious critics, while from 1523 his books begin to appear with the words 'Humiliabit Calumniatorem' on the title-page. In 1512 he addressed the Preface of his *De Concinnitate Grammatices et Constructione* 'Celeberrimo viro summaque observatione colendo magistro Stanbrigo artium magistro dignissimo', and in the course of it he anticipates the attacks of ill-natured critics. Not a book of Whittinton's appeared without some allusion either in preface or 'hexastichon', 'tetrastichon', and verses of varying length and quality 'contra invidulos', or 'in Zoilos'. The allusions are of no biographical importance, except in tracing a state of mind that seemed to increase in intensity of bitter feeling against his opponents.

[1] *Worthies*, ii, p. 335 (1840 ed.).   [2] See Bibliography.
[3] John Dorne's *Daybook*, Folio 1.

Here is the 'Hexastichon Contra inuidulos' from his 1524 edition of the *Syntaxis*:

> Inuide quum inuidia ringas : ego rideo. soli
> Pena tibi inuidia est : inuidus esto tibi.
> Estuat inuidia / turget pectus male sanum.
> Eructa inuidiam : rumpe vel inuidia.
> Iccirco inuideas : videas quod que tibi visa
> Nolles : ne invideas meme videre caue.

His edition of the *De Nominum generibus*, 1521, he dedicated to Henry, 'Angelici gloria prima soli', but even on this auspicious occasion he could not forget his invidious critics, and so he wrote a 'hexastichon dedicatorium':

> Caesarij specimen lauri / decor vne triumphi
> Phoebea vt lampas, sceptrigerumque nitor.
> Ecce tuus vates dat opus tibi iure sacrandum
> Sub duce te Laurus militet vsque ; clyens.
> Nec criticos metuet Momos, nec Rhinocerentes
> Celsis dum titulis sit redimita tuis.

This wordy warfare reached its height in 1519, and the whole controversy comes to light in the publication by R. Pynson in 1521 of a quarto volume called *Antibossicon*, a curious title. How to explain it? It is an involved story.

Horman's 'Vulgaria'. In 1519 William Horman published from Pynson's press his *Vulgaria*, edited in 1926 for the Roxburghe Club by Dr. James, Provost of Eton. Horman is an interesting figure, a member of the finest intellectual group of the day. He was a Salisbury man, went to Wykeham's School in 1468, became Fellow of New College in 1475, and in 1485 was appointed Head Master of Eton. In 1494 he accepted the Head-mastership of Winchester, returning to Eton as Fellow in 1503, and subsequently becoming Vice-Provost. He died in 1535 and was buried in the College Chapel. According to his epitaph he lived to be almost a hundred. Bale, in a long and somewhat confused list, credits Horman with some thirty works on various subjects, ranging from Grammar, Poetry, Controversial and Case Divinity, to History and Husbandry, only two[1] of which have survived the depredations of time, the *Antibossicon* and the *Vulgaria*.

[1] Possibly Horman was also the author of the black-letter tract *Introductorium linguæ latinæ*, 1495, Wynkyn de Worde. Duff (*Fifteenth-century Books*) also attributes to Horman *Dialogus lingue et uentris*, Pynson, n.d.

This last was the outcome of his work at Eton, intended for the use of the boys there and not for public circulation. The indenture between author and publisher still exists. Horman wanted eight hundred 'hoole and perfytt' copies. Payment was to be made at the rate of five shillings per printed ream, and the total cost amounted to £38 16s. Thus the cost of production was just under 10d. per copy. The *Vulgaria* of the Eton schoolmaster is far too interesting a production to pass over lightly.

It was ushered in most ostentatiously with a series of epigrams contributed by Aldrich, later Bishop of Carlisle and then Head Master of Eton, Lily, Head Master of St. Paul's, and Lily's usher, his son-in-law, John Rightwise. There is a long prefatory address from the author to William Atwater, Bishop of Lincoln, who had apparently suggested to Horman that he should not suffer to die the themes he had given the boys ('ne tyrunculis olim dictate (si qua apud me residua essent) paterer intermori aut funditus intercidere'). These, however, he had given forth 'ex tempore' ('Omnia enim (quod ipsi testari possunt) dictabam ex tempore'). They were all founded on good authors ('Semper tamen mihi cautum volui: ne quid effutirem quod e bonis authoribus non exuxissem'). So he had collected and arranged his notes without being able to recollect the authors on whose works he had based them. A weighty address by Robert Aldrich follows. The book consists of some three thousand English sentences with Latin translations under them arranged in chapters on such topics as 'De Pietate', 'De Impietate', 'De Animi Bonis et Malis', &c., the whole forming a compendium of Tudor knowledge on almost every subject. The work, printed in roman letter, is extremely entertaining, full of topical allusions and local references which add to its interest. The following sentences are selected from the section *De Pietate*:

'"Kinge Henry dothe many dyuers myracles" (Diuus Henricus non vna miraculorum specie inclarescit). The holynes of our lady pulled god out of heuen. (Sanctitas virginis deum caelo elicuit.) The sexton hath embeseled offerynge money and iewelles. Poulys styple is a myghty great thyng/and so hye that vneth a man may discerne the wether cocke. (Piramis est vastae magnitudinis/tamq*ue* prealte: vt caliget fastigium versatile.) It becometh not clerkes to haunte a nounnerye / alone nor erly nor late. Our lady hath a golden cote before but nothynge behynde. (Maria habet auream tunicam in antica parte : sed in postica nuda est.) Euery yere the prickars brynge to Poulis lyue deere. The stalles of the churche make a great noyse whan the setis be lette downe. Christis clothynge with styll werynge neuer apeyred : and with the encrease of his body / waxed larger : and so was euer mete for hym : and hadde noo seme : but all wouen lyke. Some nonnys kepe theyr virginite but easely.'

In the chapter on the human body he says:

'They that be hooke nosed haue this aduauntage that theyr spectacles shall not lightly fal fro them.'

and in that on medicines offers the information that

'Vnwasshen wolle / that groweth betwene the hynder legges of a blacke shepe is wonderful medicynable.'

The section *De Scolasticis* has a particular interest in the light it sheds on the Tudor schoolroom, its several references to Greek, and its revelation of Horman as an elementary psychologist:

'Laten speche : that was almoste loste : is nowe after longe absens recovered and come ageyne. By redynge of substanciall authours : thou shalte / brynge about or atteyne to speke elegant and substanciall laten. Thou makest this childe duller than he was : by ouermoche and to sore callynge vpon. The moste parte of techers of grammer make most of the worst authors. A man can scant beleue : how great a let and hyndraunce is wronge and fylthy latten or other speche to yonge childrens wyttis / and in especial in theyr fyrste settynge to scole. A principal poynt of a scole maister is to discerne the difference of wyttis in childrene : and to what thynge euery wytte is best disposed. We haue pleyed a comedi of greke. We haue pleyed a comedi of laten. Laten speche is almoste marred by proude folis presumynge to teche or euer they lerne. He hath founded a reder in greke for .C. ducattes a yere. I shall rede openly a lectur of greke / if so be / that honest wagis be assigned out for the yere. A dogged mynde is the worse for betynge. Tell me in laten : what he sayeth in greke.'[1]

The section *De Philosophicis* has some sound remarks on grammar :

'There is mo thynges longeynge to grammar : than semethe at the fyrste. He that wylbe taken for a very grammarion must be well broken in all faculties of lernynge. It is nat lytel maistrye to speke /

---

[1] These sentences are selected, not consecutive.

and write promptlye lattyn / or greke withoute any incongruyte / or discorde. Without knowlege of musyke grammar can not be perfecte. A grammarion muste be aqueynte with philosophy for many placis in the most parte of poetry be grounded vpon hye philosophie.'[1]

In '*De Cubicularibus*' Horman has some acid things to say about women :

'It is conuenyent / that a man haue one seueral place in his house to hym selfe fro combrance of women. He that sawe som women out of theyr aray: wolde haue lesse corage to be enamored vpon them. They whyte theyr face / necke / and pappis with cerusse : and theyr lyppis and ruddis with purpurisse. They fylle vp theyr frekyllys: and stretche abrode theyr skyn with tetanother : and plucke out theyr hearis with pynchynge yrons / & styllathre'.

A noble volume, this.

During the course of the next year Robert Whittinton's *Vulgaria* was printed by Pynson and also by de Worde. This is by no means so pretentious a book as Horman's. It is a thin black-letter quarto of forty-seven folios, arranged in four parts, the sentences illustrating the rules. His address 'Ad lectorem' Whittinton devotes to an indictment of those teachers who foolishly instruct children in Latin by imitation of authors rather than by inculcation of precepts. His little book is very well planned and his examples well chosen and of great interest. Its value as a text-book is accentuated by its richness of topical allusion. Of Henry VII he says :

Whittinton's 'Vulgaria'.

'Kynge henry the .vij. was a prynce of mooste famose memory. He was a prynce of great vertue. Wherfore the laude and prayse of that prynce floryssheth moost synguler. He was a prynce bothe of famous vyctory also wonderous pollycy. Besyde that / he was a talle persone of body / and aungelyke of contenaunce. More ouer ẙ fortune of ẙ prynce was moost merueylous. for ther coude no fraude so pryvely be conspyred agaynst his persone / but breuely it cam to lyght. And I can not ouerpasse / the stronge and myghty buyldynges / of ẙ newest and goodlyest cast whiche he made in his tyme. Also the inestimable costes of bankettes that he made to his great honour / and to al his realme. at ẙ comynge of straungers / & in especyal at the receyuyng of ẙ kyng of Castyl spoken of thorughout al realmes of crystendum. What shold I say of the goodly and sure ordynaunce of his godly entent and purpose ẙ he hath enstablysshed in west-mynster and in sauoy founded of his cost.'

[1] See note on page xxvi.

xxviii   *Introduction*

He has a reference to More that is extremely gracious and charming:

'Moore is a man of an aungels wyt / and syngler lernyng. He is a man of many excellent vertues (yf I shold say as it is) I knowe not his felowe. For where is the man (in whome is so many goodly vertues) of ẏ gentylnes / lowlynes / and affabylyte. And as tyme requyreth / a man of merueylous myrth and pastymes / and somtyme of as sad grauyte / as who say. a man for all seasons.'

There is, too, a happy reference to the visit of the French and Spanish ambassadors to London when the Mayor and Aldermen rode out to meet them and the common people lined the route and cheered; as well as a vivid description of the mutilated limbs on Ludgate Hill, and a pleasing allusion to Linacre and Erasmus. Moreover, Whittinton's schoolroom episodes are not scattered or general like Horman's. They are concentrated in a few pages and present a lively picture of the Tudor school in action.

Horman's 'Antibossicon'. The appearance of Whittinton's book so soon after his own seems to have given occasion, or rather impetus, to Horman to publish through Pynson his *Antibossicon*, the literary, if one may call it so, culmination of a protracted 'Bellum grammaticale' amongst the pedagogues. Lily and Aldrich were closely involved in the affair. The *Antibossicon* was preluded by *Epigrammata* of Lily directed against Whittinton. The book is embellished with curious woodcuts representing a bear baited by six dogs. This illustration is explained in the text. For some reason or other Whittinton had taken upon himself the pseudonym 'Bossus'. The implication was obvious—'Bos' and 'Sus'. Lily says Whittinton adopted the pseudonym because he had fallen in love with the 'Bosse' or water-tap in Billingsgate. This bosse had been built by Richard Whittington, the Lord Mayor of immortal memory, and took the form of a bear. Hence the woodcuts. It appears that Whittinton had written invectives against Lily and nailed them to the door of St. Paul's, in truly Lutheran manner, presumably for the boys of the school and all who might pass by to see. These verses have been preserved by Lily and printed in black-letter in his reply, which consists of vigorous and offensive invective castigating the 'Protovates Angliae' in a series of three 'Antibossicons'.

Horman's effort was rather more elaborate. His work contains nothing that was in Lily's except the bear and dogs, which reappear at intervals. It incorporates a rejoinder by Whittinton and an epistle in verse by Aldrich, and finally resolves itself into a prose criticism of Whittinton's grammar remarkable for its severity and ill-nature. The whole controversy was conducted in a very scurrilous vein and in language that would not disgrace the Billingsgate of to-day. The 'monstrosus Bossus' came in for some hard knocks :

GUILIELMI LILII IN AENIGMA BOSSI ANTIBOSSICON PRIMUM.
Ad Guil. Hormanum.
Non te Hormane latet, tua quod uulgaria nuper
Laudauit paucis nostra Camoena sonis
Inuidet hanc laudem tibi quidam barbarus hospes,
Inuidet et nostrum carmen habere locum.
Nec tantum lingua, qua nil petulantius una,
Verum etiam numeris carpit utrunque malis.
Nunc foribus PAULI figit sua murmura sacris,
Ebria nunc inter pocula gannit atrox
Si quaeras nomen, non vult hoc ipse fateri,
Probrosum nosci scit nimis esse sibi.
Se Bossum appellat ficto cognomine, uerum
Cęlans, stultitiae conscius ipse suae.
Monstrari digito nimium sibi turpe putauit,
Quem praui sceleris crimina tanta notant.

Labros Lacedaemonius.
Dedecus immensum pariunt tibi carmina Bosse,
Pauli quae foribus figis inepta tuis.
Squallida, manca, rudis, tua musula cespitat, et te
Inuidiae accusat, stultitiaeque simul.

I quote now from the third *Antibossicon* of Lily :

Lilius.
Tu ne ille es Whitintonus, qui Stanbrigianae
Diceris a cunctis gloria prima scholae ?
Tu ne ille Antistes Phoebi, qui nescio cuius,
Proteos aut protu, nomina uatis habes ?
Tu ne ille aegregius doctor, ludi*que* magister,
Ausus qui leges condere grammaticas :
Tam multis patriam implicuisti erroribus : ut iam
Addiscant pueri nil nisi barbariem ?

xxx *Introduction*

> Tu ne ille es Bossus : qui fixis limine PAULI
> LILIUS et HORMANUM versib*us* obrueris ?
> Tu ne ille es : populo qui te iactaueris Arcton,
> In me qui blateras, quod pudet ore loqui ?
> Certe ego si uellem tibi probra rependere probris,
> Illyrica fieres nigrior ora pice.

Horman out-Lilies Lily in his treatment of the unfortunate Whittinton, accusing him, amongst other things, of sycophancy:

> Grammaticen condit Bossus : qua nulla uagatur
> In terris peior, uel mage pestifera.
> Inficit hac pueros, qui grandes postea facti:
> Inficiunt alios. serpit ubique lues.
> Carmina compingit Bossus, celebrat*que* potentes :
> Ast homines claros, laus ea dedecorat.
> Si quicq*uam* scribant alij, faciant ue decenter :
> Bossus adest calamo, denteq*ue* liuidulo.
> Protinus infames, tunc erigit ille libellos.
> Quos lex ciuilis, fuste uel ense domat.

Whittinton's friends. There may be here an allusion to Whittinton's *Opusculum*, a collection of laudatory verses addressed to Henry VIII, Wolsey, Brandon, Duke of Suffolk, More, and Skelton, published by Wynkyn de Worde in 1519. It is obvious that about this time Whittinton had some sort of court appointment, for his *Roberti Whitintoni laureati contra Guil. Hormani inuectiuas literas responsiua* incorporated by Horman in his *Antibossicon* ends 'Ex regio palatio in Calisiens castello pridie calendas Iunios uelis equisque'. And in his Address to the Reader prefaced to his *De Nominum Generibus*, and dated 1521, he alludes to typographical errors and regrets that he has been unable to attend to the correction of the press : 'Prelo assidue adesse non licet mihi : vt qui aliorsum inter aulica negotia necessario sepius sum prepeditus.' His business at this time was probably in connexion with the henchmen or pages, and it doubtless served to increase his self-esteem and exasperate his adversaries.[1] He was friendly

---

[1] There are records of payments made to Whittinton in the capacity of 'Scholemaister of the henxmen' from Christmas 1529–September 1531. (*Extracts from the Household Book of Henry VIII* in the *Trevelyan Papers prior to 1558*. Camden Society, 1857, pp. 143, 153, 157, 160, 170, 177.) As schoolmaster to the 'henchmen' or pages Whittinton received £20 yearly. He had evidently given up the post by May, anno primo Ed. vi, when he was

Early Tudor Grammarians

with Skelton, of whom he speaks in no measured terms, calling him 'Anglorum vatum gloria', and saying of his poetry:

> Pulchrior est multo puniceisque rosis,
> Unda limpidior: parioque politior albo:
> Splendidior vitro: candidiorque niue:
> Mitior Alcinois pomis: fragrantior ipso
> Thureque panthaeo: gratior et violis.

Skelton presumably sided with Whittinton in the Antibossicon controversy, for Bale[1] credits him with a *Carmen inuectiuum in Guilhelmum Lilium poetam laureatum, lib. I*, gives the first line, 'Vrgeor impulsus tibi Lile retundere dentes', and adds the information that there were sixty-four verses. This information Bale got from Horman, so its accuracy need not be doubted. Lily held no brief for Skelton, and this is evident from his *Hendecasyllabi in Scheltonum ejus carmina calumniantem*:[2]

> Quid me, Scheltone, fronte sic aperta
> Carpis, vipereo potens veneno?
> Quid versus trutina meos iniqua
> Libras? dicere vera num licebit?
> Doctrinae tibi dum parare famam
> Et doctus fieri studes poeta,
> Doctrinam nec habes, nec es poeta,

well rendered by Fuller:

> With face so bold, and teeth so sharp,
> Of viper's venome, why dost carp?
> Why are my verses by thee weigh'd
> In a false scale? May truth be said?
> Whilst thou to get the more esteem
> A learned Poet fain wouldst seem,
> Skelton, thou art, let all men know it,
> Neither learned, nor a Poet.

The loss of Skelton's vigorous contribution, conducted, no doubt,

succeeded by John Nowell (op. cit., p. 194) 'Item, paied to John Nowell, scolemaister and instructor of the Kinges Henchmen, by vertue of the Kinges warraunt, dated the Xth day of May, anno regni Regis Edwardi sexti primo, conteigning the payment of twentie yerly, to be paied to him quarterly.'

For this reference I am indebted to the courtesy of Miss Elsa Chapin of New York.

[1] *Autograph Notebook*, p. 253.
[2] Dyce's *Skelton*, i, p. 50.

in 'Ercles' vein', to these pedagogic polemics, is greatly to be deplored.

It seems clear that Whittinton's objectionable verses called forth the first *Antibossicon*, a reply produced the second, his rejoinder to which inspired the third, but whether or no his efforts were published otherwise than piecemeal in his opponents' work is unknown. Perhaps the best comment on the controversy would be Erasmus' caustic words in his *Praise of Folly*. He was no lover of the 'pitiful profession', as he calls it, of 'Grammarian':

'Add to this that other pleasure of theirs, that if any of 'em happen to find out who was Anchises's mother or pick out of some wormeaten Manuscript a word not commonly known as suppose it Bubsequa for Cowherd, Bovinator for a Wrangler, Manticulator for a Cutpurse; or dig up the rimes of some ancient Monument, with the letters half eaten out; O Jupiter! what towrings! what triumphs! what commendations! as if they had conquer'd Africa, or taken Babylon. But what of this when they give up and down their foolish insipid verses, and there wants not others that admire 'em as much? They believe presently that Virgil's soul is transmigrated into them! But nothing like this when with mutual complements they praise, admire and claw one another. Whereas, if another do but slip a word, and one more quick-sighted than the rest discover it by accident, O Hercules! what uproars, what bickerings, what taunts, what invectives! If I lye, let me have the ill-will of all the Grammarians.'[1]

A fitting epitaph for the *Antibossicon*! And yet it must be recorded that Whittinton had the last laugh for his *Vulgaria* survived to be reprinted by the grammarian John Clarke in his *Dux Grammaticus*, 1633.

According to Bale, Whittinton was at the height of his productivity in 1530. He was certainly alive in 1532, for in a list of the Salisbury MSS., at Hatfield House, occurs the entry:

'Whitinton (Rob.)
Apophoreton, sc. poema in laudem Henrici VIII.
Whitinton (Rob.) Carmen Panegyricum in eundem.
Whitinton, poema in laudem Annae, Marchionissae Pembrochiae.'[2]

Anne Boleyn was not created Marchioness of Pembroke until

---

[1] John Wilson's Translation, 1668. Oxford, Clarendon Press, 1913, p. 102.
[2] *Hist. MSS. Com. Report*, iv, p. 201.

PLATE II

A cut of dogs baiting a bear, from Horman's *Antibossicon*.
Reproduced by permission of the H. E. Huntington Library.

1 September 1532, when she was given an annuity of £1,000 for life.

In 1530 or thereabouts Whittinton seems to have had some strong disagreement with the printer, Peter Treveris, who had published some of his work. The *De Heteroclitis Nominibus* contains in the 1533 edition some Latin verses on the back of the title-page complaining of Treveris printing the grammars badly and spoiling them:

Whittin- ton and Treveris.

Whittintonus ad lectorem.
Quod toties laceros vultus mi candide lector
   Grammatices nostrae saucia membra vides,
Id ter per peruersi faecit versutia Petri
   Treuers, inuiso cum paraphraste suo,
Anguicomae catulos dicas hos esse megaerae
   Dum mea peruertunt versat et ipsa facem,
Versutulas mentes furijs et pectora versat
   Tisiphone, ijs rabiem Cerberamque mouet
Mens agitatur inops mola ceu versatilis vsque
   Et mouet vt vertant ter male versa mea
Faucibus at tandem monstrorum erepta ferinis
   Grammatica in gremium se dedit ipsa meum
Pieridum manibus medicata, et Appollinis arte
   Iam redit incolumis, grata, venusta satis
Quae nostra est pietas in pubem iure Britannam
   Grammaticae nostrae lector amice fame,
Winandi nostri praelo, quae excusa probati
   Et nostra lima tersa recente sunt
Ac ter peruersi Treuers per adultera praela
   Causa explode tuo lector amice lare.

Herbert remarks with justness, 'Wynkyn de Worde has not supported his character, by suffering these verses especially to come forth in so incorrect a manner, whereby he must have given Treveris cause to triumph over both him and the author.' In the 1533 edition of the *De Octo Partibus Orationis* Whittinton alludes to the same subject in a hexastichon 'Ad lectorem':

Quod spersit Triuers odiosa incuria mendis
Inmineris tersum suscipe lector opus
Si tibi vel nostrae sit gratia incuria limae
Winandi ve mei praelia operosa satis
Mendosa explodas foedi exemplaria Petri
Triuers, pro meritis nostra polita fouens.

xxxiv *Introduction*

Whittinton's Translations.

Whittinton demands attention not only as an exponent of grammar but as a translator. His translations began to appear in 1532, but may have been written many years earlier, and range from Erasmus to Seneca, from Seneca to Cicero. The first to appear was his translation of Erasmus' *De Ciuilitate Morum Puerilium*—' A lytell booke of good maners for chyldren / nowe lately compyled and put forth by Erasmus Roterodam in latyne tonge / with interpretacion of the same in to the vulgare englysshe tonge / by Robert Whytyngton laureate poete '—which issued from de Worde's press in 1532. This exhibits Whittinton as a translator of some merit, with a prose style racy of the soil:

' Of the chambre.

' In the chambre sylence is laudable / with honesty. Loude speche and clattrynge is nat honest / moche more in bedde. Whether thou do thy clothes of or vpon / regarde honesty / beware thou shewe nothynge bare to syght that maner and nature wolde haue couered. If thou lye with a bedfelowe / lye styll / and make nat bare thy selfe with tumblynge / nor vexe nat thy bedfelowe with pullynge of the clothes. Before thou lay thy body downe / crosse thy forheed and thy brest with the syne of the holy crosse / & commende the to Iesu Christ with some lytell prayer.

' At Table.

' At table or at meate lette myrthe be with the / lette rybaudrie be exyled : sytte nat downe vnto thou haue wasshed / but lette thy nayles be pared before that no fylthe stycke in them / leest thou be called a slouer and a great nygarde : remembre the comen sayeng / and before make water / and if thou be gyrde to strayte to vnlose thy gyrdell is wysedome / whiche to do at the table is shame. whan thou wypest thy handes put forth of thy mynde all grefe / for at table it becometh nat to be sadde nor to make other sadde.

' Of metynge togythers.

'To turne this wayes and that / is a syne of lyght wytte. It is rudenesse ofte to chaunge countenau*n*ce / as now to wrie the nose / nowe to knytte the browes / nowe to set vp the browes / nowe to sette awrie the mouthe / nowe to gape wyde / nowe to make a narowe mouthe : these be synes of inconstance. It is also of the carte (indecorum) to shake the heed and caste the busshe / to coughe without cause / to hemme or reyche / lykwise to scratche thy heed / to picke thyne eares / to snyt thy nose / to stryke thy face / as a man that wypeth for shamfastnesse / to scrubbe or rubbe thy necke / to shrugge or wrigge thy sholders as we se in many ytalyens.'

The next to appear was 'The thre bookes of Tullyes offyces bothe in latyne tonge & in englysshe / lately translated by Roberte Whytinton poete laureate'. This was printed by de Worde in 1534 and is a diligent piece of work, but pedestrian withal. In 1535 John Byddell published 'Tullius de Senectute Bothe in latyn and Englysshe tonge Translated by Robert Whitinton poete Laureate'. Prefixed to this is a long and elaborate address 'Ad Inuictissimum Principem Henricum octauum Regem Angliae / & Franciae, Dominum Hiberniae, fidei defensorem, & Anglicanae ecclesiae in terris supremum caput, sui humillimi oratoris Roberti Whitintoni Epigramma'. After this came 'The Paradox of M. T. Cicero', 1540, and this was followed by 'A Frutefull worke of Lucius Anneus Seneca named the forme and Rule of Honest lyuynge bothe in the Latin tongue & in the Englyshe lately translated by Robert Whyttynton Poet Laureate', 1546.

'A Frutefull worke of Lucius Anneus Senecae. Called the Myrrour or Glasse of Maners and wysedome bothe in latin and in Englysshe lately Translated by Robert Whyttynton, poet Laureate', 1547, contains a very interesting 'Prologue upon the workes of Lucius Anneus Senecae Dedicate to syr Fraunceys Bryan Knyght'. This dedication to Sir Francis Bryan, the profligate poet, littérateur and friend of Henry VIII, is just another link in the long chain of evidence connecting Whittinton with court circles. That he knew Wolsey is quite possible through the prelate's term of office at Magdalen College School, and his appointment as schoolmaster to the henchmen would enable Whittinton to make the acquaintance of such men as the court favourites Brandon, Duke of Suffolk, and Francis Bryan.[1] The 'aulica negotia' must have brought him into the notice of many of the great ones, and it is a thousand pities that he, usually so vainglorious, did not boast more explicitly of his 'courtly business'.

After some weighty remarks on the pre-eminence of Seneca as a moralist Whittinton proceeds :

'All these premisses gathered togyther gentyll mayster Brian, I haue taken payne in studye to translate thre bokes of the sayde Seneca. The fyrst of maners. Seconde of the fourme of honest lyfe. Thyrde

---

[1] Bryan was 'Maister of the henxmen' 1526-47, and must frequently have been brought into contact with their schoolmaster.

of remedyes of all casuall chaunces and haue adioyned the texte of the latin, with the translacion in Englysshe, to ẙ entent that nat onely scole maysters, teachers, and reders folowynge ẙ olde tradicion of expart and excellent learned men, maye instructe theyr scolers in good and honest maners in bothe tongues. Englysshe and latin, but also all other ẙ be lettred (whiche in thys oure tyme be verye studyous of knowlege) by oft redynge of these vertuous workes : maye followe ẙ trade of morall wysedome, whiche is the nexte meane to amplyfye and encrease the com*m*en welthes. . . . And for as muche as I co*n*syder in you gentyll maister Bryan, besyde manyfolde vertues that you haue a syngler zele and delyte in workes that be pytthy and polytike, touchynge moral wysdome euer glad (as ẙ noble man of immortall laude and fame Maecenas) to sette forwarde such antique monumentes of vertue and good lernynge berynge special fauour, nat only by your beneficiall report to suche whiche be studyous to sette forthe good and vertuous workes most necessary to the knowlege of morall wysedome, wherof ensueth the auauncement of comen welthes, but also to promote suche into the fauoure of our most redoubted and bountyfull prynce kynge Henry ẙ VIII. In lyke maner as Maecenas was wonte to doo with hys souerayne Augustus Caesar ẙ puissant prynce, I am bold to dedicate this my poore lucubrations of the translacion of these thre morall workes, traducte out of the monumentes of ẙ noble philosopher Seneca, to thende that these workes goynge forth vnder the recognysaunce of your name, maye the better be accepte to al gentyll reders that hathe delyte in morall wysdome, and nat onely that, but also all other persons that be of cankerde and enuyous stomake, whose maner is to depraue ẙ studyous workes of other menne, without cause, but onely of theyr malencoly mynde replered with venym of intoxicate malyce, lyke vnto a curre dogge that barkes at euery waggynge of a strawe, shall ẙ rather refrayne theyr barkynge by deprauacion agaynst these morall monumentes, put forth vnder the tuicion of your name, and to conclude yf I by my studye in translatynge these vertuous workes haue done that thynge that may accede & come to the comen profyte of the readers herof and preferment of vertues, to hym onely be gyuen laude and prayse of whom all grace and goodness cometh.'

This is Whittinton undefiled, for notice how, like poor Dick and King Charles's head, he cannot keep his wretched critics from creeping into everything he writes. A further instalment of Seneca also saw the light in 1547—' Lucii Annei Senecae ad Gallione[m] de Remedi[i]s Fortuitorum. The remedyes agaynst all casuall chaunces.'

Whittinton was alive in 1548 according to Bale, who in the 1548 edition of his *Scriptores* gives a list of thirty authors still living, including Whittinton's name amongst them. I see no reason to doubt Bale, who was a contemporary and knew Horman, but beyond this all is uncertain. When or where Whittinton died I have, up to the present, been unable to discover.

That he was a man of considerable ability there is no question. As a translator his work, although it does not rank with Barclay's, is diligent and able, and as a schoolmaster and grammarian he was a worthy successor of the Magdalen men Anwykyll and Stanbridge. It is useless to pretend that he is a figure of literary importance, but he did extremely useful work in developing Stanbridge's plan of teaching Latin by means of English, thus, in a humble way, helping finally to enfranchise the vernacular and give it a dignity and authority that could produce the gorgeous poetry of Marlowe and the great Elizabethans.

II. VULGARIA AND LATIN TEACHING.

In the sixteenth-century grammar school Latin was a spoken as well as a written language. The culmination of written work was the Theme, and composition of verse, while the goal of Latin speaking in the schools was the Oration. Between the rudiments of grammar and this Ultima Thule lay a long and weary plain that had to be painfully traversed by the aspiring tyro. His equipment at the beginning of the century was clumsy and inadequate.[1] For grammars he would be confined to Donatus and Dolensis, Perottus and Sulpicius. He may have used the *De Utensilibus* of Alexander Neckam and the *Dictionarius* of John of Garlandia, together with the *Ortus Vocabulorum* and the useful *Promptorium Parvulorum* by way of dictionaries. 'A more obscure and repellent series of grammatical dissertations can hardly be imagined,' says W. C. Hazlitt, not, I think, without justice. Later he would have the *Compendium* of Anwykyll, Stanbridge's *Vocabula*, *Vulgaria*, and *Accidence*, not to speak of the innumerable grammatical tracts of Whittinton, text-books more adapted to the uses and understanding of schoolboys.

[1] Early vocabularies were, according to Thomas Wright, compiled by schoolmasters for their own use.

Lily's Grammar. Later still he would have a standard grammar, Lily's. This book, in reality a compilation, the work of Colet and Lily, emended by Erasmus, had a long and occasionally not undisputed reign, from its inception as the *Absolutissimus de octo orationis partium Constructione libellus*, 1515, to its appropriation as the *Eton Latin Grammar* in 1758. The earliest edition containing the King's Proclamation that all grammars but this must henceforth be eschewed appeared in 1542. It was first published in its definite form in 1574 with the title: 'A shorte Introduction of Grammar, generally to be used ; compyled and set forth for the bringing up of all those that intende to attayne the knowledge of the Latin tongue.' Henry's Proclamation is an interesting document and I quote it here :

' Henry the .VIII. by the grace of God, kynge of Englande, Fraunce, and Irelande, defendour of the faythe, and of the churche of Englande, and also of Irelande, in erth the supreme head, to al scholemaisters and teachers of grammer within this his realme, greting. Emonge the manyfold busynes and most weyghty affayres, appertaynynge to our regall auctoritie and offyce, we forgette not the tender babes, and the youthe of our realme, whose good education and godly bringynge up is a great furniture to the same and cause of moche goodnes. And to the intent that hereafter they may the more redyly and easyly attayne the rudimentes of the latyn tongue, without the great hynderance whiche heretofore hath ben, through the dyuersitie of grammers and teachynges : we wylle and commande, and straightly charge all you schoolemaisters and teachers of grammer within this our realme, and other our dominions, as ye intend to auoyde our displesure, and have our favour, to teache and learne your scholers this englyshe Introduction here ensuyng, and the latyne grammer annexed to the same, and none other, whiche we have caused for your ease, and your scholers spedye preferment, briefely and playnly to be compiled and set forth. Fayle not to applye your scholers in lernyng and godly education.'

It is supplemented by an ' Address to the Reader ' :

'For his maiestie consydering the great encumbrance and confusion of the yonge and tender wyttes, by reason of the diversitie of grammer rules and teachinges. For heretofore every master had his grammer, and every schole dyvers teachinges, and chaunging of masters and scholes did many tymes utterly dulle and undoo good wyttes, hath appointed certain lerned men meete for suche a purpose, to compyle one briefe, plaine, and uniforme grammer, whiche only (all other set a parte) for the more spedinesse, and lesse trouble of yonge wittes, his highnesse hath commaunded all scholemasters and teachers of grammer within this his realme, and other his dominions, to teache their scholers. Nowe consider you fathers in this realme how moche ye be bounde to suche a gracious kynge, whose care is not onely for you, but for your posteritie also, and your tender babes. And you scholemasters of England, to whome the cure and education of tender youth is committed, with what great study and diligence ought you to folow the example of our most gratious souerayne? You tender babes of England, shake of slouthfulnes, set wantonnes apart, apply your wittes holly to lerning and vertu wherby you may do your duety to god and your king, make glad your parentes, profit yourselves, and moch avance the common weale of your cuntrey. Let noble prince Edwarde encourage your tender hartes a prynce of great towardnesse, a prince in whom God hath poured his graces abundantly, a prince formed of suche perfectnes of nature that he is like by the grace of god, to ensu the steppes of his fathers wysedom, lernynge, and vertue, and is nowe almooste in a redynesse, to rounne in the same rase of lerning with you. For whom ye have greate cause to pray that he maye be the sonne of a longe lyuynge father.'

Whether or no Henry, in his solicitude for the 'tender babes of England', did a wise thing in substituting by force Lily for Donatus and other grammars is a matter of conjecture. There is an edition of the Grammar printed in 1557 'prelum Ascensianum' with an Address[1] to the Reader, which contains much sound advice on the teaching of Latin and deserves comparison with Brinsley.[2] *Brinsley.*

Instruction in the Accidence had to precede the business of 'making latins'. All wise minds of the period are agreed on the folly of rushing the schoolboy through his Rudiments. He must learn little by little and understand what he learns. According to the *Ludus Literarius* the usual method of 'making children perfect in the Accidence' was to let them read and repeat it and teach them the meaning afterwards. Brinsley suggests that the

1. INSTRUCTION IN THE ACCIDENCE.

[1] This Address is in the earlier edition (Lond. apud R. Wolfium, 1549), but two leaves are missing from the Bodley copy.

[2] *Ludus Literarius*, or the Grammar School, John Brinsley, 1612. Sixteenth-century grammar-school methods were conservative, and the remarks of Brinsley and his contemporaries are applicable over a wide period.

lesson should be read to the boys and thoroughly explained, that one of the class should afterwards read while the rest listen and help when necessary. He insists on continual explanation, 'apposing', and repetition. The writer of the 'Address', too, believes that 'festina lente' is the best plan for teacher and scholar:

'And when these Concordes be wel knowen unto them, (an easy & a pleasant pain, if the fore groundes be wel & thrughly beaten in) let them not continue in learning of their rules ordrely all as they lie in their Syntax, but rather learne some prety boke, wherin is conteined not only th'eloquence of the tongue, but also a good plaine lesson of honesty and godlines, (O pietas literata!) and therof take some little sentence as it lieth, & learne to make that same first out of English into Latin not seing the boke or construing it ther vpon. And if there fall any necessary rule of the Syntax to be knowen, then to learne it, as th'occasion of the sentence giueth cause that daie. Which sentence ones made well, and as nigh as can be with the wordes of the boke, then to take the boke and construe it, and so shall he be lesse troubled with the parsing of it, and easiliest carry his lesson in minde. And althogh it was saide before that the scollar shulde learn but a little at ones, it is not ment that when the maister had hard them a while, he shuld let them alone, (for that were mere negligence for both the partes), but I wold all their time they be at schoole, they shuld neuer be idle, but alwaies occupied in a continuall rehersing, loking back again to those thinges they had learned, and be more bound to kepe well their olde then to take forth any newe.

'Thus if the maister occupie them, he shall se a little lesson take a greate deale of time, and diligentlie inquiring and examining of the partes and the rules, not to be done so quickly and spedilie as it might be thoght to be: Within a while, by this use, the schollar shalbe broght to a good kind of readinesse of making, to the which if there be adjoined some use of speaking (which must necessarily be had) he shall be broght past the wearisome bitternesse of his learning.'

Hoole. Charles Hoole, in his *New Discovery of the old art of Teaching Schoole*,[1] has a significant passage on the old teaching methods used in this early stage of the game:

'After we had gone over our *Accidents* several times by heart, and had learned part of *Propria quae maribus*, we were put into this Book (*Sententiae Pueriles*) and there made to construe and parse two or three Sentences at once out of meer Latine, and if in any thing we missed, we were sure to be whipt. It was well, if of 16. or

---

[1] Dated 1660 but written twenty-three years earlier.

20. boyes two at any time could say, and that they did say right, was more by hap-hazard, then any thing that they knew; For we knew not how to apply one rule of Grammar to any word, nor could we tell what part of Speech it was, or what belonged to it; but if the Master told us it was a Noun, to be sure we said it was of the Nominative case, and singular number, and if a Verb, we presently guessed it to be of the Indicative Mood, Present tense, singular number, and third person; because these coming so frequent, we erred the lesse in them. And an ignorant presumption that we could easily say, made us spend our time in idle chat, or worse employment; and we thought it vain for us to labour about getting a lesson, because we had no help at all provided to further us in so doing. Yet here and there a Sentence, that I better understood then the rest, and with which I was more affected, took such impression, as that I still remember it, as *Gallus in suo stirquilinio plurimum potest. Ubi dolor, ibi digitus*, &c.'

2. THE MAKING OF LATINS.

The Rules mastered, either by gentle suasion or, if we are to believe contemporary woodcuts and school seals, by more drastic measures, the boy was able to proceed to the more serious business of 'making latins'. For this there would be the apparatus of vulgaria, vocabularies, and phrase-books like Udall's *Floures for Latine Spekynge*, 1533. Ascham and Brinsley have original views on Latin composition. Ascham says:[1]

Ascham.

'After the childe hath learned perfitlie the eight partes of speech, let him then learne the right ioyning togither of substantiues with adiectiues, the nowne with the verbe, the relative with the antecedent. And in learninge farther hys Syntaxis, by mine aduice, he shall not vse the commen order in common scholes for making of latines: wherby, the childe commonlie learneth, first, an euill choice of wordes, (and right choice of wordes, saith Caesar, is the foundation of eloquence) than, a wrong placing of wordes: and lastlie an ill framing of the sentence, with a peruerse iudgement, both of wordes and sentences. Those faultes, taking once roote in yougthe, be neuer, or hardlie, pluckt away in age. Moreover, there is no one thing, that hath more, either dulled the wittes, or taken awaye the will of children from learning, then the care they have, to satisfie their masters, in making of latines. For the scholar is commonlie beat for the making, when the master were more worthie to be beat for the mending, or rather,

---

[1] *Scholemaster*, 1570, Arber's reprint, p. 25. Vives anticipates Ascham by nearly fifty years.

marring of the same: The master many times, being as ignorant as the childe, what to saie properlie and fitlie to the matter. Two scholemasters haue set forth in print, either of them a booke, of soche kinde of latines, Horman and Whittington. A childe shall learne the better of them, that, which an other daie, if he be wise, and cum to iudgement, he must be faine to vnlearne again.'

Whittinton and Horman.

However unprofitable, the Horman-Whittinton method was one that prevailed for many a long year at Eton and Winchester, and was in full swing at Westminster in 1560. Whittinton's *Vulgaria*, 1520, is, as I have pointed out earlier, peculiarly rich in topical allusions which give it a fineness of flavour and temper its stolid scholasticism, and it was thought worthy of inclusion in his *Dux Grammaticus*, 1633, by John Clarke, although to be sure, he says it 'is meerely for *children*, and too meane for better capacities.' Whittinton belonged to the old school and believed in thorough inculcation of 'precepts'. His book is divided into four parts— De Concordantiolis, De Constructione Nominum, De Constructione Verborum, and De Constructione Impersonalium. It is a very workmanlike volume, the Precepts in English, then in Latin verse (to be found again in his *De Concinnitate* and *Sintaxis*), followed by adequate and illuminating Examples. Sometimes, where there is need, he quotes his authority and cites, not always correctly, Virgil, Sallust, Terence, Cicero. The quality of his Latin is neither here nor there : it has all the faults and some of the virtues of the written Latin of the period. From the pedagogical point of view the work is sufficiently well constructed to warrant its adoption as a school book. Horman treated it with great contempt in his *Antibossicon*. Characteristically he prints Whittinton's remarks in black-letter and his own in roman :

'*In Vulgaribus.*

W. Prima pars de concordantiolis.
H. Verum est quia parua et iniqua concordantia.
W. Mi puer diligenter inuigilato his preceptiunculis.
H. Imo potius ijs indormi ut rectis preceptionibus inuigiles.
W. Quem inuenias (saltem expertum) qui probabili ratione hoc refragetur.
H. Neminem inuenies rudimenta grammatices uel summis labris expertum qui diceret : hoc refragetur. sed huic refraget.

Vulgaria and Latin Teaching

W. Quicunque nihil absolutum legit, &c.

H. Pro eo quod est legendo nihil absoluere dicis ineptissime. nihil absolutum legere. Multi enim Ciceronem et Vergilium absolutissimos legunt. sed lectionem non absoluunt. . . .

W. Moribus vel mores (pro tempore) approbatis : propius accedere sese comparet puer.

H. Dic mihi magister grammatices / dic mihi magister in artibus in vtopia create : dic mihi o protouates Anglie : quale hoc latinum moribus vel mores approbatis. Sed tua stultitia fatigat solem.

Ex immenso tuorum errorum pelago : haec pauca tibi proponere volui : vt noscant homines : me talem tibi diem dixisse non ex animi vicio / aut priuata offensa (quae tamen satis contumeliosa fuit) sed potius vt rei literariae : quae tuis pessimis auspicijs ferme pessum ierat / suppetias ferrem. Idque afferre paratus sum / nihil penitus in tuis vulgaribus esse reliquum (modo tuum sit) quod puerum didicisse profuerit. Abyssum vero errorum / quibus tua scatet grammatica : nihil attigi. Superant enim numero & vicijs omnem modum / nisi apud eum / cui vel suppetit ocium ad horas male collocandas : vel ad id agendum. Diuitis stipendi / proposita est conditio. Argumento sit / qui in primo grammatices vestibulo / & in eius ipsius grammatices definitione turpiter per inscitiam erraueris : dicens grammatica componi ex gramma : & ita quo dici potest nihil ridiculosius. Restat hoc solum : vt duplici epigrammati : quo mea vulgaria celbrasti unum reponam in tuorum omnium operum praeconium.'

He ends his attack with the biting

Epigramma in opera Whitintoniana.

Quisquis in illius vatis / qui nomine protos
   Dici vult Anglis : dogmate fidis homo :
Ex his quę scripsi / poteris bene noscere : qualem
   Ad claras artes legeris ipse ducem.
Praecipit hic alijs / quem nil didicisse patescit :
   Quod puero prosit quod ue uirum deceat
Nanque nocet : secunque trahit pars magna venenum
   Quo puer imbutus vix resilire potest.

The ordinary way of 'making latins' is clearly described in the following quotation from Brinsley's *Ludus Literarius* :

I haue giuen them vulgars, or Englishes, such as I haue deuised, to *Brinsley.* be made in Latine : and at the first entrance I haue taught and heard them, how to make euery word in Latine, word by word, according to their rules. After a while I haue onely giuen them such uulgars and appointed them a time, against which they should bring them made in Latine : and at the perusing and examining of them, I haue beene wont to correct them sharply, for their faults in writing, and for their negligence; and so haue giuen them new Englishes, and it may be that I haue told them the Latine to the hardest words.'

'Double' transla-tion. This time-honoured method of acquiring the Latin tongue was repudiated by Ascham,[1] and, following him, by Brinsley. Ascham proposed a system of 'double' translation, recommending a model book to be used for the purpose, Sturm's *Selection of Cicero's Letters*, 1539:

'Therefore, in place of Latines for yong scholers, and Paraphrasis for the masters, I wold haue double translation specially vsed. For, in double translating a perfite peece of Tullie or Caesar, neyther the scholar in learning, nor ẙ Master in teaching can erre. A true tochstone, a sure Metwand lieth before both their eyes. For all right congruitie: proprietie of wordes: order in sentences: the right imitation, to inuent good matter, to dispose it in good reason, to expresse any purpose fitlie and orderlie, is learned thus, both easelie and perfitlie. Yea, to misse somtyme in this kynde of translation, bringeth more proffet, than to hit right, either in Paraphrase or making of Latins.'

Ascham's system is an excellent one and, requiring the use of three paper books, marks the transition from the oral to the purely written method of Latin teaching. He aimed a deadly blow at Horman's and Whittinton's vulgars, so arbitrary and unclassical.

One of the most interesting pronouncements on sixteenth-century education came from the pen of the grammarian John Palsgrave, translator of Fullonius' *Acolastus*. The title-page of the work, dated 1540, deserves to be quoted:

Palsgrave. 'THE Comedye of Acolastus translated into oure englysshe tongue, after suche maner as chylderne are taught in the grammer schole, fyrst worde for worde, as the latyne lyeth, and afterwarde accordynge to the sence and meanyng of the latin sentences: by shewing what they do value and counteruayle in our tongue, with admonitions set forth in the margyn, so often as any suche phrase, that is to say, kynd of spekyng vsed of the latyns, whiche we vse not in our tonge, but by other wordes, expresse the sayd latyn maners of speakinge, and also Adages, metaphores, sentences, or other fygures poeticall or rhetoricall do require, for the more perfyte instructynge of the lerners,

[1] J. L. Vives in his *De Tradendis Disciplinis*, 1531, anticipates Ascham's idea of paper note-books and 'double' translation.

Vulgaria and Latin Teaching

and to leade theym more easilye to see howe the exposytion gothe. and afore the seconde sceane of the fyrst acte, is a brefe introductory to haue some general knowledge of the dyuers sortes of meters vsed of our auctour in this comedy. And afore Acolastus balade is shewed of what kyndes of meters his balade is made of. And afore the syxte sceane of the fourthe acte, is a monition of the Rhetorycall composytion vsed in that sceane, and certayne other after it ensuynge.'

The Introductory Epistle, addressed to Henry VIII, is full of good things.

He speaks of 'How great a damage it hathe heretofore bene, and yet is, vnto the tender wyttes of this your noble realme, to be hyndred and confounded with so many dyuers and sondry sortes of preceptes grammaticall', and approves of a uniform grammar, but proceeds :

' I wyshed, that vnto this moch expedient reformation of your schole maisters vnstayd libertis, which hytherto haue taught such grammers, and of the same so dyuers and sondry sortes, as to euery of theym semed best (and was to their fantasies mooste approued) : myght therto also folowe and succede one stedy and vnyforme maner of interpretation of the latyn authours in to our tonge, after ỹ the latyn principles were by your graces youth ones surely conned and perceyued. Upon the want and defaute wherof, besydes the great and euydente inconuenience (of whiche the effecte is to moche in euerye place espied) that is to say, the playnly apparant ignorance & want of a required sufficiencye of many, whiche in priuate places take vpon theym to teache, afore they be theyr craftes maisters. To whome the beste grammaticall rules, that euer were or could be deuised, can not vaylably be sufficient : I haue by experyence lerned, that there be dyuers other occasions, rysynge vppon the schole maisters parties, whereby your graces youth is not a lyttell hyndered. For some instructers of youre hyghnes youth, for want of a perfyte iudgement in this behalfe, so moche desyre to seme affectately curiouse, that hauyng no due consyderation to the tender wyttes, whiche they take vnder theyr charge to teache in the stede of pure englyshe wordes and phrases, they declare to their chylderne one latyne worde by an nother, and confounde the phrases of the tongues : And thus not a lytell do hynder their yong scholers, while they wold seme for their own partes to haue a knowledge and erudition aboue the common sort. And som other ageyne there be, whiche hauynge vndoubtedly, lernyng ynoughe, vaylable and sufficiente, yet whyle they by sondry wayes and maners of speakynge vsed in our tongue, labour to expresse suche latyn auctours myndes, as they do take vppon them for the tyme to interprete, and for to seme therin more dilygent, than the common sorte, dyspende in maner hole forenoones and afternoones, in the declarynge of a fewe lynes of suche latyne authours, as they for the season haue in hande (as to confesse the very truthe, the schole maisters hole dilygence tendeth in maner chiefely to that effecte and purpose) they do by that meanes not only ryght lytell for the tyme further their yong audience, but also by that wayes do oppresse and ouerlaye the tender wyttes, the whiche they wold so fayne further, with their multitude of sondry interpretations, confusedly by them vttered. So that fynally theyr yong scholers, to helpe their memory with, be forced to falle a glosynge, or rather a blottyng of their latyn bokes, and as theyr chyldyshe iudgement dothe for the tyme serue them, of dyuers englishe wordes in our tongue beinge synonymes, or of dyuers maners of interpretations vsed by theyr mayster, they chuse moste commonly the very worste, and therewith scryble the bokes of theyr latyne auctours. And somme other furthermore there be, whiche thoughe they haue by their greatte studye, at youre graces Unyuersities, soo moche prouffyted in the Latyne tongue, that to shewe an euydente tryalle of theyr lernynge, they canne wryte an Epistle ryght latyne lyke, and therto speake latyne, as the tyme shall mynyster occasyon, very well, yea and haue also by theyr diligence atteyned to a comly vayne in makynge of verses: yet for all this, partly bycause of the rude language vsed in their natyue countreyes, where they were borne and firste lerned (as it happened) their grammer rules, & partely bycause that commyng streyght from thense, vnto some of your graces vniuersities, they haue not had occasions to be conuersaunte in suche places of your realme, as the pureste englysshe is spoken, they be not able to expresse theyr conceyte in theyr vulgar tonge, ne be not suffycyente, perfectly to open the diuersities of phrases betwene our tonge and the latyn (whiche in my poore iudgemente is the veray chiefe thynge that the schole mayster shulde trauayle in).'

Palsgrave cites six advantages that would ensue from accurate and representative translation:

1. Stabilising of the language,
2. Improvement of standards of scholarship,
3. 'Thirdly, for than shulde the wyllynge scolers, whiche hadde all redy gotten their grammaticall principles, be so euidently encouraged to go forwarde, that they shulde be great callers vpon theyr felowes whiche by theyr negligence wolde dragge, be sydes that the maysters them selfes shulde haue no small prouocation, to vse for theyr owne parties a good dylygence, leste theyr scholers of theyr owne mynde

Vulgaria and Latin Teaching   xlvii

shulde call for more of theyr auctour to be declared vnto them, then perchance they had prepared to reade vnto them before: where as nowe the scholers, be they neuer so well wyllynge to be furthered, they haue no maner remedy, but vtterly and holly to staye vpon theyr maysters mouthe. Fourthely, for than shulde all suche as be alredy departed from the grammer scholes, and afterwarde be taken with a repentance of theyr yong time negligently by them ouerpassed, whiche aforetyme were forced to dispayre, thoughe theyr wylles afterwarde waxed neuer so good, nowe by this meanes easely recouer them selfes agayne. Fyftely, for than shulde younge scholers, with small paynes, engrose the hole argumentes of the latten autours in theyr memory, where as heretofore, after they haue redde the latyne auctours in the schole, they haue not perceiued what matter they entreated of: yea and than theyr furtherance and spedy encrease shoulde be so notable, that with pleasure in maner, and with bannyshynge of all seruile rudenes out of grammer scholes, they shulde soner be able perfytely to go then they could afore tymes be able to creepe. Syxtely, for whan the schole maysters, and also the scholers, shuld by this meanes be eased in maner of .iii. partes of theyr paynes, than shuld the masters haue both tyme and better occasion, to open theyr farder lerning, & to shew vnto theyr scholers the great artifice vsed of the auctors, in the composition of theyr workis, which afore tyme they had no suche opportunitie to do.'

This excellent appreciation of the value of good translation is the more remarkable coming, as it did, only twenty years after Whittinton and Horman.

Brinsley improved and elaborated Ascham's method. He calls his system 'Grammatical' translation and gives a detailed description of it in his *Ludus Literarius*. Before construing, the artificial or rhetorical order in the Latin was to be replaced by the purely grammatical: *'Grammatical Translation.'*

'An Example of Dictating in English, and setting downe both English and Latine, and the Latine both plainly and elegantly.

Dictating according to the naturall order	Ordo Grammaticus	Ordo Ciceronianus
No man hath been euer great without some diuine inspiration.	Nemo fuit vnquam magnus sine afflatu aliquo Diuino.	Nemo magnus sine aliquo afflatu diuino vnquam fuit. de Natura Deor.'

Curriculum.

For Brinsley, who always speaks with authority from the experience of a schoolmaster, this method is the complete panacea for all ills in connexion with the 'making of latins'. What was to be translated depended very much on what was being read in class. I have already given in detail Wolsey's curriculum for his school at Ipswich. At Eton the first form read the *Disticha de Moribus* of Dionysius Cato and the *Exercitatio Linguae Latinae* of J. L. Vives. The second read Terence, Lucian's *Dialogues*, and Aesop's *Fables*; the third, Terence, Aesop, and Sturm's *Selected Letters of Cicero*; the fourth, Terence, Ovid, Martial, Catullus, and Sir Thomas More; the fifth, Ovid, Horace, Cicero's *Epistles*, Valerius Maximus, Lucius Florus, Justin, and the *Epitome Troporum* of Susenbrotus. In the sixth and seventh forms the boys read Caesar's *Commentaries*, Cicero, *De Officiis* and *De Amicitia*, Virgil, Lucan, and the Greek grammar. At Canterbury Grammar School of the new foundation, 1541, the reading of Latin authors began in the second class with Cato, Aesop, and *Familiar Colloquies*. The third read Terence's *Comedies* and Mantuan's *Eclogues*; the fourth, stories of the poets and familiar letters of learned men; the fifth, the best poets and historians; and the sixth, *De Verborum Copia ac Rerum*, Horace, and Cicero. It would perhaps be opportune at this point to mention a curious

Kempe. educational treatise written in 1588 by William Kempe, called *The Education of Children in Learning*. Kempe was master of Plymouth Grammar School, and described his work as 'a verie profitable matter, and most necessarie to be urged in this secure and licentious generation'. Kempe is very detailed in the statement of his methods. He divides learning into four degrees. The first is purely rudimentary and concerns spelling and orthography. The second is Grammar. The first form learns the parts of speech, the second practises the precepts of grammar and reads the Dialogues of Corderius and Castellion. The third and fourth read Sturm's *Cicero* and practise imitation of authors, while the fifth reads Terence's *Comedies*, Cicero's *De Amicitia* and *De Senectute*, with Ovid, *De Tristibus*. At this time the boys were twelve years of age! The third degree of schooling meant Logic, Rhetoric, and more perfect understanding of Grammar. Logic and Rhetoric were to occupy one-sixth of the scholar's time, and the rest was to be devoted to the study of

Vulgaria and Latin Teaching

good authors, Tully's *Offices* and *Orations*, Caesar's *Commentaries*, Virgil's *Aeneid*, Ovid's *Metamorphoses*, and Horace. This amount of scholarship took three years to acquire, but of the fourth degree, Arithmetic and Geometry, he writes that boys 'may easely passe through these Artes in halfe a yeere'.

Hoole[1] had very different ideas on what should be read in the various forms. Form II could read Corderius and Cato's *Distichs*; Form III, Aesop's *Fables* and Mantuan; Form IV, the Latin Testament, Terence, and Ovid, *De Tristibus* and the *Metamorphoses*; Form V, Aphthonius, Livy, Justinus, Caesar's *Commentaries*, Lucius Florus, Virgil, the *Historiae Variae* of Aelianus, and Epictetus; while Form VI had a plethora of authors, Horace, Juvenal, Persius, Lucan, Seneca, Martial, Plautus, Lucian's *Select Dialogues*, Tully's *Orations*, Pliny's *Panegyrics*, and Quintilian's *Declamations*. The influence of the Renaissance is strong in the insistence on classical authors. Colet's Statutes for St. Paul's School, insisting on such *Christian* authors as 'Lactantius, prudentius and proba and sedulius and Juuencus and Baptista Mantuanus', stamp him as a reactionary, and wise as they are in other respects, are not in this too salutary.[2]

When the boy could construe without difficulty, and had mastered the art of 'making latins', he passed on to the harder exercise of 'imitation', that is, of classical authors. This imitation of classical style, which was a subject of contention between Whittinton and his rival schoolmasters, meant, as a preparation for the 'Theme', the adaptation of classical vocabulary and phrasing to the exigencies of contemporary thought on all subjects. Cicero and Terence were the models, and the form the exercise took was the writing of letters. That this exercise may have degenerated into 'something approaching transcription' is quite possible (and Brinsley lays great stress on proper examination and correction of exercises), but it was a necessary and most useful preliminary to the culmination of all written work in schools, the Theme, which required not only a knowledge of classical phrase and idiom, but an acquaintance with the rules of Rhetoric.

3 'IMITA-TION.'

[1] *New Discovery of the old art of Teaching Schoole*, 1660.

[2] In this emphasis on Christian authors Colet approaches Vives rather than Erasmus.

1   Introduction

Letter-writing.

Hoole summarizes his method of teaching Letter writing:

'1. Ask one of your boyes to whom, and for what he is minded to write a letter, and according as he shall return you an answer, give him some general instructions how to do it.

2. Then bid him and all his fellows let you see which of them can best indite an English letter upon that occasion, and in how short a time.

3. Let them every one bring his own letter fairly written that you may show them how to amend the imperfections you finde in it.

4. Take his that hath done the best, and let everyone give you an expression of his own gathering, for every word and phrase that is in it, and let it be different (if it may be) from that which another hath given already before him.

5. As they give in their expressions, do you, or an able Scholar for you, write them all down, in a paper, making a note that directeth to the place to which they belong.

6. Then deliver them the paper and let everyone take such words or phrase, as is most agreeable to the composition of an Epistolary style (so that he take not the same that another useth), and bring the letter writ fair, and turned out of English into Latine. And thus you shall find the same epistle varied so many several wayes, that every boy will seem to have an epistle of his own, and quite differing in words from all those of his fellowes, though the matter be one and the same.'

Brinsley describes the usual method of teaching letter writing in his *Ludus Literarius*:

'I have done this. I have read them some of Tully's epistles and some part of Macropedius or Hegendorphinus de Conscribendis Epistolas. I have directed them that they are to follow the rules set down in the several kinds of Epistles there mentioned, and made the examples plain unto them. Moreover, I have used to put them in mind of this, that an epistle is nothing but a letter sent to a friend, to certify him of some matter, or to signify our mind plainly and fully unto him. And, therefore, look how we would write in English, so to do in Latin. These and the like are the helps which I have used; and I take them to be the most that are done in ordinary schools.'

Rhetoric.

For use in the study of Rhetoric, a knowledge of which was essential for Theme writing, Hoole suggests:

'William Dugard's Elementa Rhetorices, Charles Butler's Rhetoric, Thomas Farnaby's Index Rhetoricus, Susenbrotus, Thomas Horne's

Compendium Rhetorices together with the more advanced Partitiones Oratoriae of Vossius, Tesmari Exercitationes Rhetoricae, Caussinus, and Paiot, De Eloquentia.'[1]

'However technical and stilted the training in Rhetoric may have been', says Foster Watson, 'the subject in the hands of judicious teachers must have largely increased the vocabulary of words, of metaphors and similes. It must have drawn attention, in many ways, to the value of forms of statement and to effective statement. The wealth of imagery in authors read must have been, when the teaching was thorough, a valuable possession, and a sense of alertness in discovering the various tropes and figures could not but be an excellent school discipline.'[2] So prepared and fortified with an adequate understanding of Latin and Rhetoric, the boy could enter on the final business of Theme writing. The collection of matter was a prime difficulty. Commonplace books into which everything went, arranged under appropriate headings, to be referred to as occasion required, were a necessity and every boy had one. Hoole gives a detailed account of the manner and method of Theme writing:

'Now the manner I would have them use them, is thus; Having a Theme given them to treat of, as suppose, this, *Non aestas semper fuerit, componite nidos*. Let them first consult what they have read in their own Authors concerning Tempus, Aestas, occasio, or opportunitas, and then,

4. THEME WRITING.

2. Let everyone take one of those books forementioned and see what he can find in it for his purpose, and write it down under one of those heads in his Commonplace book; but first let the Master see whether it will suit with the Theme.

3. Let them all read what they have written before the Master and everyone transcribe what others have collected, into his own book; and thus they may always have store of matter for invention ready at hand, which is far beyond what their own wit is able to conceive. Now to furnish themselves also with copy of good words and phrases, besides what they have collected weekly, and what hath been already said of varying them; they should have these and the like books reserved in the School Library.... After you have shewed them how

[1] Brinsley suggests Reusner's *Symbola* for variety of matter and the *Progymnasmata* of Aphthonius for the form of the Theme.
[2] *Curriculum and text-books of English Schools, in the first half of the seventeenth century*. Bibliographical Society's Transactions, vi, pt. ii.

to find matter, and where to help themselves with words and phrases, and in what order they are to dispose the parts, and what Formulas they are to use in passing from one to another, propound a Theme to them in English and Latin, and let them strive who can soonest return you the best Exordium in English, and then who can render it into the best Latin, and so you may proceed to the Narration, and quite through every part of a Theme, not tying them to the words of any author, but giving them liberty to contract or enlarge or alter them as they please ; so that they still contend to go beyond them in purity of expression. This being done, you may dismiss them to adventure to make every one his own exercise in English and Latin and to bring it fair written, and be able to pronounce it distinctly *memoriter* at a time appointed. And when once you see they have gained a perfect way of making Themes of themselves, you may let them go on to attain the habit by their own constant practice, ever and anon minding them what places in their Authors (as they read) are most worthy notice and imitation, and for what purposes they may serve them.'

John Clarke.

How complicated in reality the writing of Themes could become is easily inferred from a glance at John Clarke's *Formulae Oratoriae in usum Scholarum concinnatae*.[1] In general there were five parts to a Theme—Exordium, Narratio, Confirmatio, Confutatio, Conclusio. These could be elaborated [2]—Propositio, Ratio, Confirmatio, Similitudo, Exemplum, Testimonium, Conclusio. Clarke gives these Formulae for the making of a Theme :

1. Narrandi sive proponendi.
2. Partiendi.
    Distribuendi vel Dividendi.
3. Confirmandi in genere.
    2. Per Causam, offering reasons and arguments.
    3. Contrarium.
    4. Similitudinem.
    5. Exemplum.
    6. Testimonium, citing words of ancients.
4. Objiciendi.
5. Confutandi.
6. Concludendi. 1. In genere. 2. In specie, through Recapitulation.
    2. Pathopoeam in exclamatione.
            interrogatione.
            admiratione.

---

[1] Fourth edition, 1632.
[2] Foster Watson, *Bibliographical Society's Transactions*, vi, p. 244.

Vulgaria and Latin Teaching

As a side-light on contemporary Rhetoric the following quotation from Palsgrave's translation of Fullonius' *Acolastus* is enlightening:

'He vseth also in this syxt sceane specially anxesis, exclamation, dubitation, collation of contraryes, simulation, precision, correction, exaggeration, argumentation, epyphonoma. And in his composition and desposynge of these matters, he vseth also these schemes rhetorycal, as dissolution, interpretation, complexion ex repetitionibus, subiection, and conduplication : and sometyme vseth euident imitation of the auctours aboue rehersed, in suche places as they haue vsed the lyke artifyciall composition, all whyche thynges in the margyne, I shall set forth, as theyr places shall gyue me occasion.'

Small wonder that Locke and Milton should denounce the folly of expecting work so advanced and difficult from boys who were little more than children.

Verse composition, particularly recommended by Brinsley and taught concurrently with Theme writing in the schools, incurred the strong disapproval of Locke,[1] who says : 'If he has no Genius to Poetry, it is the most unreasonable thing in the World, to torment a Child, and waste his time about that which can never succeed.' Composition of verses, however, remained part of the regular curriculum in the Grammar School down to the present day, and, like the Theme, was the culmination of written work. *Verse Composition.*

The real aim of the Grammar School was to make Latin live again as a spoken language. So great was the insistence in early Tudor schools on the necessity of Latin speaking that children forgot their English. According to Brinsley, 'The surest course for entring young schollars to speake Latine' was— 5. LATIN SPEAKING.

1. Examining and answering every peece of a rule or sentence in Latine, to make them their owne. So in their Authours.
2. To utter before them what they cannot.
3. Daily practice of Grammaticall translations ; chiefly reading bookes of Dialogues out of English into Latine, which is nothing but such talking.
4. To talke together in the wordes of the Dialogues, each sentence first in English, then Latine.
5. Translating and uttering every morning a peece of their Accedence in Latine.

---

[1] *Some Thoughts concerning Education*, 1693.

Introduction

6. Accustome (them) to parse wholly in Latine.
7. Daily practice of disputing.

The 'Custos'.

Continual practice was naturally essential and in order to enforce it the early sixteenth-century schoolmaster resorted to the expedient of employing spies. These were known in schools as 'custodes' or 'asini', and correspond to the 'lupi' appointed by the Masters in the Universities to inform against 'vulgarisantes' who spoke their mother tongue. The duties of the 'custos' are clearly defined in the Statutes for Westminster School, 1560.[1] 'That boy shall be made custos in each class who has spoken in English, or who cannot repeat one of the rules he has learnt without making more than three mistakes, or through neglect of writing perfectly has made three mistakes in spelling in his notes. . . . Then all the classes shall say by heart what has been read to them in this order, viz. the Custos shall always begin and shall carefully observe the rest saying it afterwards. . . .' The practice of this method of securing information against offenders had its abuses which Brinsley was quick to recognize:

'That is a usuall custome in Schooles to appoint Custodes, or Asini (as they are tearmed in some places) to observe and catch them who speake English in each fourme, or whom they see idle, to give them the Ferrula, and to make them Custodes if they cannot answere a question whiche they aske.

'But I have observed so much inconvenience in it, as I cannot tell, what to say in this case: for oft-times, he who is the Custos will hardly attend his own worke, for harkening to heare others speake English. Also there falleth out amongst them oft-times so much wrangling about the questions, or defending themselves, that they did not speake English, or were not idle, that all the whole fourme is troubled. So likewise when the Custodes are called for, before breaking up at dinner and at night, there will be so much contention amongst them, as is a disquieting and trouble to the Master. Besides all these, I doe not see any great fitnesse, that one schollar should smite another with the Ferula; because much malicing one another, with grudges and quarrels do arise thereupon.'

Whittinton has this sentence in his *Vulgaria*, 'If thou accuse me of spekynge englysshe / I shall complayne vpon the for fyghtynge in the maysters absence. set the one agayn the other', which throws light on the practice.

[1] A. F. Leach, *Educational Charters*, p. 517.

In the 1557 edition of Lily's Grammar it is suggested in the 'Address':

'A great helpe to further this readines of making and *speaking* shalbe, if the Maister give him an English boke, and cause him ordinarily to turne every day some part into Latin. This exercise can not be done without his rules: and therfore doth establish them and ground them surely in his mind for readinesse, and maketh him more able to speake sodeinly, when so ever any present occasion is offered for the same. And it doth helpe his learning more a great deale, to turne out of English into Latin, then contrariwise. Further we se, many can understand Latin, that cannot speake, and when they reade the Latin word in the boke, can tell you th'English therof at any time : but when they have laide away their bokes, they can not contrariwise tell you for th'English the Latin again, when so ever ye will aske them. And therfore this exercise helpeth this sore well, and maketh these wordes, which he understandeth to be ready by use unto him, and so perfecteth him in the tongue handsomely.'

Kempe insists that the boy's 'exercise of speaking Latin shall be first in common and easie matters, as of his lesson, of orders in the Schoole, of dinner and supper, etc. Afterwards in all matters, heed being taken that he be reformed when he useth barbarous words, or trippeth in his speach.'[1] Locke looked upon Latin 'as absolutely necessary to a Gentleman', and approximates to Colet in his common-sense view of the way in which it should be taught, both as a spoken and written language :

'And I would fain have anyone name to me that Tongue, that anyone can learn, or *speak* as he should do by the Rules of Grammar. Languages were made not by Rules, or Art, but by Accident, and the common Use of the People. And he that will speak them well, has no other Rule but that; nor anything to trust to, but his Memory, and the habit of speaking after the Fashion learn'd from those, that are allow'd to speak properly, which in other words is only to speak by roat. ... Languages are to be learn'd only by reading, and talking, and not by scraps of Authors got by Heart.'

Latin speaking was taught by means of the Colloquy, and the *Colloquies*. Colloquies most in use were those of Erasmus, Vives, Corderius, and Castellion. As Foster Watson points out,[2] a study of these Colloquia and Dialogi had two results ; it purged Latin speaking of many of the barbarisms that had vitiated the Latin of the

---

[1] Vives insists on the necessity for correct speaking in the vernacular.
[2] *English Grammar Schools to 1660.*

lvi   *Introduction*

Middle Ages, and it helped to bring the schoolroom into touch with the life and thought of the outside world, for these Colloquia were rich in topical interest, and their diction was, within limits, the diction of Terence and Cicero.

School Plays.

The school play was a subsidiary and extremely useful way of teaching and improving Latin speech. There are allusions to school plays in Horman's *Vulgaria*: 'We have played a comedi of greke. We have played a comedi of Latten', and at Westminster the custom of giving a Latin play at Christmas has persisted to the present day:

'Quo juventus majori cum fructu tempus Natalis Christi terat, et tum actioni tum pronunciationi decenti melius se assuescat : statuimus, ut singulis annis intra 12m. post festum Natalis Christi dies, vel postea arbitrio decani, ludimagister et praeceptor simul Latine unam, magister choristarum Anglice alteram comoediam aut tragoediam a discipulis et choristis suis in aula privatim vel publice agendam, curent. Quod si non praestiterint singuli, quorum negligentia omittuntur decem solidis mulctentur.'

6. THE ORATION.

As the object of Latin writing in the school was the composition of Themes, so in the case of Latin speaking the goal was the Oration, reached only through frequent practice in disputing.

The pronunciation of Latin at this time is a point that deserves consideration. Whittinton says in the *Vulgaria*, 'Thy nyse and newfangled pronunciacyon after ẙ Italyans fason fedeth delycate eeres ẘ wonders pleasure', from which one might assume that at his day Italian pronunciation of the vowels was a new thing. As late as 1543 the vowels were still pronounced at Cambridge in the Italian manner. To quote J. E. Sandys:[1]

Pronunciation.

'The Reformation made it no longer necessary for the clergy to use the common language of the Roman Church, and, partly to save trouble to teachers and learners, Latin was gradually mispronounced as English. The mischief probably began in the grammar schools, and then spread to the Universities. Coryat, who visited Italy and other parts of Europe in 16c8, found England completely isolated in its pronunciation of long i. At Leyden, in 1608, Scaliger received a visit from an unnamed English Scholar, and, after listening to his "Latin" for a full quarter of an hour, and finding it as unintelligible as Turkish, was compelled to bring the interview to a close by

[1] *History of Classical Scholarship*, p. 233.

apologising, in perfect good faith, for his inadequate knowledge of English. The isolation of England had doubtless extended still further by the time of Milton, who holds that "to smatter Latin with an English mouth is as ill a hearing as Law-French", and recommends that the speech of boys should " be fashion'd to a distinct and clear pronuntiation as near as may be to the *Italian*, especially in the vowels".'

And now the wheel has come full circle and, after years of characteristic isolation, England has returned once more to the Italian 'fason' of pronunciation.

The models for Latin speech as for Latin writing were Terence and Cicero, and the Colloquies in general use were based on classical usage. Not only were these Colloquies storehouses of classical phrase and idiom adapted to the purposes of everyday speech, but they gave first-hand information about teaching methods. The Dialogues of J. L. Vives,[1] for many years an honoured school text-book, were intended as 'a first book of practice in *speaking* the Latin language'. In his thirteenth Dialogue Vives gives a picture of a ' Disputation' in progress:

'SPUDAEUS. TYRO.

S. Let us go down. They are "batelarii", going to the disputation. *Disputa-*
T. Please lead us thither. *tions.*
S. Step in, but quietly and reverently. Uncover your head and watch attentively all, one by one, for there is a discussion beginning on weighty matters which will conduce greatly to one's knowledge. That one whom you see sitting alone in the highest seat is the president (praeses) of the disputation and the judge of the disputes, so to say, the Agonotheta. His first duty is to appoint the place for each of the contenders, lest there should be any disorder or confusion, if one or other should want to take precedence.
T. Who is that thin and pallid man they all rush upon ?
S. He is the propugnator, who will receive the attack of all, and who has become thin and pale by his immoderate night-watches. He has done great things in philosophy and is advanced in theology. But now you must be quiet and listen, for he who is now making the attack is accustomed to think out his arguments most acutely and subtly, and presses most keenly the propugnator, and, in the opinion of all, is compared with the very highest in this discipline, and often compels his antagonist to recant. Notice how the latter has tried to elude him, but how the oppugnator has met him effectively by his

[1] *Tudor Schoolboy Life*, Foster Watson.

irrefutable reasoning, and how the propugnator cannot escape him! This arrow cannot be avoided.... The propugnator cannot protect himself and soon will give in unless some god suggests a subterfuge to his mind. Behold, the question is brought to an end by the decision of the judge.'

In his *Vulgaria* Whittinton says:

'Was thou present at the dysputacyon?
They were as ferre asondre the one fro the other/as London is dystaunt out of my countre. whiche be a hondred myle asondre.
Herdest ẙ what they commened of bytwene them?
After the one was concluded he ascrybed to hymselfe / or toke vpon hym great ignoraunce.
It wyll teche hym to be wyse how he compareth with his better for ever.
He gaf hym noo lesse than a dosen chekmates or they had done.
It shall profet hym moche yf he be wyse and make hym to loke better vpon his booke.'

Fitz-stephen.   Fitzstephen's delightful account of schoolboys disputing in the twelfth century deserves to be quoted once again:

'In London the three principal churches have celebrated schools of privilege and ancient dignity. Often, however, through personal favour to some noted philosopher more schools are allowed there. On feast days the masters celebrate assemblies at the churches, en fête. The scholars hold disputations, some declaiming, others by way of question and answer. These roll out enthymemes, those use the better form of perfect syllogisms. Some dispute merely for show as they do at collections, others for truth, which is the grace of perfection. The sophists using the Socratic irony are pronounced happy because of the mass and volume of their words; others play upon words. Those learning rhetoric, with rhetorical speeches, speak to the point with a view to persuasuon, being careful to observe the precepts of their art, and to leave out nothing that belongs to it. The boys of the different schools vie with each other in verses; or dispute on the principles of grammar, or the rules of preterite and supines. Others in epigrams, rhymes and verses, use the old freedom of the highway, with Fescennine licence freely scourge their schoolfellows without mentioning names, hurl abuse and fun at each other, with Socratic wit gird at the failings of their schoolfellows, or even of their elders, or bite them more deeply with the tooth of Theon in audacious dithyrambics. The audience, "ready for much laughter wrinkle their noses as they redouble their shaking guffaws".'[1]

[1] A. F. Leach, *Educational Charters*, p. 83.

Vulgaria and Latin Teaching   lix

Stow apparently saw disputations in progress in 1598, and in 1580 the Statutes of Sandwich School provide for them to be held. Stow's amusing description [1] is too good to be missed.

Stow.

' I remember there repayred to these exercises amongst the Maisters and schollars of the free Schooles of S. Paules in London, of Saint Peters at Westminster, of Saint Thomas Acons Hospitall: whereof the last named commonly presented the best schollars, and had the prize in those dayes.

' This Priorie of S. Bartholomew, being surrendered to Henrie the 8. those disputations of schollars in that place surceased. And was againe, onely for a yeare or twaine, in the raigne of Edward the 6. revived in the Cloyster of Christs Hospitall, where the best Schollers, then still of Saint Anthonies schoole, were rewarded with bowes and arrowes of silver, given to them by Sir Martin Bowes, Goldsmith. Nevertheless, howsoever the encouragement fayled, the schollers of Paules, meeting with them of S. Anthonies, would call them Anthonie pigs, and they againe would call the other pigeons of Paules, because many pigions were bred in Paules church, and Saint Anthonie was always figured with a pigge following him: and mindfull of the former vsage, did for a long season disorderly in the open streete prouoke one another with Salve tu quoque, placet tibi mecum disputare, placet: and so proceeding from this to questions in Grammar, they usually fall from wordes to blowes, with their Satchels full of bookes, many times in great heaps that they troubled the streets, and passengers: so that finally they were restrained with the decay of Saint Anthonies schoole.'

Skill in disputing was essential to any student who aspired to a degree, and the work done in the Grammar Schools was a very necessary and useful preliminary to the more advanced and intricate disputations held at the Universities. Brinsley approves of disputing as a daily exercise, and recommends the study of John Stockwood's *Grammatical Disputations*. According to John Clarke's *Formulae Oratoriae*, Oratorical Disputations, developing from Grammatical Disputations, were delivered by defendens, opponens, moderator, and laurifer. The speeches were constructed in the same way as a Theme. Clarke gives a list of subjects which range from classical matters to subjects of general interest:

Oratorical Disputations.

[1] *Survay of London*, 1603, p. 75.

lx   *Introduction*

'Ajaci potius quam Ulysso, Achillis arma deferri debeant?
Diogenis dolium, an Alexandri solium expetibilius sit?
Lucretia bene fecit, quando seipsam interfecit?
Honesta mors turpi vitae sit anteferenda.
Qui ducit uxorem, libertati valedicit?
Educatio publica privatae praeferenda sit?
Magnates sint magnetes?
Praestat aquam an vinum bibere?
Dominetur regibus aurum?'

and so on, all equally and appallingly academic and unprofitable.[1] The modern counterpart is the debate, which still flourishes, not only in schools, but at the Universities, particularly in America.

Richard Sherry.   Richard Sherry has some illuminating remarks on the subject in his 'Treatise of the Figures of Grammer and Rhetorike, profitable for al that be studious of Eloquence, and in especiall for suche as in Grammer scholes doe reade moste eloquente Poetes and Oratours', 1555. 'Every good and eloquent oration must have three principall virtues,' he says, 'that it be pure, playn, and garnished. To these there are as many contrary vices. Barbarous, dark, and ungarnished.' In the section 'De Inornato', 'Of ungarnished', he enumerates the following faults:

Pleonasmus, Perittologia, 'a superfluous addyng of woordes', Tautologia, Periergia, 'when in a small matter we spend many words', Macrologia, 'when ... the whole oration ... is lenger then it should be', Tapinosis, 'when a weighty and high matter is brought downe by basenes of a worde', Bomphiologia, 'when light and tryfling matters, are set out with gaye and blasing wordes', Asiatismus, 'full of figures and wordes, lackyng matter', A*r*schrologia, 'when through the fault of ioynyng wordes together, some uncleanly meaning may be gathered', Cacemphaton, 'when letters and syllables hang evil favouredly together', Cacozelia, 'a pevishe desyre to folowe suche a kynde of wrytyng as thou arte not mete for', Aschematon, 'when in the oration there is no varietie'. The intricacy and difficulty of the exercise are only too apparent.

It would be, as Foster Watson says, an 'interesting enquiry to discover the processes whereby the teaching of Latin as a spoken

---

[1] Vives protests against this and demands that the matters debated should have some relevance to life.

language gave way to Latin as a written language'. The process was a gradual one, affected greatly by the growth in importance of the vernacular, the procurability of text-books, and the increasing cheapness of books and paper. When text-books had been inaccessible, incomprehensible, and, in smaller schools, perhaps unprocurable, when paper had been expensive and the art of writing not easily acquired, then teaching had to be entirely oral, and the medium between teacher and pupil was the language required of every scholar and of most substantial persons—Latin. But when Anwykyll and Stanbridge began to teach Latin at Magdalen College School by means of English, they dealt a blow to its supremacy as a spoken language, and by using the vernacular in conjunction with Latin they, with their successor, Whittinton, helped to give the English language stability and dignity and make it a speech fit 'for English men'.

VULGARIA STANBRIGIANA

PLATE III

Title-page of Stanbridge's *Vulgaria*, printed by Wynkyn de Worde in 1519. Reproduced by permission of the H. E. Huntington Library.

UULGARIA STA*N*BRIGIANA[1]

SInciput et vertex caput occiput et coma crinis

    Hoc sinciput /is   the fore parte of the heed.
    hic vertex /is   the crowne of the heed.
    hoc caput /is   for a heed
5 hoc occiput /is   the hynder parte of the heed.
    hec coma /e   for a busshe.
    hic crinis /is   for heer.

Cincinius cranium cerebrum sutura pilusq*ue*.

    hic cincinius /i   for a locke.
10 hoc cranium /i   for the brayne panne.
    hoc cerebrum /i   for the brayne.
    hec sutura /e   for the seme in the heed
    hic pilus /i   heer.

O[s][2] facies oculus acies albugo / pupilla.

15 hoc os /is   for a mouth
    hec facies /ei   for a face.
    hic oculus /i   for an eye.
    hec acies /ei   for the syght of the eye.
    hec albugo /is   for the whyte of the eye
20 hec pupilla /e   for the apple of the eye.

Frons intercilium gena barba supercilium.

    hic frons /tis   for the foreheed.
    hoc intercilium /i   the space bytwene   browes
    hec gena /e   for the eyelydde
25 hec barba /e   for a berde.
    hoc supercilium /i   for the browe aboue.

Palpebra nigrum oculi / cilium / sic angulus hircus.

    hec palpebra /e   for the eyelydde.
    hoc nigrum oculi   the blacke of the eye.

---

[1] The somewhat irregular punctuation of the original has been followed to the end of the lists of words.   [2] *Text* Of

2 Vulgaria Stanbrigiana

hoc cilium /i the brye of the eye.
hic angulus /i for the corner of the eye.
hic hircus /i idem.

Tempus os : et bucca / cartilago quoque mala.

hoc tempus /is for the temple of the heed 5
hoc os ossis for a bone
hec bucca /e for the cheke
hec cartiligo /is for a grystell.
hec mala /e for the ball of the cheke.

Uultus / maxilla / mandibula / ruga / molaris. 10

hic vultus /us for a countenaunce.
hec maxilla /e for a cheke
hec mandibula /e for the holow parte of ẙ cheke.
hec ruga /e for a wrynkle proprely in ẙ face
hic molaris /is for a gome tothe. 15

Interceptum / interfinium / [gi]ngiua[1] palatum.

hoc interceptum /i for the brydge of the nose.
hoc interfinium /i idem.
hec [gi]ngiua[1] /e for the gome.
hoc palatum /i for the rofe of the mouthe. 20

Dens / latus / duplex / intersticium / genninus.

hi[c][2] dens /tis for a tothe.
Dens latus for the tothe before.
Dens duplex for the gome tothe
hoc intersticium for the space bytwene ẙ tethe. 25
hic genninus for the gome tothe.

Dens colu[m]elaris[3] / maxillaris / et caninus.

Dens colu[m]elaris[3] ẙ rounde tothe next ẙ eye tothe
Dens maxillaris for the gome tothe.
Dens caninus for the eye tothe. 30

Lingua / nares / nasus / labrum / labiumque / labellum.

hec lingua /e for a tongue
hec naris /is for the nosethryll

[1] *Text* iungiua [2] *Text* his [3] *Text* colunelaris

Vulgaria Stanbrigiana

hic nasus /i   for the nose
hoc labrum /i   for a lyppe.
hoc labium /i   idem
hoc labellum   idem

5 M[u]cus[1] sic mentum collum guttur iugulusque.

  hic mucus /i   for the snyuell
  hoc mentum /i   for a chynne
  hoc colum /i   for a necke
  hoc guttur /is   for a throte
10 hic iugulus /i   idem

Ceruix arteria sublinguium gurgulioque.

  hic ceruix /is   the nappe of the necke
  hec arteria /e   the wynde pype
  hoc sublinguium   the wynde flappe
15 hic gurgulio   idem

Auris et auricula glans et tonsillaque iunges.

  hic auris /is   for the organ of the ere
  hec auricula   for a lytell ere
  hec glans /is   for a wexe kernell
20 hec tonsilla /e   idem

Unula faux rictus frumen tergum gula dorsum.

  hec vnula /e   for ẙ flap ẙ couereth ẙ wynde pype
  he[c][2] faux /cis   for a cheke
  hic rictus /us   for ẙ compace of ẙ mouthe.
25 hoc frumen /is   for the throte bolle
  hoc tergum /i   for the backe
  hec gula /e   for the meet pype.
  hoc dorsum /i   for a backe

Spiritus anhelitus halitus cutis caro pellis.

30 hic spiritus /us   for the brethe
  hic anhelitus   for the pantynge
  hic halitus /i   for brethe
  hec cutis /is   for skynne

---

[1] *Text* Mocus   [2] *Text* he

4 Vulgaria Stanbrigiana

hec caro /is	for flesshe
hec pellis	for a skynne

Uena / membrana / sanguis / cruor / atqᵘᵉ varix dic

Hec vena /ne.	for a vayne	
Hec membrana /e.	for ẏ lytell skynne in the flesshe.	5
hic sanguis /inis.	for blode.	
hic cruor /oris.	idem	
hic varix /cis.	for the vayne in the thyge	

Atrabilis / colera / sputum / pituitaqᵘᵉ flegma

Hec atrabilis	for the melancoly	10
hec colera	for the coloure	
hoc sputum /ti.	for the spytell	
hec pituita /te.	for the fleume or the pyppe	
hoc flegma	for fleme.	

Spinaqᵘᵉ / cum scapula / pectus / torax / humerusqᵘᵉ.   15

Hec spina /ne.	for the backe bone	
hec scapula.	for the sholder blade	
hoc pectus /oris.	for a brest	
hic torax /cis.	for a chest	
hic humerus /ri.	for a sholder	20

Interscapilium / latus / alaqᵘᵉ / costa / papilla.

hoc interscapiliuᵐ	for ẏ space bytwene ẏ sholders.	
hoc lat[us] /ris ¹.	for a syde	
hec ala /le.	for an arme hole	
hec costa /te.	for a rybbe.	25
hec papilla /e.	for a pappe heed.	

Mamma / mamilla / simul vber / compago / medulla

Hec mamma /e.	for a pappe.	
hec mamilla.	for a lytel pappe / or for ẏ teet.	
hoc vber /is.	idem	30
hec compago /is.	for ioynynge .ij. Ioyntes togyder.	
hec medulla /le.	for mary.	

¹ *Text* later.

Vulgaria Stanbrigiana

Brachium / & gybber / cubitus / manus / vlna lacert*us*   A. iii

Hoc brachium /i.	for the arme
hoc gibber /ris.	for ẙ brawne of the arme
hic cubitus /ti.	for a cubyte
5 hec manus	for a hande.
hic lacertus	ẙ space bytwen ẙ sholder to ẙ elbowe

Muscul*us* / et call*us* / pugn*us* / digit*us* / vola / palma.

hic musculus	for the calfe of the legge
hic callus	the hardnes in ẙ hande or fote.
10 hic pugnus	for a fyste
hic digitus	for a fynger
hec vola	the holownes in the hande
hec palma	the basse in the hande.

Nodus / et articulus / vnguis / fissuraq*ue* neruus.

15 Hic nodus	for a Ioynt
Hic condylus	for a knokle.
hic articulus	for a too
hic vnguis	for the nayle of a man.
hec fissura	ẙ space bytwene the fyngers & toos
20 hic neruus	for a senowe

Ac internodium / pulsus / brachialeq*ue* / pollex.

Hoc internodium	the space bytwene the ioyntes.
hic pulsus	for betynge of the vaynes
hoc brachiale	for a wrest
25 Hic pollex	for a thombe

Index / et medicus / anularis / et auricularis

Hic index	for the formest fynger.
hic anularis	for the mydle fynger
hic medicus	for the leche fynger
30 hic auricularis	for the lytell fynger

Cor / epar / atq*ue* iecur / fel / splen / precordia lien.

hoc cor	for a herte
hoc epar	for a lyuer.
hoc iecur	for a mawe

6 Vulgaria Stanbrigiana

hoc fel	for a gall
hoc splen	for the mylte
In plurali hec precordia.	for the herte strynges
hoc lien	for the longe gutte

Pulmo / rien / stomachus / ren / omentum dyafragma.

hic pulmo	for the longe
hic rien	for the raynes of the backe
hic ren	idem
hic stomachus	for the stomacke.
hoc omentum	for the kell.
hoc diafragma	for the mydryf

Intestinum / vmbilicus / cincturaque / venter

Hoc intestinum	for a bowell
hic vmbilicus	for a nauel.
hec cinctura	for the gyrdle stede
hic venter	for a bely.

Ilia / vesica / fibre / renunculus / aluus

In plurali hec ilia	for the small ropes
hec vesica	for the bladder
He fibre	for small vaynes.
hic renunculus	for the kydney
hec aluus	for a bely or paunche

Sumen / coxa / nates / podex / lumbus / quoque pubes

hoc sumen	for the fatnesse of the flanke
hec coxa	for a hyppe
hec nates	for a buttocke
Hic podex	for an ars hole.
hic lumbus	for a loyne
hic pubes	for a share.

Inguen / vrina / locium / penis / membrum genitale.

Hoc inguen	for the share
hec vrina	for pysse.
hoc locium	idem
hic penis	for a mannes yerde
hoc membrum genitale.	idem.

Vulgaria Stanbrigiana

Ramex / aquaticus / vrine fistula / tubus

    hec ramex   for the codde
    hic aquaticus   for the bladder
    hec fistula vrine   the pype in a mannes yerde.

5 Scortum / testiculus / vterus / crus / vuluaq*ue* matrix

    Hoc scortum   for the codde
    hic testiculus   for a stone
    hic vterus   for a bely.
    hoc crus   for a thyghe
10 hec vulua   locus vbi puer concipitur
    hec matrix   idem

Est genitura / femur / semen / strea / dic quoq*ue* sura

    Hec genitura   for nature of a man
    hoc femur   for a thyge.
15 hoc [s]emen.[1]   for the sede of a man.
    hec strea   for a shynne
    hec sura.   idem

Tibia / sicq*ue* genu / poples / pes / malleolusq*ue*

    hec tibia   for a legge
20 hoc genu   for a knee
    hic poples   for a hamme
    hic pes   for a fote
    hic malleolus.   for an ankle.

Vertebra / sic digitus pedis / et calx / plantaq*ue* subtal.

25 Hec vertebra   for the whyrlebone.
    hic digitus pedis.   for a too
    hic calx.   for a hele
    hec planta   for the sole of the fote
    hoc subtal.   idem

30   Finis.

[1] *Text* femen.

8   *Vulgaria Stanbrigiana*

    o/garment   e/clothe   i/idem   i/apparayle.
Dic indumentum / vestis / vestitus / amictus.

    i/idem   i/idem   i/idem.
Ornatus simul / apparatus amiculus idem.

          i/a cappe   e/a hatte   idem. 5
Ista caput gestat / apes / caliptra / galerus.

o/a cappe i/idem i/an hood o/idem.
Biretum / pilius / cucullus / capiciumq*ue*.

e/gowne shorte idem longe idem.
Toga / subducta / curtata / dimissa / talaris. 10

  Syngle   lyned   furred   o/gowne.
Simplex / duplata / pellita / pallium adde.

e/lynynge i/bosom full of plytes e/plyte e/idem.
Duplatura / sinus / sinnosus / plicaq*ue* / ruga.

e/a hemme e/coler   e/purfle e/idem i/idem. 15
Fimbra / collaris / simul instica / fascia / limbus.

i/a cloute o/idem o/idem.
Penulus vel penuculum / penuculamentum.

i/doblet e/cote e/petycote e/iaket. i/mantell.
Deplois / et tunica / tunicella / tunicula clamis. 20

e/sleue i/cloke o/a shorte gowne
Manica / bardiacus / hemitogium / bardocucullus.

e/a sherte e/breches e/a gloue e/a sherte i/a gyrdlestede.
Interula / bracce / cyrotheca / subucula / cinctus.

o/gyrdell e/purse o/idem. e/gyrdle e/idem. 25
Cingulum / crumena / marsipium / zonula / zona.

  to lace e/a lace to lace togyder vnlace.
Fibulor / et fibula / confibulor refibulorq*ue*.

  shorte e/hose i/e/o/to the knee longe.
Curtate / calige / cincturales / quoq*ue* longe. 30

e/a poynt e/a lace e/lachet i/a pynson.
Cordula / cum ligula corriga / calceolusq*ue*.

i/a sho e/slypper i/a buskyn e/bote i/socke.
Calceus / et crepida / cothurnus / & occrea / soccus.

  e/a stomacher e/pynne o/tache e/ne[dl]e.[1] 35
Fascia pectoralis / acicula / spinter / et acus.

    o/garter   o/idem.
Hijs subligaculum / necnon et subligar adde.

o/blade o/hafte o/idem e/shethe
Ferrum / manubrium / capulus / vinaq*ue* cuspis. 40

e/edge i/knyfe dull parelles sharpe.
Acies / cultellus / obtusus / infestus / acutus.

[1] *Text* nelde

Vulgaria Stanbrigiana 9

   o/a frontlet   o/kall   o/bonet   o/kall   e/payre of burlettes.
Mundum / reticulum / mitrum / crinale / mitella.

   o/keuerchef   o/idem   e/idem   fyllet   o/an apron.
Flameum / flaminium / rica / vitta / gremiale.

5 i/rynge   e/broche   o/an agnus dei   o/a seale.   e/a rynge for the eere.
Anulus / armilla / monile / sigillum / martis.

   o/a napkyn   e/a lytell keuerchefe.   o/a napkyn.
Lintheolum / simul et ricula / sudariolumq*ue*.

   o/idem   e/a pyncase.
10 Sudarium iungas simul acicuraria theca

   o/bedde   e/chambre   i/bedde   o/inerchambre   o/idem.
Stratum / cubiculum / lectus / penitrale / penates.

   o/bedde   i/idem   i/chambre   e/bedborde   a bedfote.
Cubile / thoras / thalamus / et spondaq*ue* / fulcrum.

15 o/strawe   o/idem   o/bolster   e/federbede   i/blanked.
Stramen / stramentum / ceruical / culcitra / lodix.

   o/matres   o/saye   o/pylowe   e/shete   a couerlet.
Tormentum / stragulum / puluinar / linthea / thoral.

   e/case   o/ testour   e/curtayne   o/idem.
20 Teca / canopium / peristroma / peripetasma.

   o/benche   o/stole   e/pyspot   e/idem   e/sege.
Scamnum / scabellum / matula / matella / latrina

   o/pyse   e/idem   comyn sege   a/tourde.
Locum / vrina / cum forica / facio / stercus.

25   idem   idem   a farte stynke   shyte   pysse.
Donsorio / cacco / fedo / feteo / cumo / mingo.

   o/brusshe   o/combe   o/glasse   to brusshe   to combe.
Uericulum / pecten / speculum / verro quoq*ue* / pecto.

   o/dore   e/locke   e/keye   e/nayle.   o/dorebarre.
30 Hostium / sera / clauis / clauus / quoq*ue* pessulum adde.

   e/wyndowe   o/glasse   i/lattyse   i/a lytell keye.
Fenestra / vitrum / cancellus / clauiculusq*ue*.

   e/matche   i/flynt stone   e/boxe   candell   e/idem.
Sulphurata / silex / pixis / candela / lucerna.

35 o/a candelstyck   i/torche   i/taper   e/lanterne   o/talowe.
Candelabrum / lichinus / cereus / lanterna / sepumq*ue*.

   o/a presse   or a wardrop   i/a wardrope keper   to folde   clothes.
Estq*ue* / vestiarium / vestispicus / complico / vestes

   o/a courte   an hall   o/parlour   o/hall.
40 Atrium / et aula / cenaculum / tricliniumq*ue*.

   i/a courtyer   i/idem.
Hinc et atriales / simul alicus. esse feruntur.

   o/a preuy chābre   e/a carpet   i/coborde   o/carpet   hangynge.
Conclaue / tabes / abacus / tapetum / aulea.

10   *Vulgaria Stanbrigiana*

                e/borde
e/borde clothe e/table i/trestell o/quysshyn e/chayre clothe.
 Mapula / mensa / tripos / puluinar / cathedra mappa.

o/a towell o/napkyn o/lauer o/basyn.
 Mantile / mantilielum / gutturum / labrum.

o/a water basyn o/salte o/saller o/spone a dysshe. 5
 Manilium / sal / salinum / coclear quoq*ue* discus.

e/platter o/saucer dysshe e/sa[u]cer[1] plater.
 Lanx et cytabulum / patina / scutella / perapsis.

  i/for a sewer   chamberlayne.
 Ciborum appositor / simul architriclinus eis das. 10

e/pantre e/idem   botre.
 Cella / penaria / sic seruisiaria dicas.

e/a spence o/wyneseller e/idem i/butler.
 Penarium / et celarium / apoteca / promusq*ue*.

to drawe to drawe out to tunne e/tankarde barell. 15
 Promo / depromo / dolium / et amphora / cadus.

o/pype o/tunnynge dysshe e/spygot o/wyne.
 Doliolum / infundibulum / et clipsedra / vinum.

i/bottell e/idem i/drynke e/dreges e/ale   e/ryall.
 Uter / obba / potus / fex / seruisia quoq*ue* spuma. 20

i/tankarde e/flat pece i/standynge pece e/couer.
 Cantarus et patera / crater / acorona.

i/a cuppe o/a potte / or a cup o/couer e/crome i/breed.
 Cyphus / et poculum / operculum / et mica / panis.

i/chese o/crust o/gobet o/a lytell bytte. 25
 Caseus / et crustum / frustum / frustibulum adde.

  o/crust o/broken meet e/basket e/idem i/frayle.
 Crustellum / fragmentum / sistella / fiscina / corbis.

i/coke e/kechyn e/woman coke e/kechyn e/idem.
 Coquus / coquina / coqua / popina / culina. 30

i/e/scolyn e/synke   idem   i/fyre idem.
 Lixa / lauitrina / aquariolum / et focus / ignis.

i/chymney i/furneys o/the thowell of a chymney flambe.
 Caminus / fornax / infumibulum / quoq*ue* flamma.

i/smoke e/sote e/spercle e/bronde e/idem. 35
 Fumus / fuligo / fauilla / titio / torris.

e/a lytell bro*n*de o/spercle e/bronde e/cole i/idem i/asshes.
  Facula / sintilla / fax / pruna / carbo / cinisq*ue*.

  o/wood o/stycke   o/andyron e/chyppe i/tonges.
 Lignum / ligniculum / ipopirgium / assula / forceps. 40

i/bellous e/fyreforke o/idem   e/chyppes.
 Follis / furcilla / rotabulum / quisquillieq*ue*.[2]

     [1] *Text* sancer   [2] *Text* quisquilliesq*ue*.

Vulgaria Stanbrigiana 11

e/porte   o/caudron   i/idem   e/posnet   to broche.
Olla / calearium / cacabus / et ollula / veru.

e/flesshehoke e/fryengepanne e/slyse to sethe frye sethe.
Fuscina / sartago / spatula / coquo / frigo / elixo.

5 o/caudron   i/idem   e/pan   e/lytell pan   e/gyrdyron.
Ahenum / lebes / patilla / patillula / crates.

skumme   make redy   pople   idem   rost.
Dispumo / paro / ebulit / escuat / asso.

to drawe byrdes / clense   vnscale fysshe   to plucke byrdes.
10 Euisero / purgo / desquamo / iunge deplumo.

o/a morter e/pestell o/wortes o/grewell o/mustarde.
Mortarium pistulus / olus / ius / sinapiumq*ue*.

o/garlyke o/vergyous o/sauce.
Allium / acetum / condimentum / cimeusq*ue*.

15 cates or meet   i/cater   e/flesshe   vele.
Obsonium / obs[o]nator[1] / carnes / vituline.

befe   mutton   kydde   porke.
Boui[n]e[2] / simul ouine / heduline / porsine.

                                                             i/a ren*n*ynge
o/dragge i/well e/boket i/well i/ryuer i/lake water.
20 Haustru*m* / fons / situla / puteus / riuus / lacus / amnus.

i/a lytell ryuer e/water e/fysshepole o/ponde e/water.
Riuulus et lympha / piscina / stagnum / et aqua.

Herbarum nomina.

e/sage e/borage e/rosemary e/columbyne e/rue.
25 Saluia / borago / libatonis / brassica / ruta.

i/floure delyce i/ysope o/percely blacke worte.
Hyrios / ysophus / petrocilium / olisatrum.

e/crowfote o/tyme e/endyue o/fenell.
Acedula / timum / endiuia / feniculumq*ue*.

30 o/marygolde e/lettuce e/betony e/malous.
Et oliotropium / lactuca / betonica / malua.

e/holyhocke e/plantayn e/sauerey e/daysy.
Althea / plantago / saturgia / consolidaq*ue*.

o/sothernewood e/moderworte e/hertes tongue o/herbeton.
35 Abrotinum / artemesia / scolopendria / baccar.

o/lyly o/smallage e/ramys o/wormewood i/wake robyn.
Lilium / et apium / ramisis / absinthium / aron.

o/tansey e/stoncrop e/lauender.
Tansetum / paritaria / lauendula iunge.

40 e/myntes o/horsmynt watercresses e/horehounde.
Menta / mentastrum / nastaricium / cinoglossa.

---

[1] *Text* obsenator   [2] *Text* Bouiue

Nomina piscium.

o/salte fysshe   fresshe fysshe.
Est salsamentum simul et piscis fluuialis.

e/creuys   i/crab[b]e[1]   i/mullet   seelfysshe.
Licusta / cancer / mullus / vitulusq*ue* marinus.   5

e/porpos   i/storgyon   i/macrell   i/dolphyn.
Phoca / cum rombus / scombeus / sic quoq*ue* delphin.

e/cocle   i/cabege   e/oyster   i/c[o]nger.[2]
Coclea / sic capito / iungas simul ostrea / congrus.

salmon   i/morte   e/sprote i/hornkeke   e/cocle shell fysshe.   10
Salmo / mugil / apoa mutilus / et coclea concha.

o/herynge   e/thornebagge   i/pleys   i/whale   e/whyrlepole
Allec / radagia / pecten / cetusq*ue* / balena.

e/tenche   o/cheuyn i/e/dogfysshe   i/pyke   e/pykerell.
Loligo / clepa / canis / lupus atq*ue* lupillus.   15

i/barble   e/ele   e/shale   e/fynne.
Barbatilus / simul anguilla / squama / quoq*ue* pinna.

B. i   De pertinentibus ad equum.

o/sadle   o/brydle   e/rayne   o/styropeleder.
Epiphium / frenum / habena / sca*n*cilelorumq*ue*.   20

e/gyrthe   e/poytrell   e/croper   e/packsadle.
Cingula / antelo / postela / clitella.

e/packe   e/fardell   i/a dryuer of clothe.
Sarcina / sarcinale / hinc sarcinarius addas.

e/a male   e/a boget   hors combe   hors locke   25
Mantica / manticula / addas strigilis / quoq*ue* compes.

e/houe   e/pastoures   i/packe hors e/mane   e/idem.
Lingula / suffragines / clitellarius / iuba / caprona.

i/geldynge   e/mare   i/hors   ballocked
Cantherius / [e]qua[3] / simul equus / testiculatus.   30

i/cable   i/colte   i/a breker of a hors   to tourne to breke.
Caballus / pullus / agas[o][4] / flectoq*ue* domo

i/ambler   i/idem   i/trotter.
Gradarius / volutarius / successariusq*ue*.

to trotte   courser   to trotte   amble.   35
Succutio / sompus / simul et succutio / voluto.

to smell   touche   sobbe   to couche the coughe.
Olfacio / tango / singultio / tussio tussis.

here   taste   smellynge   vnderstan*de* touchynge.
Audio / gusto / simul olfactus / sentio / tactus   40

---

[1] *Text* crable   [2] *Text* canger.   [3] *Text* rqua   [4] *Text* agasa

Vulgaria Stanbrigiana·

<pre>
     herynge   i/seynge   i/vnderstandynge i/touchynge to se.
     Auditus / visus   /   sensus   / gustus videque

       gape   nese   i/stutter   to stutte i/lysper.
     Ossito / sternuto / balbus / balbutio / blesus
  5 to syghe or sobbe   spyt   to wagge the heed   to wynkle.
     Singultio   /   screo / conquinisco / conniueoque
                    e/a gogle eyed
    i/gogle eyed   woman   i/blere eyed i/spurblynde   e/idem.
     Strabo   /   straba   /   lippus /   luscus / iungesque cocles
         deef   squynt   blynde   he that loketh a squynte.
 10 Et surdus / petus / sic cecus   /   cecutiensque.
         dombe   lame   croked   idem   idem.
     Et mulus / et claudus / varus / curuusque / vietus.
         longe   tall   propre   vpryght   lytell   hye.
     Longus / procerus / elegans / rectus / breuis / altus.
 15   a dwerfe   idem   idem   idem.
     Homullus / nauus / homuntio / pomilioque.
         brode   consumed   fatte   idem   lene.
     Latus / abesus / crassis / pinguis / macrilentus.
         fatte or lene   small   lene   to belene.
 20 Sic corpulentus / gracilis / macerque / marcesco.
         fatnes   slowe or slacke   lene.
     Et pinguedo / cessabundus / sic maciesque.
          taryenge   slowe   idem   quycke.
     Sic cunctabundus / et signis / tardus / acutus.
 25   ¶ Finis.
</pre>

¶ The auctour.

All lytell chyldren besely your style ye dresse.
Unto this treatyse with goodly aduertence
These latyn wordes in your herte to impresse
30 To [t]hende¹ that ye may with all your intelligence
Serue god your maker holy vnto his reuerence
And yf ye do not / the rodde must not spare
You for to lerne with his sharpe morall sence
Take now good hede / and herken your vulgare.

35 Vulgaria quedam cum suis vernaculis compilata iuxta
       consuetudinem ludilitterarij diui pauli.
   Good morowe. Bonum tibi huius diei sit primordium.
   Good nyght. Bona nox / tranquilla nox / optata requies.

---

¹ *Text* hende

Good spede. Bona salus / salue / saluus sis / optata sal*us*.
How fares thou. Qua valitudine predit*us* es / vt vales.
Qua valitudine afficeris / vt te habes.
I fare well thanked be god.
Bene me habeo altithrono sit gratia. 5
Whyder goost thou. Quo tendis.
I go to syege. Ad foricam pergo.
Vulga. I shall bere the company. Comm[i]tabor[1] te / sociabo te.
sta*n*. I shall wayte on the. Obseruabo te / dabo tibi operam.
B. ij
I shall quyte the. Refera*m* tibi gratias / par pari refera*m*. 10
How doth my fader. Ut pater se habet.[2]
He was at the poynt of deth. Ferme moriens erat.
God be here. Assit deus.
Thou art welcome to me. Grat*us* est michi tuus adue*n*t*us*.
How is it with the. Ut tecum est. 15
Gyue me breed. Cedo mihi panem.
Thou shalte haue ony thynge that I haue.
Quicquid meum est obtinebis.
I am well at ease if I had dyned.
Bene me habeo si pransus essem. 20
Drynke fyrst and I wyll nexte.
Bibe prior et ego bibam posterior.
Drynke agayne. Gemina haustum.
Laye thy pledge. Depone pignus.
Laye thy shotte. Pone simbolum. 25
It is a gret helpe for scollars to speke latyn.
Non nihil conducit discipulis loqui latine.
I am sure ẙ louest me not. Co*n*stat mihi te me no*n* amare.
I was set to scole whan I was seuen yere olde.
Datus sum scolis cum septemnis eram. 30
From ẙ daye hiderwarde I was neuere kepte fro scole.
Ab eo tempore hucusq*ue* nunq*uam* a studio detentus sum.
Scolars must lyue hardely at Oxforde.
Scolasticos [o]xonij[3] parce viuere oportet.
Ther is one at the dore wyll speke with the. 35
Quidam apud hostium te conuentum expetit.
I praye the come se me at home. Reuise me domi queso.
What dooth he. Quid nam agit.

---

[1] *Text* Commutabor   [2] *Text* habeat.   [3] *Text* exonij

Vulgaria Stanbrigiana

He is waken. Uigilia tenet hominem.
He is a slype. Somnus opprimit eum.
He is fallen a slepe. [Iniuit]¹ somnum.
Garlyke maketh a man to slepe. Alium suadet homini somnum.
5 They go arme in arme. Insertis brachijs incedunt.
I wyll wrastle with the. Luctabor tecum.
If thou wrastle with me I shall laye the on thy backe.
Si mecum luctatus eris humi te prosternam.
I holde the a peny. Depono denarium tecum.
10 What hast thou done. Quid fecisti.
I haue dronke a ferthynge worthe of ale.
Exhausi ceruisiam quadrantis.
Leue thy chattynge. Desiste a tuis superbis gressibus.
I perceyue by many tokens thou arte not my frende.
15 Multis argumentis comperio te non meum amicum fore.
I was beten this mornynge. Dedi penas aurora.
The mayster hath bete me. Preceptor a me sumpsit penas.
I haue shewed the all my counseyle.
Tradidi tibi omnia mea consilia.
20 I haue loket longe for ẙ. Expectaui tuum aduentum iam diu.
For his folysshenes he may were a bable.
Ob stulticiam precium ferri potest.
I am lefte ale. Desertus sum.
Profred seruyce stynketh.
25 Ministerium oblatum sordescit.
It semeth a scolar to were a syde gowne.
Decet discipulum vti toga longa.
Wype thy nose. Munge nasum.
Snuffe the candell. Emunge lucernam.
30 I am rydde of my mo[n]eye.² Emunctus sum pecunia.
Syt awaye or I shall gyue the a blowe.
Amoue sedem / sinautem colaphum male addam.
Sayst thou this in ernest or in game.
Ioco an serio loqueris.
35 I may not holde³ my handes fro the.
Non possum manus a te continere.
We must note ete flesshe. A carnibus nobis abstinendum est.

¹ *Text* Innuit.   ² *Text* momeye.   ³ *Text* sholde

It is fastynge daye commaunded by the chyrche.
Est dies ieiunus indictus ab ecclesia.
It is halfe a daye.   Est dies inter scalaris.
He clypped me about ỹ myddle.   Me medium amplexus est.
I loue the as my lyfe.   Afficio te amore eque atque animam.
All my felowes hate thy company.
Omnes condiscipuli mei fastidiunt contibernium tuum.
My mynde gyueth me.   Animus mihi presagit.
I shall gyue the that I promysed the.
Reddam tibi quod pollicitus sum.
I praye the tell me whan the caryers come.
Queso fac me certiorem quum tabellarij venerint.
Fare well for this nyght.   Uale in hac nocte.
He hath taken my boke fro me.   Eripuit mihi librum.
Goo hens.   Confert te hinc / abi / discede / recede.
I goo in the cyte.   Confero me in vrbem.
I wyll bere the company.   Sociabo te / commitabor te.
Come hyther.
Ades / accede / aduenies / appropinqua / aggredere.
He came stelynge vpon me.   Adortus est me.
He came openly vpon me.   Aggressus est me.
It longeth to a scollar to speke latyn.
Att[ine]t[1] ad discipulum loqui latine.
All my trust is in the.   Tota mea spes in te est sita.
He is a secrete man.   Uir taciturnus est.
Tary me at home tyll I come.
Operire me domi donec venero.
I cane my rule without the boke.
Possum meum preceptum memoriter.
Thou stoppest my lyght.   Interpellas lumen.
Fetche me water for my handes.   Affer aquam manibus.
Drynke agayne.   Gemina haustum.
Reche me breed.   Porrige michi panem.
I am a thruste.   Sitis me tenet.
I am wery of study.   Tedet me studij.
I am wery of my lyfe.   Tedet me vite mee.
My mayster commaundeth hym to you.
Herus meus salutes tibi impertit.

[1] *Text* Attenit

Vulgaria Stanbrigiana

What countre man arte thou. Cuias es tu.
I am an englysshe man. Sum anglicus genere.
My fader is an aged man.
Pater meus est grand[e]uus.¹
5 I haue a grete waye to go. Grandis via mihi restat.
My purse is heuy with monye.
Crumena mea est nummis referta.
I lye in a feder bedde euery nyght.
Quiesco in culcitra plumali singulis noctibus.
10 He is a boystous man. Uir rudis est.
What parte synges thou. Qua voce cantas.
Thou spekest softly. Summisse loqueris.
Speke out. Aperte loquere.
I am almoost beshytten. Sum in articulo purgandi viscera.
15 Thou stynkest. Male oles.
I beshrowe the. Mala sit tibi gratia.
Well mote thou fare I praye god.
Ut bene valeas deum oro
I trow I shall be a good grammarian within a shorte whyle.
20 Puto me fore preceptum grammaticum breui spacio.
Yf ẙ take not hede to thy lernynge ẙ wylte neuer thryue.
Si libris non incumbueris nunquam rem facias.
What mynde arte ẙ in / to be a preest / or a wedded man.
Quid animi habes ad sacerdot[i]um² / an ad nuptias.
25 Laye the table. Sterne mensam.
Set salte and spones. Pone salinum et coclearia.
Thou arte a false knaue. Perfidus es.
My berde is not growen.
Barba mea nondum excreta est.
30 The fatte stycketh to the rofe of my mouthe.
Pinguedo carnium heret palato meo.
I haue not dyned. Impransus sum.
He is well washed. Est bene potus.
He is dronke with ale. Est captus ceruisia.
35 He is blynde. Est captus oculis.
He is madde. Est mente captus.
One sought for the at the door.
Unus quesiuit te apud hostium.

¹ *Text* grandiuus   ² *Text* sacerdotum

Vulgaria Stanbrigiana

I haue taryed for the an hole houre.
Parcontatus sum te integra hora.
I haue dyned.   Pransus sum.
I haue souped.   Feci cenam.
I haue broken my fast.   Feci ianctaculum.   5
Moche good do it you.   Proficiat vobis cibus.
Souper is done.   Cena est completa.
I am hongry.   Sum familicus.
I thruste.   Sitio.
The coke is a good seasoner of meet.   10
Cocus est bonus curator ciborum.
He is an outragyous ladde.   [S]celestus est.[1]
Lende me the copy of thy latyn and I shall gyue it the agayne by and by.
Comoda mihi exemplar materie latine : illico tibi reddam.   15
Thou playest the knaue.   Inhoneste te habes.
My fader hath had a grete losse in the see.
Pater meus magnam naufragium iacturam habuit.
Thou arte worthy to be hanged.   Dignus es furcis.
I had gret angre for ẙ.   Tuam ab amorem cepi inimicitias.   20
He his fallen a slepe.   Iniuit somnum.
I knowe it not.   Latet me / preterit me / fugit me.
I knowe not the mater.   Res clam me est.
I am sure of this mater.   Sum certus huius rei.
He is cunnynge in syngynge.   Peritus est cantandi.   25
I haue done as moche for the as thou for me.
Tuis beneficijs respondi.
I gyue the the maystry.   Concedo tibi.
I shall matche the at all games.
Equiparabo te singulis in ludis.   30
I am content with thy answere.
Placet mihi tuum responsum / cordi est mihi tuum responsum.
Thou hyttes the nayle on the heed.   Rem ipsam tangis.
I haue bespoken a payre of shone agayn sondaye.
Stipulatus sum calceos in diem dominicam.   35
Be the daye neuer so longe at last cometh euensonge.
Quantumuis dies prolixa sit / vespere tandem succedunt.

---

[1] *Text* Celestus

Vulgaria Stanbrigiana

He is euyll a colde that gooth naked in the frost.
Male frigescit qui nudus frigore incedit.
I haue pyte on the. Miseret me tui.
I am sente for to dyner. Accersor ad prandium.
5 Thou blames me without a cause.
Me accusas immerito.
Thou answered me not as thou sholde do.
Male mihi respondes.
His mouth is a wrye. Os sibi distrorsum est.
10 His nose is lyke a shoynge horne. Simus est homini nasus.
My throte is hoors. Guttur meum est raucum.
My brest is shryll. Uox mea est sonora.
My heed is full of lyce.
Caput meum est plenum pediculorum.
15 My heed aketh. Caput meum dolet.
Tourde in thy tethe. Merda dentibus inheret.
My heed is curled. Caput meum est crispum.
He is euer chattynge. Omni[n]o[1] garrit.
Bere out the dust. Effer puluerem.
20 Drawe water. Haure aquam.
I haue pleynte of wyne. Est mihi vini copia.
His speche pleased me not.
Sermo suus non est mihi cordi.
This wyne is of verdure. Hoc vinum est acre.
25 Hoc vinum confe[c]tum.[2] For ypocras.
The mayster gaue me a blowe on the cheke.
Preceptor colaphum male addit.
The tree hangeth full of apples.
Mala crescunt arbore referta.
30 The waye renneth full of shepe.
Oues curcitant via plena.
He is sowsed in water. Submergitur aqua.
The hors trottes. Equus succutit.
Chere thy gestes. Exillera conuiuas.
35 It lyeth not in my power. Non penes me est.
Take no thought. Securus sis.
Be mery and flee care. Gaude & curas fuge.

[1] *Text* omnio   [2] *Text* confestum

The fader is gladde to here his sone praysed.
Pater filium laudari libenter audit.
Thou hast begyled me.   Dedisti mihi verba.
What the deuyll does thou here.
Quid malum hic agis.   5
Thynke this of a surete.   Hoc pro certo habeto.
Thou strykest me that dare not stryke agayne.
Me percutis que referire non audeo.
If I were thy matche I wolde not dye in thy dette.
Si tibi equalis essem no*n* inultus morirer.   10
Thou shall not shape quyte.   Non impune abibis.
It is shrewed to Iape with naked swerdes.
Dubium est ioca strictis gladijs exercere.
He is croke backed.   Scapularis est.
He hath taken shyppe.   Con[s]cendit[1] nauem.   15
I shall kyll the with my owne knyfe.
Proprio gladio te interimam.
I hadde no leser to ete nor drynke.
Haud mihi potestas fuit comedendi aut bibendi.
My shoes ben broken.   Calcei sunt detriti.   20
I am wete shodde.   Pedes humect[a]nt.[2]
I were slyppers and pynsons.   Utor crepidis calceolis.
He came from hors euyn now.   Iam ab equo descendit.
He is boted and spurred and redy to ryde.
Ocrijs et calcaribus induitur et ad equum accingitur. 25
My handes breke out.   Manus pruriunt.
He is a kokolde.   Alter supponit vxorem suam.
He is moche in dette.
Multum est obnoxius ero alieno.
He hathe maryed a wyfe.   Duxit vxorem.   30
I shall mary my doughter to the.
Collocabo tibi gnatam.
I fere the mayster.
Timeo preceptorem vel a preceptore.
Thou spekes many wordes to me but nothynge to ẏ purpose. 35
Multa in verba facis sed nihil ad rem.
I force not.   Mea nil refert.
The meet is rawe.   Cibus est crudus.

[1] *Text* concendit   [2] *Text* humectunt

Vulgaria Stanbrigiana

The mete is soden ynough.   Cibus satis est coctus.
The flesshe is rosted ynough.   Carnes sat assantur.
The latyn is full of fautes.   Materia latina est me*n*dosa
I haue blotted my boke.   Obleui librum.
5 I pray the wryte me my latyn.
Ex[a]ra¹ materiam latinam oro.
The chyldre*n* be sterynge about in the maistres absence.
Absentia preceptoris paruuli inquietes sunt.
I do this by my nature.   Meapta hoc facio.
10 It is gyuen the of kynde to shote well.
Tuapte bene [s]agittas.²
He rynseth the pottes.   Euacuat ollas.
He drynketh well bothe on $\stackrel{e}{y}$ faders syde & moders syde.
Ex vtroq*ue* parte aptus a[d]³ bibendum nascitur.
15 He is deed.   Obijt morte*m*.   Defunctus est.   Mortuus est.
Expirauit animam.   Mundo ademptus est.
Humanis reb*us* eximit*ur*.   Emisit spiritu*m*.   Efflauit spiritu*m*.
A mayster i*n* scole.   Preceptor & didascul*us*.   Monitor.   Instructor.   Gimnasiarcha.   Pedotripes.
20 A mayster.   Herus.   D*omi*n*us*.   Mandator.   Magister.
A ussher.   Ipodidasculus.
They be at dyryge.   Missa pro defunctis celebratur.
Saye de profundis.   Dicantur preces pro defunctis.
Thou fedest me forth with wordes.   Me tenes verbis.
25 I praye the vtter not this mater.
Oro ne hec res palam fiat.
Yf I scape this dau*n*ger I wyll neuer aue*n*ture somoche.
Si hoc malu*m* diuitauero nu*n*q*uam* vsq*ue* adeo p*er*iclo me obijcia*m*.
Proue me wheder I loue the or not.
30 Fac periculum ante prosequor amor necne.
I coniecture in my mynde what thou menes.
Facio coniecturam quid tibi queris.
What menes thou.   Quid tibi vis.
Appoynte me where I shall mete with the.
35 Statue mihi tempus quo te conueniam.
I wyll not begyle the.   Haud te fallem / haud te decipia*m*.
Syth I went hens I was neuer mery.
Ex quo hinc profectus sum nunq*uam* affectus sum leticia.

¹ *Text* Exera   ² *Text* fagittas   ³ *Text* ab

I am at my wyttes ende. Sum incertus animi.
Thou arte a blabbe. Futilis es.
I loue the. Te amore amplector / te amore complector.
This potte wyll holde no water. Hec colla effundit aquam.
He kepeth his feest to daye. Celebrat conuiuium hodie. 5
Tary not. Ne moram facias. Ne moram trahas.
Thou hast serued me gentylly. Tractasti me liberaliter.
I haue money. Est mihi pecunia.
I haue breed. Est mihi panis.
I remembre not my lesson. Immemor sum lectionis. 10
We must go to the feldes on thursdaye.
Petendum est nobis agros in die iouis.
I was not borne to a helfpeny. Neutiquam heres natus sum.
We were borne in one countre. In vno solo nati sumus.
Therfore we must loue well togyder. 15
Mutuo nos igitur amare oportet.
Ryot is the destruccyon of all yonge men.
Intemperantia adolescentum omnium pernicies est.
He standeth in is owne conceyt. Hic magni se precij putat.
He craketh of his noble actes. Hic gloriatur de preclaris gestis. 20
He is ȳ veryest cowherde ȳ euer pyst. Imbellissimus est omnibus.
He is euyll fauoured. Informis est. Deformis est.
He is fallen a slepe. [Iniuit]¹ somnum.
Beggers be regged & baudy. Mendici scuti & squalidi sunt.
Brusshe thy gowne. Verre togam tuam. 25

Vulga. Rake ȳ fyre. obrue ignem. garter thy hose. subliga caligas.
stan.
C. i Clapse thy gowne. Consibulare togam.
Tye thy poyntes. Noda cordula.
Untye thy poyntes. Enoda cordulas.
It is the properte of a woman to vse scoldynge. 30
Ingenium est mulierem conuicia exercere.
I shall be bete. Dabo penas / sumam supplicium.
Thou hast quyt thyselfe well. Strenuum virum te prebuisti.
Let me alone a lytell whyle.
Mitte me parumper. Sine me parumper. 35
I haue made a loue daye bytwene theym.
Feci fedus inter eos. Reddidi eos amicos.
Archery is gyuen to me of nature. Sagittatio mihi innata est.

¹ *Text* Innuit

Vulgaria Stanbrigiana

Though peper be blacke it hathe a good smacke.
Tamen si piper nig[ri]¹ coloris sit bene sapit tamen.
Bende thy bowe. Tende arcum.
I wyll shote at buttes / pryckes / or rouers.
5 Sagittabo tecum ad metas / limites certos / aut incertos.
Thou arte harde herted. Admodum difficilis es.
I am let with other besynes. Alijs curis impedior.
I can not wayte upon the. Nequeo te obseruare.
He hath ordeyned a staffe for his owne heed.
10 Laqueum sibi ipsi perauit. Wheder away. Quorsum tendis.
Se how lyke the one broder is the other.
Vide quam uterque frater alteri similis est.
He is a man borne of this towne. Est ciuis natus.
It is ẙ gretest madnes of ẙ world to loue & be not loued agayne.
15 Extrema dementia est non amantem afficere amore.
I gaue no occasyon. Non optuli tibi occasionem.
He lay with a harlot al nyght. concubuit cum pellice tota nocte.
I sate at the table with the mayre and the sheryues.
Discubui in mensa cum prefecto ac vicecomitibus.
20 Thou hast bewrayed my conseyle. perdidisti consilium meum.
Yf thou be angry with me without a cause / thou shall be made
   at one without a mendes.
Si abs re mihi succensueris immunis reconsiliaberis.
I shal fynde the ynough to do to day. Hodie te exercebo.
25 Without a cause. Abs re / iniuria / immerito / iniuste.
Thou takes ẙ best morsell thyselfe / & leuest me ẙ worst.
Morsus lautissimos tibi carpis & mihi pessimos relinques.
Thou lyes. Fingis. Deliras a veritate. Commentum facis.
Erras / non recte dicis.
30 I am dyspoynted of an hors. Defraudor equo.
I am faderles and moderles. Orbor parentibus.
I am mased in my mynde. Confectus sum in animo.
Attonitus sum in animo. Consternatus sum in animo.
My fader hathe a backe hous. Patri meo pistrina est.
35 Let me alone or I shall complayne on the.
Mitte me sin autem querar de te.
Thou hast conforted me wel. Pulchre animum releuasti.
Tourne on the ryght hande. Verte dextrorsum.

¹ *Text* niger

24   *Vulgaria Stanbrigiana*

Ryght forthe on thy nose.   Recta via incede.
Take not my wordes to herte.   Ne egre feras dicta mea.
My tethe ben on edge.   Dentes obtupescunt.
Take hede to thy selfe.   Caue tibi / obserua teipsum / prospice tibi / consule tibi / cura teipsum.
Fyrst.   Primum ad tempus / primo ad locum.   5
I loue ⁊ as well as ony man.   Nem*i*ni se*cu*ndu*s* su*m* re in ama*n*do.
Agere gra*ti*as / ve*r*bis habere gra*ti*as / a*n*i*m*o referte gratias in re.
I am ⁊ best louer thou has[t].[1]   Tu[i] [2] amantissimus sum.
I haue made mery this daye.   Hunc diem in leticia degi.
To lyue.   Agere vitam / degere vitam / ducere spiritum.   10
The waye is foule.   Via cenolenta est.
Vulga. The waye is fayre.   Via puluerulenta est.
sta*n*.
C. ij Y̊ waye is slabby.   Via labilis e*st*.   ⁊ arte unky*n*de.   i*n*grat*us* es.
I haue spent in wast.   Cantriui.   Abliguriui / dissipaui.
If ony man aske for me / saye thou sawe me not.   15
Si quis me querat negate me vidisse.
Nyght is comen vpon me.   Nox me oppressit.
There is a smyth on the other syde of my faders house.
Fabrica est opposita edibus paternis.
My moder lyeth in hale.   Mater mea iacet in decubijs.   20
Herken.   Audi / ausculta / aduerte / arrige aures / hauri.
I am syke.   Eger sum / egrotus sum / male me habeo / valetudinarius sum.
Come out.   Exi / egredere.
I haue dyspoynted hym of his purpose.   25
Reddidi animum eius incertum.
I haue a good cause to chyde with the.
Est mihi iusta causa obiurgandi tecum.
Thou arte worthy to be bette.   Dignus es plagis.
My nose leueth bledynge.   Nasus sistit sanguinem.   30
Drawe a cuppe of ale.   Propine ceruisiam cypho pleno.
I am angry w*ith* ⁊.   Irascor tibi / stomachor ti*b*i.   Succe*n*seo ti*b*i.
Hold vp thy heed.   Tolle caput.   make a kne.   curua genu.
Holde vp thy handes.   Tende manus.
Stoupe downe.   Flecte genu.   35
Tourne the spytte.   Rota verutum.
He wepeth.   Effundit lachrymas.

[1] *Text* hase   [2] *Text* Tue

Vulgaria Stanbrigiana 25

Thou mockes me.
Irrides me / illudis mihi / derides me / ludificaris me.
Stande out of my waye. Cede mihi [/] concede mihi. da mihi locum
He is redy to fyght.   Paratus est ad pugnam.
5 It is my propyte.   Mea natura est / meum est ingenium / mos
  meum est.
He is po[y]soned.¹   Interfectus est veneno.
Hec nouerca. A stepmoder. Hec quadra. A trenchour.
He burste in the myddle.   Crepuit medius.
10 Hic & hec patruelis / an vncle or aunte on ẙ fader syde.
Hic & hec matruelis / on the moders syde.
He lened on me.   Declinauit in me / hesit mihi cubitis.
He plucketh me by the nose.   Vellit nasum meum.
I am seuen yere olde.   Septemnis sum.
15 I lacke a boke.   Deest mihi liber.
Thou hast take my goodes fro me.   Priuasti me bonis.
Yelowe. Fulnus. Grene virudis. Cerules. Blew / blodius.
Crymsyn / purpureus / coccineus.   scarlet Ruteus.
Sad colour.   Color intensus.   Lyght colour / color remissus.
20 Motley / polimitus.   How olde arte thou.   Quotennis es.
He smote me with a dager.   Me pugione percussit.
He is a lyue. Superstes est / res agit humanas / spiritus suos
  regit / aura vestitur ethera / anhelat spiritum / humanis par-
  ticipat / vita manet / cor homini viuendum est.
25 The henne sytteth on the egges.   Gallina incubat ouis.
The corne rypeth fast.   Seges candescit.
I haue knowen hym sythe he was borne.
Ab incunabilis hominem noui.
He ranne awaye without leue.   Si[ne]² copia aufugit.
30 The henne hathe layde an egge.   Galina exclusit ouum.
It is euyll with vs whan the mayster apposeth vs.
Male nobiscum est cum preceptor examinat nos.
Here be many praty maydes.
Hec sunt multe lepide puelle.
35 Lyfte vp bothe thy handes to god.
Ambas palmes ad celum tolle.
It is out of my mynde.   Excidit a memoria.
Egressum est a memoria.

¹ *Text* ponsoned   ² *Text* Siue

26   Vulgaria Stanbrigiana

<small>Vulga.
sta*n*.
C. iij</small>
What trust is now a dayes.
Hijs diebus cui est fides adhibenda.
He is a nygarde.   Parcus est.
He is a waster.   Profusus est pecunie.
He dyde it for the nones.   Ex industria fecit.   5
He is dylygent.   Obsequiosus est.
I am so feble that I can not stande on my fete.
Adeo sum impotens q*uam* pedibus stare nequeo.
Thou takest me otherwyse than I speke.
Me aliorsum capis q*uam* loquor.   10
Be ware in welthe or thou be wo.
Secundis in rebus caue anteq*uam* aduerse co*n*tigerint.
I haue no leaser to conne my latyn.
Non est mihi ocium sciendi materiam latinam.
Thou has done me wronge.   Intulisti mihi iniuria*m*.   15
Thou byleues me not.   Non adhibes mihi fidem.
I trust not the.   Non est mihi fides apud te.
His face is meruaylously chaunged.
Vultus eius admodum immutatur.
Iacke napes maketh a mowe.   Simea os distorquet.   20
He is besy in askynge questyons.   Curiosus est.
It is accordynge.   Equu*m* est / pax est / co*n*uenit / congruit.
Consonum est.   Dignum est.   Decet.
Stande styll.   Siste gradum.   Resiste.   Fuge gradum.
He is a pacient man.   25
Vir leuis est.   Vir facilis est.   Vir procliuus est ad venia*m*.
Put awaye all fere thou hast no cause to be aferde.
Amoue metum non est tibi timendi occasio.
I coughed all nyght.   Tussebam tota nocte.
My nose bledeth.   Nasus effundit sanguinem.   30
He is a noble man of warre.
Egregius est armis.   Bellicosus est.
It is a goodly woman.   Est mulier egregia forma.
It is a grete whyle sythe.   Non nihil temporis est.
[Thou]¹ make to longe talkynge.   Omnis prolixa oratio tua.   35
Make an ende.   Impone dicendi finem.
He hathe spued all in his bely.   Om*n*ia comesta reiecit.
I shall shewe the in fewe wordes.   Paucis dicam.

¹ *Text* I

Paucis soluam. Expediam.
We must go to the feldes. Petendum est agris.
My fader is a grete man of landes.
Pater meus est ample possessionis.
5 My fader is thryfty. Pater meus frugi homo est.
Chyldre*n* be brought vp w*ith* gret cost of ẙ fader & moder.
Liberi magno sumptu parentum educantur.
It is not for nought. Non timere est.
I knowe not the mater. Res clam me est.
10 I haue the maystry. Concedo mihi palmam.
They make a fraye in the strete. Turbatur in platea.
I am fallen in the maysters conceyte.
Iniui gratiam preceptoris tui.
I haue gete the maysters fauoure.
15 Conciliaui gratiam preceptoris.
I was not borne to a fote of lande.
Neutiq*uam* natus sum.
A gyuen hors may not [be][1] loked in the tethe.
Donati equi non respicere licet.
20 Not yet. Non dum. Necdum.
On this halfe. Istorsum.
My fader dwelleth in the countre.
Pater meus rure commoratur.
It is out of my mynde. A memoria exigit.
25 I wyll not leue the.
Non te distituam. Non te derelinq*uam*. Non te deseram.
It is a c[h]yldysshe[2] thynge. Puerile est.
I haue bredde. Est mihi panis. Preditus sum pane.
I haue forgete my lesson. Immemoria sum lectionis.
30 I go to the cytee. Peto vrbem.
He playeth well at organs. Bene pulsat organa.
I am as good as y̎ in grammer. Equip*ar*abo te [in][1] gram*m*atica.
Equiualeo tibi in grammatica.
This gowne is mete for me. Hec toga mihi conuenit.
35 He is drunke.
Ebrius est. Tamulentus est. Victus est ceruisia.
He is an euyll coke that can not lycke his owne lyppes.
Fatuus est cocus qui nescit lambere labia.

[1] Omitted in text.   [2] *Text* cyldnysshe

Vulgaria Stanbrigiana

Malaperte. Elegant. Curiosus.
I am sory for the deth of my fader.
Obitus paternus est mihi molestus.
Mors paterna me male habet.
I brynge the good tythynges.   Res bonas tibi a[p]porto.¹   5
It is almost ten of the clocke.   Instat hora decima.
I had leuer thou had gyuen me no thynge than to cast me in the tethe withall.
Malo te nil mihi dedisse q*uam* beneficia mihi obijcier.
I haue all the tethe that nature gyueth me.   10
Omnes dentes habeo quos natura mihi tribuit.
Thou takest more vpon the than thou can bere.
Plus tibi tribuas q*uam* vales.
I shall make good that I sayd.   Dicta mea prestabo.
This man is totheles.   Hic edentulus est.   15
Thou hast serued me ge*n*tylly.   Humanit*er* mecu*m* tractasti.
I haue money.   Sum preditus pecunia.
I haue a dull wytte.   Obtuso ingenio preditus sum.
I haue a sharpe wytte.   Sum preditus ingenio acuto.
He hathe but a small housholde.   20
Paruam familiam sustentat.
This is a grete sclaunder to the.   Hec res tibi infamie est.
Thou goos awaye fro thy sayenge.   Deflectis.
Put out the wrathe out of thy stomacke.
Expectora omnem iracundiam.   25
I haue boosted out thy mater.
Exploraui rem / expiscatus sum.   Cribraui.
The ayere is full of cloudes.
Celum est nubilosum.   Celum est ductum nubibus.
By my trouth I lyed not.   Me hercule nihil falsi dixi.   30
He speketh for the nones.
Loquitur ex animo / loquitur ex industria.
He hathe broke his heed ayenst the wall.
Allidit caput contra parietem.
Wolde god we myght go to playe.   35
O si nobis potestas laxendi anim[u]s ² esset.
I was borne in ỹ see cost.   Maritimis in locis nat*us* su*m*.
I was borne in the feldes.   Ca*m*pestrib*us* in locis nat*us* su*m*.

¹ *Text* asporto   ² *Text* animos

Vulgaria Stanbrigiana 29

I was borne in the marres countree.
Palustribus in locis natus sum.
I was borne in $\bar{y}$ wodes. Siluestrib*us* in locis nat*us* sum.
Sette my gowne. Roga togam.
5 My heed curles. Caput meum crispat.
The dayes be longe in somer. Dies sunt tardi in estate.
The dayes be shorte i*n* [w]ynter.¹ Dies su*n*t veloces i*n* hyeme.
The dayes waxe lo*n*ge. Dies crescunt. Lux p*er*trahitur.
I ete browne brede. Vescor atro pane.
10 My clothes be blacke. Vestimenta mea sunt pulla.
He hathe all the maners of a gentylman.
Cunctos mores nobilitatis habet.
Thou lokest on me as thou wolde ete me.
Torto vultu me respicis.
15 He dyed sodeynly. Mors ho*min*em improuiso occupauit.
I am aboute. Paro. Conor. Nitor. Melior.
He hathe layde watche for me. Parauit mihi insidias.
I laboured in thy cause. Dedi opera tua in causa.
I cast in my mynde. Coniecturo. [Conijcio].²
20 Hoc in animo hariolor.
I shall begyn my grammer on mundaye.
Hauspicabor grammaticam in die lune.
I haue taken my Iourney.
Meum iter arripui. Ingressus sum iter.
25 We be but of a shorte aquayntaunce.
Noticia inter nos recens est.
Inter nos parua familiaritas fuit.
I trowe we shall be better aquaynted.
Spero inter nos maiorem familiaritatem esse.
30 I haue begyled hym. Seduxi hominem.
I beshrowe suche loue.
Detestor huiusmodi amorem.
Thou hast slepte ynough yf the deuyll be not in the.
Ni malum tibi insit sat dormisti.
35 I hadde leuer go to my boke than be bete.
Mallem libris incumbere *quam* vapulare.
I maye curse the tyme that euer i came hyther.
Possum deuouere horam qua huc me contuli.

¹ *Text* vynter ² *Text* Conuitio

Vulgaria Stanbrigiana

Thou pynchest me. Vellis me.
Thou plays the foole. Ineptis.
I haue goten is good wyll.
Suam beniuolentiam na[c]tus¹ sum.
Thou plays the madde man. Insanis.   5
I am the worst of all my felowes.
Indoctissimus sum discipulorum.
I shall hele thy dysease. Tuo morbo medificabor.
My my*n*de is not set to my boke. Anim*us* a studio abhoret.
My gowne is the worste in all the scole.   10
Toga mea in toto ludo deterrima est.
Wysshers and wolders be small hous holders.
Affectantibus diuitias modica*m* hospitalitate*m* obserua*n*t.
I go my waye. Adeo. discedo / recedo.
Wyll thou commaunde me ony seruyce.   15
Nunquid mecum vis.
Nothynge but god perserue you.
Nil preterq*uam* vt valeas.
Our lorde be with you. Muniat / protegat / custodiat / tuetur te deus / dominus dux vel custos tibi sit.   20

Finis.

Imprynted at London in Flete strete by Wynkyn de Worde at the sygne of the sonne. The yere of our lorde. M.CCCCC. and .xix.

¹ *Text* natus

Uulgaria Roberti Whitintoni Lichfeldiensis / et de institutione grammaticulor*um* Opuscul*um* : libello suo de concinnitate Grammatices accommodatum : et i*n* quatuor partes digestu*m*.

Eiusdem distichon.
Quid frustra Inachidos queris vestigia lustris ?
Non quesita (viden ?) se ne reperta tulit ?

Wynkyn · de · Worde

PLATE IV

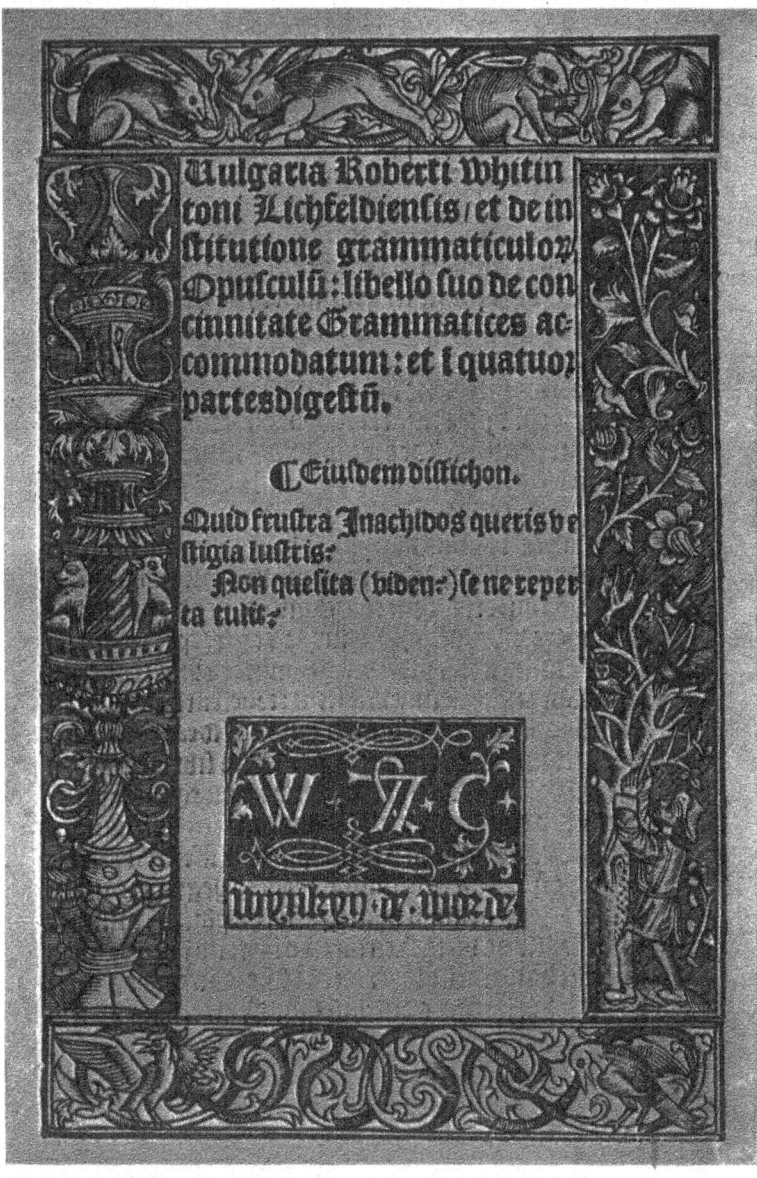

Title-page of Whittinton's *Vulgaria*, printed by Wynkyn de Worde in 1520.
Reproduced by permission of the H. E. Huntington Library.

Ad lectorem.

Cum sepius mecum nonnullos grammaticulorum instituendorum studiosos consydero : qui quanquam inferioris sunt doctrine / diligentioris tamen industrie opere precium duximus pijssimi
5 eorum laboris onus (his tanquam fulcimentis) aliquantulum leuare. Collectaneum hoc quadripertitum / de vulgaris & quotidiani sermonis exemplaribus excogitauimus : preceptiunculis nostri de concinnitate grammatices libelli accommodatum. Ea demum gratia / vt pijs lectoribus (vel doctulis) apertior pueris (grammatice
10 rudimentis) imbuendis & enucleatior fiat introitus. Atque vt alia id genus (tanquam ad exemplarium ducta) marte suo (vt dici solet) commodius elucubret quiuis. Deprompsimus isthec lectoribus / non tetricis / superciliosis / & plus iusto sibi placentibus qui sue odiose ambitioni / ampullate ostentationi : & affectate
15 curiositati potius obnoxij / quam discipulorum vtilitati sunt addicti. Neque subticere possum eorum insolentiam / qui authorum imitationem preceptis anteponendam (quod sibi soli sapere videantur) affirmant vt preceptores preposteri. Immo nulla precepta grammaticulis tradenda sed solam authorum imitationem cecu-
20 cientem amplectendam pugillatice contendunt. At quis non rideat eorum inscitiam? vt clauum clauo trudunt / & vorsuram sibi soluunt. In hac enim palestra suo cum errore aliquandiu colluctantes / plus iusto desudantes. & licet stomachum secum dissimulantes : Sisyphi tamen saxum satis diu voluisse videantur.
25 Quippe qui sibi conscii sub quodam ceco ex peregrinis oris nuperrime allato (quia aliquid noui semper affert Aphrica) militare iurarunt. sue ne vicis sacietate : an immerito in quendam odio impulsi haud facile dixerim. At sine. Siles (vt aiunt) habent labra lactucas. Gellium sane de noctibus atticis cum suo phauo-
30 rino huic ceco cum suis obsoletis mercibus licitatores dari exoptem. Quid dixi ? Gellio ipso haud est opus. A duce enim suo ceco peditentim (quam breui?) labascentes deficere / & furtim sese subducere moliuntur. exploratum est. Ut qui erumnose sue molestie & labyrinthee sollicitudinis pertesi : Ixionis (qui se
35 sequiturque fugitque) volubilis rote supplicio miserrime afficiuntur.

D

34 Vulgaria Roberti Whitintoni

Nec longe abest (quantum presagire videor) cum ijs et eiusmodi vsuveniat illud Flacci. Tantalus a labris fugientia flumina captet. Quippe qui precepta abijcienda & negligenda censuerit : priscos illos et illustrissimos grammaticos / Diomedem. Donatum. Phocam. Honoratum Seruium. Priscianum : & (recentiores ne sileam) Sulpitium. Perottum. & de latine lingue elegantijs meritissimum Laurentium vallensem frustratos labores / & quasi laterem lauisse iudicant. Adeo ut tantorum virorum memoriam extinguere : immo artem ipsam grammatices explodere (quamuis cerete cera digni) videantur. Quantus in pueris educandis est eorum error : luce clarius perspicitur. Multiplici enim lectione & sese et discip[u]los [1] delassant : per longas & cecas imitationis ambages (tanquam Herculani nodi inuolucra) misellos deducunt discipulos. Umbraticum latini sermonis vsum / per immensos labores hinc inde vagantes / vulgo queritare cogunt. Grammatices artem parui curantes dummodo late qui splendeat vnus / & alter Assuitur pannus. At quorsum isthec ? ni vt indoctulis & credulis parentibus persuadeant / fucatam puerorum eruditionem. de ijs probe cecinit Satyricus. ad populum phaleras. Quodsi eorum discipulos de ipsis grammatice rudimentis examines vel anginam patiuntur / vel (hallucinantis in morem) suam balbutiunt ignorantiam. Postremo (vt paucis absoluam) vos adhortor candidi lectores / vt maiorum more (& probatissimorum quidem) preceptiunculis grammaticulos imbuatis. Neque dubium : quin ad fertiliorem frugem quam sola imitatione cecucienti facillime sint emersuri. Hoc igitur opusculum de grammaticulorum institutione (probatorum desyderijs) in tyrunculorum literarie militie vsum edidimus. Quare si illud (vt alia nostra) vobis gratum fore perspexero : pietati nostre / nedum vestre expectationi fecisse satis videbor. authore deo / cui debetur omnis honor. A M E N.

Vulga. whitin. A. ij

[1] *Text* disciplos.

Grammaticulorum institutio.

Prima pars de concordantiolis.

Precept.

The verbe shall accorde with his nominatyfe or vocatyue case in persone and nombre / as appereth here folowynge by rule and example.
Verbum cum recto casu quinto ve coheret
Persona et numero. docet vt Maro / marce doceto.

Example.

My chylde gyf dylygent hede to this instruccyons.
Mi puer diligenter inuigilato his preceptiunculis.
Imitacyon of autours without preceptes & rules / is but a longe betynge about the busshe & losse of tyme to a yonge begynner
Imitatio authorum sine preceptis est nisi temporis procrastinatio / & iactura grammaticulo.

Precept.

The adiectyue shall agre with his substantyue in case gendre / & nombre : as appereth here after.
Cum substantiuo concordat mobile. &c.   Example.
It is a wast labour / yf a carpenter / without compas / rule / lyne & plummet sholde attende to square tymbre frame and reyre ony buyldynge.
Frustrata est opera / si faber lignarius absque circino / regula / linea / & perpendiculo / materiem dolare aliquod edificium fabricare & extruere niteretur.

Precept.

The relatyue of substance shall accorde with his antecedent / in gendre / nombre / & persone / as appereth here folowynge by rule. &c.
Antea cedenti debet quadrare relatum
Substantis genere sic persona numeroque.

Example.

That teycher setteth the cart before the horse that preferreth imitacyon before preceptes.
Preposterus est ille preceptor / qui imitationem preceptis anteponit.

Precept.

The relatyue of accidence shall accorde with ẙ substantyue that cometh after hym in case / gendre / and nombre / as appereth here after.
Cum substantiuo iungi comitante relatum
Uult contingentis / genere et casu numeroque.

Example.

Chyldre brought vp only by imitacyon wandre bloundrynge as a blynde man without his staffe or guyde.
Pueri sola imitatione educati errant tenebrosi / qualis cecus sine baculo aut duce.
Tendre wyttes with suche derke ambage be made as dull as a betle.
Ingeniola his cecis ambagibus redduntur obtusa / qualis est pistillus.
The labour is as greuous as the burden of Athlas.
Hic labor est grauis / quantum onus Athlanticum.
A scholer by suche tryfullynge hath as moche losse in one daye / as he getteth profet in .iiij. dayes.
Tyrunculus his nugis die iacturam facit / quotuplum fructum quatriduo vix queritat.
His eyes be clere as crystall yet he seeth no thyng.
Oculi eius sunt lucidi / qualis cristallus / ceci tamen.
His lyppes be as wan as lede.
Labella sunt liuida / quale est plumbum.

Precept.

Whan ther cometh a nominatyf case bytwene ẙ relatyue of substance / ẙ nowne interrogatyfe / infinyte / and ẙ verbe. than the relatyue / interrogatyue / or infynyte shall be suche case as ẙ verbe wyll haue after hym / as appereth here after by rule and example.

Vulgaria Roberti Whitintoni

Quu*m* rectus situs est inter verbu*m* atq*ue* relatu*m*
Substantis / quere*n*s / infinitum ve / erit illud
Eius que*m* verbum casus post se rogitabit.

Example.

5 This is a waye whiche ÿ shalt fynde bothe redy / and expedyent to the bryngynge vp of scholers.

Hic modus est que*m* et apertu*m* & com*m*odum ad institutione*m* pueroru*m* experieris.

Whome canst thou fynde at the lestwyse experte ỷ can by good
10 reason denye this.

Quem inuenias (saltem expertu*m*) qui probabili ratione hoc refragetur.

Whome so euer I maye here saye nay to hit / I repute hym ignoraunt & blynde in lernynge.

15 Que*m*cunq*ue* isthuc oppugnare audiam hunc ignaru*m* et sciolu*m* reputabo.

Precept.

But whan there cometh no nominatyf case bytwene ỹ relatyue / interrogatyue / infinyte / & ỹ verbe. than the relatyue / interro-
20 gatyue / infinyte shal be nominatyue case vnto the verbe / as appereth here after.

Cu*m* intersit nullus / tu*n*c rectus verbo aut eris illud.

Example.

Who is he (as Tully sayeth) ỷ in gyffynge or techynge no preceptes
25 dar call hymself a phylosopher.

Quis eni*m* (vt inq*uit* Cicero) est : qui in nullis trade*n*dis preceptis audeat se philosophu*m* dicere.

He that laboureth no thynge holy / but catcheth a patche of euery thynge / is mete t[o][1] pyke a salet.

30 Quicu*n*que nihil absolutu*m* legit / immo vndecunque paululu*m* quid diuellit : moretu*m* hunc excerpere decet.

Precept.

If it be a verbe impersonal ỷ is ioyned vnto the relatyue / interrogatyue / or infynyte. than the relatyue interrogatiue or infinite Fo. iij

---
[1] *Text* te

shall be suche case as the verbe impersonall gouerneth / as appereth here after.

Si impersonale est verbum cui iungitur / illo
Tum casu ponas: quem impersonale reposcit.

Example.

Many fresshe wyttes by that blynde imitacyon be deceyued / all labour and cost lost : wherof theyr teychers may be bothe sory & ashamed.

Multa ingeniola clara illa labyrinthea imitatione eluduntur / labores et sumptus frustantur : cuius suum preceptorem & pigeat & pudeat.

Precept.

This nowne Quis qui is not alway gouerned of ẙ verbe ẙ foloweth next hym but somtyme of the infinytyue mode folowynge / as appereth here after.

A verbo haud semper quis qui comitante regetur
Sed de infinito quandoque modo comitante.

Example.

The comen way ẙ our elders dyd vse is by preceptes.
Uia peruulgata qua maiores nostri vti solebant est per precepta.

Precept.

Somtyme quis qui is gouerned of the partycyple. Somtyme of ẙ nowne. Somtyme of the gerundyfe. Somtyme of ẙ aduerbe. Somtyme of the preposicyon. Somtyme it shall agre with a substantyue in case / gendre & nombre. Somtyme it is put in the ablatyue case absolute / as appereth here after.

Nunc a participo / nunc nomine / nuncque gerundo
Nunc ex aduerbo / nunc preposito sibi iuncto.
Nunc fixo quadret genere et casu numeroque
Ponitur et sexto casu quandoque soluto.
Intellecto (non expresso) participante.

Example.

It is a token of obstynacy whan a man wyll not recognyse his faute / of ẙ whiche he is oft tymes warned.
Est pertinacie indicium / vbi errorem de quo es admonitus crebro non corrigas.

Vulgaria Roberti Whitintoni 39

It is a spyce of peuysshe pryde (y̆ many be infecte with) whan a man wyll take a synguler waye by hymselfe.
Inepte arrogantie (cui obnoxij sunt non pauci) est argumentum. cum solus videri affectat quisquam.
5 It is a lewde touche / whiche no wyse man hath desyre to vse.
Est res improba / qua vtendi desyderium habet nemo.
He is a man whome I wolde not mete with.
Uir est cui obuiam ire nolim.
For he is euer inquisityue of suche maters whiche I am wery to
10 here of.
Est enim curiosus inuestigator rerum de quibus audire fastidio.
He is ful of tongue / by reason of the whiche vyce fewe men regarde hym.
Linguax est / cuius flagitij causa / fidem huic adhibent rari.
15 Rolle vp these thynges in thy mynde / whiche perfytely done / thou shalt get good lernynge.
Has res memoriter ediscas / quo accurate facto : eruditionem fructuosam assequeris.
He is the man whiche lyuynge thou canst not lacke.
20 Is est (quo viuo) indigere nequis.

Precept.

Whan ther cometh a verbe bytwene .ij. nominatyue cases of dyuerse nombres whiche betokeneth one maner of thynge : y̆ verbe may accorde with the nominatyue case before hym / and
25 somtyme with the nominatyue case that foloweth hym / thoughe it be seldomer as appereth here after folowynge.
Si binos inter rectos. &c.   Example.
Preceptes is the chefe and moost expedyent bryngyng vp of a yonge grammaryon.
30 Precepta / grammaticuli prima & precipua est institutio.
This besy ambages of imitacyon is an extreme payne to the teycher & no profet or small to the lerners.
Ille inextricabilis imitationis ambages preceptori odiosa est molestia / et discipulis nullus aut rarus fructus.

35   Authoryte.

The variaunce of louers (sayth Terence) is the renuynge of loue.
Amantium ire / amoris redintegratio est.

Thy commaundementes (sayth the prophete) is my meditacyon and study.

Mandata tua (inquit propheta) meditatio mea est.

Precept.

Whan ther cometh an adiectyue bytwene two substantyues of dyuerse gendres belongyng bothe to one thynge / the adiectyue may agre wit*h* the substantyfe before. And somtyme wit*h* ẙ substantyfe ẙ foloweth / though it be seldome / as appereth here after folowynge.

    Mobile si quando medium est inter duo fixa
    Diuersi generis. &c.   Example.

Lernynge semeth vnto me a tresur moost excellent.

Eruditio mihi thesaurus visus est summus.

Ryches worldly semeth to me as a floure ẙ soone fadeth and falleth / where lernynge wyll abyde.

Diuitie temporarie mihi flos cito marcescens & caducus est visus. vbi eruditio herebit.

Connynge (be it neuer so moche) semeth no burden to hym ẙ hath hit.

Cognitio rerum (quantumuis multa) habenti onus non est visum.

Pryde with some men is called clenlynes.

Fastus vestium apud quosdam mundicia est nuncupata.

Authoryte.

Pouerte semed neuer to me as nowe / a burden bothe wretched and greuous.

Teren. Paupertas nunquam eque atque nunc onus mihi est visum et miserum et graue.

After that the marshall dyd tast of the water tourned into wyne.

Postquam architriclinus (vt scriptum est) gustauerit aquam vinum factum.

Vulga. whitin. B. i

Precept.

Whan a relatyf of substaunce cometh bytwene two substantyues of dyuerse genders be longynge bothe to one thynge / yf they be nownes appellatyfe. The relatyf may agre indyfferent in gendre wit*h* eyther of them / but yf the one be a nowne propre ẙ relatyfe must euer agre wit*h* hym only / as appereth afterwarde.

Vulgaria Roberti Whitintoni

Diuersi generis si inter duo fixa. &c. Example.

Grammer whiche is the welle of scyences lyberall is groundely to be loked vpon.

Grammatica que vel qui fons est liberalium artium radicitus est
5 amplectenda.

Idelnes whiche is the nourysshe of all vyces is to be auoyded / specyally in youthe.

Ocium / quod vel que omnium vitiorum est altrix / abigendum est : precipue in tenera etate.

10 Authoryte.

The study of wysdome whiche is called philosophye.

Tullius. Studium sapientie / que philosophia dicitur.

Example whan the one substantyue is a nowne propre.

I was borne in the chefe cyte of Englande whiche is called
15 London.

In prima Anglie ciuitate / quod Londinum appellatur : sum natus.

Ther renneth by my faders dore a goodly water that is called Temmes.

Paterna fores preterfluit gratissimum flumen / qui tamisis nuncu-
20 patur.

Authoryte.

There is a place in the pryson that is called Tullyan.

Salustius. Est locus in carcere quod Tullianum appellatur.

Precept.

25 Whan the relatyue of substaunce / or the adiectyue is referred to the hole sentence or reason goynge before ẙ relatyue or adiectyue shal be put in the neutre gendre syngler & ẙ thyrd persone. Also yf ẙ relatyf be referred to .ij. sentens or more than it shall be the plurell nombre.

30 Ad totum sensum preeuntem quando relatum   Fo. v
Substantis referas. &c.

Example of the relatyue.

I haue spend all my youthe in exercyse of lernynge / whiche is nowe to me bothe profet and pleasure.

35 Teneram etatem in discendi exercitatione prorsus transegi : quod quidem et vtile et gratum nunc est mihi.

I haue set apart all pastans / & pleasur / for loue of lernynge: whiche maketh me now to be taken in fauour before other.
Ludicra & oblectamenta doctrine studio postposui: quod gratiam pre ceteris mihi conciliat.

Example of the adiectyue.

Yf a man take great labour / and haue nother profet / nor thanke therof: it is greuous vnto hym.
Si graues labores susceperis: neque fructum neque laudem merearis, molestum est tibi.

Example of the relatyue referred vnto .ij. sentence.

Thou wyll not labour. other thou must begge or stele of the whiche the one bryngeth a man to mysery / the other to an haltre.
Laboribus subire nolis. aut mendicare / aut latrocinari debes. quorum alterum miserias / alterum laqueum parit.

Example of the adiectyue.

To do nought or support nought. be cosen germanes.
Flagitium committere / aut flagitium fouere sunt eque improba.

Authoryte.

I in lykewyse am a lost man / whiche is to me a derer thynge.
Terentius. Ego quoque vna pereo / quod mihi carius est.
To rule thy countre & thy bryngers vp: though thou may do it / & correcte thyn owne fautes / yet is it vnsyttynge and dangerous.
Salustius. Nam vi patriam & parentes regere quanquam possis / & delicta corrigas: tamen importunum est.
Cicero. Uereor ne aut eripiatur a nobis causa regia / aut differatur / quorum vtrum minus velim non facile possum existimare.

Precept.

Whan $\breve{y}$ verbe is referred vnto the hole sentence or ony worde $\breve{y}$ is put materyally: $\breve{y}$ is to saye / for $\breve{y}$ selfe voyce of $\breve{y}$ worde & not $\breve{y}$ sygnificacyon / it shall be the thyrde persone and synguler nombre. But yf $\breve{y}$ verbe be referred to .ij. or dyuerse sentence / or wordes put materyally it shall be the plurell nombre.

Vulgaria Roberti Whitintoni

Ad totum sensum verbum. &c.   Example.
To walke moderately after meet conforteth naturall heet and helpeth dygestyon.
Modeste ambulare post refectionem / naturalem recreat calorem /
5 & concoctionem maturat.
To study immedyatly after replecyons plucketh vp vapours to the hed and hurteth the brayn.
Studio incumbere continuo post saturitatem vapores capiti attrahit : & cerebro officit.
10 Example of the verbe referred to two sentence or dyuerse.
To refresshe the mynde with myrthe / exercyse $\stackrel{e}{y}$ body with labour / & to vse temperate dyet. be the chefest phisicyons for a student.
Animum solacijs acuere / corpus exercitatiunculis versare : et
15 temperata refectiuncula frui : sunt studenti medici presentissimi.

Authoryte.
To besy thyself in vayne / & to get no thyng elles in werynge thyself / but grudge : is an extreme foly.
20 Salustius. Frustra autem niti / & nihil aliud te fatigando nisi odium querere : est extreme dementie.
Cicero. Quasi ipsos induxiloquentes : ne inquit / & inquam sepius interponerentur.

Precept.
25 Whan a nowne demonstratyue is referred to $\stackrel{e}{y}$ hole sentence folowynge / it shall be the neutre gendre synguler nombre / yf it be referred to .ij. or dyuers sentence / it shal be the plurel nombre / as appereth by this rule.
Ad totum sensum comitantem. &c.   Example.
30 This I wyll laye for myn excuse to my mayster / that I was letted Fo. vj with straungers.
Hoc preceptori causabor : me prepeditum aduenis / vel hospitibus.
These or lyke / he wyll lay agayne to my charge : this is a con-
35 trefet excuse / what wytnes hast thou?
Hec / aut similia obijciet mihi : figmentum est istud. [quos][1] testes adducas.

[1] Omitted in text.

Authoryte.

I iudge this moost profytable in this lyfe y̐ y̍ set not thy mynde ouermoche or toto vpon ony thynge.

Terentius. Id arbitror apprime esse vtile in vita / vt ne quid nimis supplefacias.

Teren. An hec dicent mihi? inuitus feci / lex coegit.

Precept.

Lyke as the relatyue maye be nominatyue case vnto the verbe / so he maye be substantyf vnto the adiectyf.

Rectus vt esse potest verbi. &c. Example.
He is a man / whiche is bothe wyse and well lerned.
Uir est / qui et ingeniosus et eruditus est.

Authoryte.

Cicero. Nihil enim stabile / quod infidum est.

Precept.

An adiectyue somtyme comynge without a substantyue may be put in the neutre gendre lyke a substantyue as appereth by this rule.

In genere ornate neutro. &c. Example.
It is wysdom to loke before what maye fal here after.
Scitum est / ante initium exitus cogitare.
It is foly to spron agaynst the prycke.
Stultum est aduersus stimulum calcitrare.

Authoryte.

He asketh ryght.
Terentius. Equum postulat.

Precept.

An adiectyue ioyned with y̐ sygnificacyon of this nowne Res / may ofte tymes be set in y̐ neutre gendre lyke a substantyue / this nowne res lefte aparte.

Adiectum iunctum cum sensu nominis huius
Res. &c. Example.
I haue many thynges to do.
Multa facienda habeo.

Vulgaria Roberti Whitintoni

I haue a fewe thynges to rekken with the.
Pauca tecum raciocinanda habeo.
What thynges be those / shewe at fewe wordes.
Que sunt ea paucis expedito.
5 They be thynges touchynge thy profet.
Sunt tibi vtilia.

Authoryte.

Terentius. Omnia habeo neque quicquam habeo.

Precept.

10 Whan .ij. substantyues or moo come togyder immedyatly / whiche belonge to one thynge or be sayd of the same thynge they shall be set in the same case as ẙ fyrst is.
Quum duo conueniunt fixa. &c.   Example.
Ryot the moder of all maner of sykenes abbreuiateth & shorteneth
15 many a mannes lyfe.
Crapula / omnium egritudinum mater / multis vitam diminuit.
Contrary wyse good dyet : ẙ preseruatyue of healthe augmenteth or encreaseth a mannes lyfe.
Rursus temperantia / sanitatis custos / homini dies adijcit.
20 So he that foloweth temperaunce / chefe guyde of nature / gouerner of healthe : nedeth no physicyons.
Itaque / qui moderatiam / primam nature ducem / sanitatis reginam obseruat / medicis non indigebit.

Authoryte.

25 Uirgilius. Nate mee vires mea magna potentia solus.

Precept.

The nowne partityue as aliquis / quisquam : & euery nowne set as a nowne partyue shall agre with ẙ genytyue case folowynge in gendre only / as aliquis virorum.

30 ### Precept.

Nownes ẙ be set partytyfly be these : nownes distributyues : as Fo. vij
nullus / neuter. Uirg : Nulla tuarum audita mihi ne visa sororum.
Nownes infinyte / as quisquis quicunque. Ouidius. Quisquis fuit ille deorum.

Precept.

Nownes interrogatyue: as quis / vter: vt quis hominum.
Nownes of comparatyue degre: vt duorum fratrum / tu maior.
Nownes of the superlatyf degre. Uirg. Maxima natarum priami.
Uult partitiuum. &c.

Exempla satis patent.

Precept.

The nominatyue case of a nowne collectyue maye haue somtyme after hym a verbe of the plurell nombre ornately. whiche verbe doeth accorde with the intellecte or sygnificacyon & not with ẙ voyce. And this is by a fygure of construccyon called Synthesis. Singlaris rectus collecti. &c.

Example.

Parte be fledde this waye / part that waye.
Pars hac / pars illac fugierunt.
All the world wondreth & cryeth out of this penury & scantnes of all thynges.
Plebs (ad vnum) clamitant de hac vniuersali rerum penuria.

Authoryte.

Uirgilius. Pars in frusta secant verubusque trementia figunt.
Ouidius. In me turba ruunt luxuriosa proci.

Precept.

The adiectyf / lykewyse ẙ relatyf somtym may agre in gendre & nombre with intellecte or significacyon of ẙ nowne collectyf: also of ẙ nowne of the epycene gendre and the worde that is set materyally.

Nominis interdum collecti. &c.   Example.

There is an vngracyous company mette togyder.
Turba proterui vel flagitiosi istic conuenerunt.
People redemed be glad & mery that lyfe is gyuen vnto vs by a vyrgyn.
Uitam datam per virginem gentes redempti plaudite.
An hare bagged maye not away / but is soone ouertaken.
Lepus gra[u]ida[1] effugere nequit / immo cito arripitur.

[1] *Text* granida.

A broody goose is lothe to go from her nest.
Anser feta a nido egre excitatur.
A fysshe in spawnynge tyme wyll couet to the calme watre.
Piscis ouipara vel fetuosa / tranquillum appetit stagnum.
5 R / is rough in pronuncyacyon.
R / est aspera in pronunciatione.

Authoryte.

Uirgilius. Pars hominum validi turres et menia scandunt.
Esopus. Anser erat quondam precioso germine feta.

10   Precept.
Two nominatyue cases or dyuerse with a coniunccyon copula-
tyue comynge betwene requyre a verbe of the plurell nombre.
Bini vel plures recti. &c.   Example.
Continual healthe and abundaunce of ryches (as sayth saynt
15 Agustyne) be moost euydent tokens of damnacyon.
Sanitas continua / & rerum abundantia (vt inquit Augustinus)
eterne damnationis sunt maxima indicia.

Authoryte.

Ouidius. Non bene conueniunt : nec in vna sede morantur.
20 Maiestas et amor.

Precept.

A nominatyue case and an ablatyue with this preposicyon cum
put in ẙ styd of ẙ nominatyue case with this coniunccyon & /
wyll haue a verbe plurell.
25 Cum sexto adiuncto / vult et vice poni aliquando.   Fo. viij

Example.

Lernynge with vertue auaunseth a man.
Eruditio cum virtute exornant quenquam.
The mayer and the alder men syt in counseyle.
30 Preses vrbis cum senatoribus consultant.

Authoryte.

Uirgilius. Remus cum fratre Quirino. Iura dabunt.

Precept.

Whan an adiectyue / or a relatyue be referred to dyuerse substantyues hauynge lyfe with a coniunccyon copulatyf bytwene / of ẙ whiche one is of ẙ masculyne gendre / the other of ẙ feminyne or ẙ neutre / tha*n* ẙ adiectyue or ẙ relatyue shalbe ẙ masculyne gendre.

Si iungi adiectu*m* contingat. &c. Example.

Bothe my fader & my moder be so te*n*dre & choyse vpon me / ẙ they wyl not suffre me to be punysshed whome therfore I in tyme to come vtterly may curse.

Et pater et mater adeo mihi sunt indulge*n*tissimi : ne me castigatu*m* patiantur : quos igitur olim deuoueam.

Myn vncle / his wyfe / & his seruau*n*t mette me comynge / whome I must go speke with.

Auu*n*culus / vxor sibi / & mancipiu*m* : mihi venienti fueru*n*t obuij : quos conuenire habeo.

Authoryte.

Uirgilius. Ascaneumque patre*m*q*ue* meu*m* iuxtaq*ue* creusa. Alteru*m* in alterius mactatos sanguine cernam. Idem. Superest ne creusa Ascaneusq*ue* puer quos omnes vndiq*ue* graij. circuerant acies.

Precept.

Whan an adiectyue or a relatyue be referred to dyuerse substantyues hauynge lyfe with a coniunccyon copulatyue betwene / of ẙ whiche one is of the feminyne gendre / the other of the neutre / the adiectyue or the relatyue shalbe of the feminyne gendre.

Si iungi adiectum. &c. Example.

Beestes and cattell that we haue seen to be plenteous here in englande were neuer so scaunte as nowe.

Pecudes et pecora quas copiosas hic in Anglia vidim*us* / nunq*uam* eque atq*ue* nunc fuerunt rare.

Precept.

Whan an adiectyfe or a relatyf is referred to diuerse substantyues not hauynge lyfe / with a co*n*iunccyon copulatyue betwene : of what ge*n*dre so euer they be : other of dyuerse gendres / or lyke / the adiectyue and ẙ relatyue shall be of the neutre gendre.

Vulgaria Roberti Whitintoni

Diuersis fixis si mobile. &c. Example.
I thynke all the cost & labour that I haue made well bestowed:
now that I haue my purpose.
Su*m*ptus et molestias q*ue* pertuli / equa iudico : nu*n*c cu*m* insti-
5 tuti co*m*pos sum.

Authoryte.

Salustius. Diuitie / decus / gloria / in oculis sita sunt.
Terentius. Spes opesq*ue* in te vno sita sunt.
Uirgilius. Arcum fregisti et calamos / que tu donata vidisti.

10 ### Precept.

Whan the verbe is referred vnto dyuerse nominatyue cases / of
ỹ whiche one is of ỹ fyrst person / an other of ỹ seconde or the
thyrd / ỹ verbe shalbe ỹ fyrst persone.
Ad rectos verbu*m* dyuersos. &c. Example.
15 Thou and I be lyke of one age.
Tu et ego sumus coetanei vel coeui.
Thou and I and thy broder haue be brought vp togyder of lytle
babes.
Tu et ego et germanus tuus / ab incunabulis vna educati fuimus.

20 ### Precept.

Whan a verbe is referred to dyuerse nominatyfe cases / of the
whiche one is of the second persone / ỹ other of the thyrd / ỹ
verbe shalbe the seconde persone.

Example.

25 Thou & all thy frendes shall neuer be able to make me amendes
/ for the hurt that thou hast done vnto me.
Tu et tui ad vnu*m* necessarij / damnu*m* quod mihi intulistis /
redimere vel resarcire potestis nunq*uam*. Fo. ix

Precept.

30 Whan a relatyue is referred to dyuerse substa*n*tyfes of the
whiche one is the fyrst persone / an other of ỹ seconde or the
thyrd / ỹ relatyue shall be the fyrst persone.

E

Quando relatiuum fixa. &c. E[x]ample.¹
It is unsyttynge y̆ thou & I whiche be felowes of one schole shold holde one agaynst an other.
Dissentaneum est / vt tu et ego qui condiscipuli sumus : dissentiamus inuicem. 5
What answere shall me bedfelowe / ẙ / & I make whiche be accused vnto the mayster.
Quid respondebimus conthoralis meus / tu / et ego? qui ad preceptorem accusamur.

Precept. 10

Whan a relatyue is referred to dyuerse substantyfes of ẙ whiche one is the seconde persone / ẙ other ẙ thyrd the relatyue shalbe the seconde persone.

Example.

Thou and thy seruaunt be well met. 15
Tu et famulus tuus estis non dissimiles.
Thy company and thou / that can bothe forge & lye be two mete marchauntes / to vttre ware in buklersbury.
Tu et tibi consocius / qui et fabricare et mentiri nostis : inter pharmacapolas ad antidota² vendenda / maxime estis idonei. 20

Precept.

Whan a verbe is referred to dyuerse nominatyue cases / also an adiectyue or a relatyue to diuerse substantyues / the verbe somtyme shall agre with ẙ nominatyf case nexte vnto hym : lykewyse ẙ adiectyf & ẙ relatyue shall accorde with the substantyue y̆ is 25 next vnto them.

Ad rectos verbum diuersos. &c. Example.

Other thou / or I shal dere bye this bargen : & perauenture bothe of vs.
Aut tu / aut ego ob hoc facinus penas luam : fors vterque nostrum. Uel sic 30
Aut tu / lues penas ob hoc facinus / aut ego : fors vterque.
Nother my fader / whome I ought to loue before all other / nor my moder is more welcom to me than ẙ art.
Neque pater / qui mihi egregie preter ceteros est carus / neque 35 mater : te mihi magis grata aduenit. vel sic. Neque pater /

¹ *Text* Eample.   ² *Text* antitoda

Vulgaria Roberti Whitintoni 51

sed neq*ue* mater / que egregie preter ceteros mihi est cara :
te mihi gratior aduenit.

Authoryte.

Uirgilius. Hic illius arma : hic currus fuit. Idem. Nec deus
⁵ hunc mensa / dea nec dignata cubili est.
Ap*osto*lus. Hebrei sunt et ego.
And this maner of construccyon is by a fygure called zeugma /
whiche is a reduccyon of the verbe or the adiectyue or relatyue to
dyuerse substantyues.

¹⁰ Precept.

The antecede*n*s many tymes is ioyned elegantly in case with
his relatyue leuynge his verbe & his adiectyfe and oratours put y̆ͤ
antecedens after the relatyf. Albe it poetes somtyme put the
antecedens before. And in co*n*struccyon y̆ͤ antecedens shal be
¹⁵ reuersed into his due case : or elles we shall repete the antecedens / as in this example of virgil. Urbem qua*m* statuo vestra
est. Whiche this wyse maye be co*n*strued. Urbem (.i. vrbs)
qua*m* statuo / est vestra. or elles (supple vrbs) quam vrbem
statuo / est vestra. And this is to be vnderstande of all other
²⁰ cases / & after some men this maner of speche is by a fygure
called Antithesis : whiche is wha*n* one case is put for another.

Sepe relatiuo co*n*nectitur antea cedens
In casu ornate. &c. Example.
The lettres which you sende vnto me last were to me very
²⁵ pleasaunt.
Quas ad me proxime dedisti literas mihi periocunde fuerunt.

Example of the nominatyue case.

And the more pleasaunt bycause I se the olde amyte whiche
hath betwene you and me dayly to renue.
³⁰ Eo iocundiores / q*uia* pristinam : que mihi tecu*m* (a pueris)
intercessit amicitia / indies accrescere perspicio.

Example of the genityue case.

And in especyall y̆ ye haue ended the lytygyose mater whiche I
desyred you for in my last lettres.
³⁵ Et in primis q*uia* litigiosam cuius rei postremis literis eram
cupidus expedisti.

Example of the datyue case.

For by this humanyte you haue made ẙ man to whome I was in daunger specyall frende vnto me.
Hoc eni*m* officio / cui viro obnoxius eram effecisti mihi amicissimum.

Example of the ablatyue case.

Wherfore I wyl be a frend vnto you / whome you shal boldely vse at all nedes.
Unde quo (vbiuis) familiariter vteris amico / paratissimus tibi ero.

Authoryte.

Terentius. Populo vt placerent quas fecisset fabulas. Uirgilius. Nam que p*r*ima solo. Ide*m*. Urbem quam statuo vestra est subducite naues.
Cicero pro ligario. Sed hoc no*n* co*n*cedo. vt quibus rebus gloriemini : in vobis easde*m* reprehendatis.

Precept.

As ofte as the significacyon of a nowne substantyfe is ioyned immedyatly w*ith* this nowne quis qui / or with his compoundes whether he be a relatyue / interrogatyue / or infinyte : the substantyue shalbe set in ẙ same case with this nowne quis qui / or his co*m*poundes.

Cu*m* quis qui quoties (vel natis) immediate
Fixum coniu*n*ctu*m* est / casu illi iungito fixum.

Example.

What state & what condicyon your maters be in / this messenger shall shewe you by mouthe.
Qui status / et que co*n*ditio / tuaru*m* sit reru*m*. Hic internuncius tibi verbis aperiet.
The processe therof is to longe to wryte of / by reason of ẙ whiche thynge I com*m*ytte all to his credence.
Sum*m*a reru*m* est longior q*uam* vt literis co*m*plectar : cui*us* rei causa om*n*ia huius com*m*itto fidei.
I wolde ye shold enquyre of the messenger what besynes we haue had withall.
Perconteris velim a tabellario. quas molestias inde cepimus.

What man is it? but he wold merueyle to here therof.
Quisnam homo est? qui non admiretur si inde audiat?

Authoryte.

Terentius. Quod remedium eius inueniam iracundie. Idem.
5 Quam causam reperient demiror. Idem. Quo ore patrem compellabo?

Precept.

Whan the verbe is ioyned to one hole thyng / which afterwarde is diuyded in partes / than the partes shall be put in the same
10 case with theyr hole. But yf the verbe be ioyned with the partes / than the hole shalbe put in the genityue case.

Toti diuiso in partes. &c.

Example whan ẙ verbe is ioyned with the hole.

Your frendes that you put in truste with the cause be: some
15 fast / some full slacke and feynte.

Amici in hac re sunt: alij fidissimi / alij remissi et languentes.

Example whan the verbe is ioyned with the partes.

Albe it your aduersaryes some appere wery of theyr parte / some (thoughe they make a face outward) they wolde gladly shake
20 theyr handes therof honestly.

Aduersariorum tamen pars videntur sue vicis pertesi: pars autem (quamuis vultum simulent) se honeste fore dimissos: cupidi.

Precept.

This coniunccyon quod many tymes ornately shall be exclude
25 with chaungynge ẙ worde whiche semeth to be ẙ nominatyue case into the accusatyue / & the verbe into ẙ infinytyue mode of the same tens / as it sholde haue be / yf this coniunccyon quod had be expressed / as whan barbarous and vnlerned men say / gaudeo quod tu vales Latyn men say: gaudeo te valere.

30 Excludetur quod coniunctio. &c.   Example.   Fo. xi

I am glad that all thynge goeth forwarde accordyng to your mynde & your last lettres.

Gaudeo omnia succedere ex optato tuis postremis literis.

I coniectured & thought in the begynnynge ẙ the mater wolde
35 growe to this conclusyon.

Conijcitabam (ipsa prima fronte) rem huc esse redituram.

Authoryte.

Cicero in Ep*ist*ola prima. Ego q*u*ia idem in tua causa facere nequeo: vita*m* mihi acerba*m* esse putem. Terentius. Meu*m* gnatu*m* rumor est amare.

Precept.

This *con*iu*n*ccyon q*uod* not withstandyng somtyme is expressed in latyn tongue / as whan it is take for this coniunccyon q*u*ia / or elles whan propterea cometh before it / or elles whan it is set in the fyrste begynnynge of an Epistole or a sente*n*ce.

Example.

That ye wryte that you haue merueyle / you herde nothynge fro hens many a daye / is bycause you be ferre dystaunt / also by the reason fewe cometh betwene.

Quod scribis te admirari / hinc diu ad te allatum nihil: fit tum q*u*ia longe hinc abes / tum propterea q*uod* rari intercursant nuncij.

Authoryte.

Cicero ad Brutu*m*. Augebat etia*m* molestia*m* / q*uod* magna sapientiu*m* / ciuiumq*ue* bonorum penuria iam in ciuitate esset. *id. est.* q*u*ia magna. &c.
Terentius. Propterea q*uod* mihi seruiebas liberaliter.
Cicero. Quod scribis quid de exitu belli sentiam.

Finis prime partis.

Secunda pars de constructione nominu*m*.

Precept.

A Nowne that betokeneth possessyo*n* / or a thyng had in possessyon requyreth a genytyfe case of the hauer / or owner: or elles his possessyf ioyned with the hauer in case gendre and nombre. And somtym in ẙ styd of the genityue case he wyll haue a datyue.

Possessum rogitat possessoris. &c.

Breuitatis causa (deinceps) precepta omitto / lectore*m* ad libellu*m* nostru*m* de Co*n*cinnitate gra*m*matices recurrere volens: preceptoru*m* tame*n* hemistichia pro indice inseruimus: eo vt exempla et vulgaria preceptis applicet.

Vulgaria Roberti Whitintoni

Example. This is my faders seruaunt.
Hic est famulus patris / patri / vel paternus.
She is my broders wyf.   This is the kynges horse.
Ea est vxor fratris / fratri / vel fraterna.   Hic est equus regis /
regi / vel regius.

Authoryte.

Ouidius. Iam patrem famulumque patris lucemque timebam.
Terentius. Oro vt in commune consulas. ita vt si ego pater essem Pamphilo / et tu huic nostro.

Precept.

The hauer or the owner gouerneth somtyme a genityue case of ẽy thynge y̆ is had / & somtyme a datyue.
Possessi interdum. &c.   Example.
He is lorde of this grounde.
Is est dominus huius fundi / vel huic fundo.
He is a great lord of woddes & waters / as ony within this partys.
Est amplus dominus syluarum et aquarum / vel syluis et aquis : qualis hic locorum quisquam.
Authoritates & precepta in nostro libello de concinnitate satis patent.

Precept.

Nomen significans affinem. &c.

Exempla de affinitate.

My maysters fader in lawe wyll be here to daye.
Socer heri vel hero affuturus est.   vel aderit hodie.
This is my broders moder in lawe.
Hec est socrus fratris / vel fratri.
She is doughter in lawe to myn vncle.
Illa est genera patrui / vel patruo.
He dealeth with my as hardely / as I were his stepsone.
Perinde duriter me tractat acsi essem priuignus illius / aut illi.
His stepmoder is more harde vnto hym than his stepfader.
Eius vel ei nouerca est seuior illi / quam victricus.

Exempla de co*n*sanguinitate.

The patrymony ẙ his fader / graundfader / & his auncytres / tyme out of mynde haue kepte at theyr wyll / he hath folysshely lost.

Patrimonia que illius vell illi pater / auus / et parentes / maiores (vltra memoriam hominu*m*) possiderunt : is stulte perdidit.

Fo. xij So that his sone / his neuewe / with all his posteryte / and yssue shall curse hym.

Adeo vt eius vel ei filius / nepos / et tota progenies et posteritas illum deuoueant.

He loueth me better tha*n* his fader moder broder syster and all the kynne that he hath.

Amat me vehementius / q*uam* illius aut illi patrem / matrem / fratre*m* / sorore*m* / et totam cognationem.

Exempla de preeminentia.

He is mayster of the ordynaunce.
Est preses machinaru*m* bellicaru*m* / vel machinis bellicis.
He is graunde capten / or chefe capten of the hoost.
Est primus vel precipuus dux exercitus vel exercitui.
Myn vncle is one of the alder men of the cyte.
Auunculus meus est vnus ex primatibus vrbis vel vrbi.

Exempla de n*omi*ne ad aliquid dicto.

Who is fader of this chylde?
Quis est pater huius pueri vel huic puero?
He is worthy to be a teycher of scholers ẙ instructeth them as well in good maners as lernynge.
Hic dignus est discipuloru*m* vel discuplis esse preceptor : qui tum moribus / tum scientia eos instruit.
It becometh hym euyll to be a mayster vpon seruau*n*tes that can not ordre hymselfe.
Iniquu*m* est hunc. famuloru*m* / vel famulis esse dominu*m* : qui sibi dominari nescit.

Preceptu*m*.

Nomen siginificans excellere. &c.

Vulgaria Roberti Whitintoni

Exempla de nominibus excellentie.

He is kynge of kynges that made all thynges.
Ille rex est regum / qui omnia creauit.
He is a man by hymselfe.
5 Est homo perpaucorum hominum.
The rose is a floure of floures.
Rosa est flos florum.
Of all pleasures this is a pleasure by itselfe.
Omnium voluptatum ea demum est voluptas.
10 Of all paynes this is a payne.
Omnium dolorum hic dolor est.

Exempla de nominibus ponderis.

A pounde of wexe is at .ix. pens.
Libra cere nouenis denarijs estimatur.
15 Bye me halfe a pounde of saffron / a quarteren of cynomom .ij.
  vnces of peper.
Emas mihi selibram croci. quadrantem cinamomi. dextantem
  piperis.

Exempla de nominibus mensure.

20 A quarter of malt was at .viij. scyllynges in the market to daye.
Corus ordei tosti in hodierno mercato octenis solidis / siue aureis
  estimabatur.
A busshell of whete was holde at .xij. pens.
Modius tritici duodenis denarijs pendebatur.
25 A stryke of rye at .x. pens.
Semodius secalis denis denarijs.
A mette or an hoope of oote mele at foure pens.
Semodiolus auenatie farine quaternis denarijs.
A galon of swete wyne is at .viij. pens in London.
30 Lagena vel congius dulcis vini octenis denarijs Londini venditur.
A galon of ale is at.i. peny & ferdynge.
Lagena ceruisia denario cum quadrante.

Preceptum.

Exposcunt genitum verbalia. &c.   Exempla.
35 He is a louer of vertue.
Est amator virtutis. vel amat virtutem.

58 Vulgaria Roberti Whitintoni

He is a bolsterer of fals maters.
Iniuriaru*m* est defensor.   vel iniurias defendit.
Surfet is the nouryssher of all sykenes.
Crapula est altrix om*n*iu*m* egritudinem.

     Preceptu*m*.   5
   In genitum mutant verbalia. &c.

He is a couetyse man of other mennes good / and a waster of his owne.
 In ens.   Est alieni appetens sui profusus.
He hath be euer a keper of iustyce.   10
 In ans.   Iusticie semper fuit obseruans.
He is an expert man in many thynges.
 In tus.   Multaru*m* reru*m* est expertus.
He careth not what he spendeth all the whyle he hath ony thynge in his purse.   15
 In sus.   Qua*n*tu*m*uis nu*m*moru*m* sit profusus / nihil pensi habet : du*m*modo sibi supersit quicqua*m*.
He wolde spende goddes coope yf he had it.
Tantaleas opes profunderet : vel tantalearu*m* opu*m* profusus foret : modo ijs potiat*ur*.   20
He gadreth and stoureth vp ryches for hym / y̆ shal full soone spende them.
Opes recondit vel cumulat illi : qui eas breui profundet : vel earu*m* profusus erit.
I am p*er*plexe / or doutefull in this mater / to what ende it wyll 25 growe at lenght.
 In xus.   Sum huius rei perplexus : quo ea euadet tandem.
He standeth in suche doute of hymself that he wote not whiche waye to tourne hym.
Adeo est sui perplexus : vt quo se vertat ignoret.   30
He casteth awaye his money vpon suche whiche yf he haue nede of helpe can nought do for hym.
 In gus.   Nu*m*moru*m* prodigus est in eos qui (si subsidij indigus fuerit) ei opitulari̇ non valent.
He knoweth not what prudence is / that casteth not before that 35 thynge whiche may come here after.
 In ius.   Prudentie est inscius / qui futuroru*m* non est prescius.

Vulgaria Roberti Whitintoni 59

He is so desyrous of glorye ẙ he knoweth not hymselfe.
   In dus. Glorie adeo est auidus / vt suijpsius sit ignarus / vel seip*su*m ignoret.
He is suche a nyggarde of his purse / that noo man coueyteth
5 his company.
   In rus. Num*m*oru*m* ita est auarus : vt sue conuersationis cupidus sit nemo. vel suam familiaritatem cupiat nemo.
A man that regardeth honestye / must somtyme be lyberall of his purse : and somtyme sparynge therof / as tyme requyreth.
10 In or. In cus. Honesti vel decori memor / nunc sumptuu*m* (vel impensaru*m*) liberalis / nu*n*c aut*em* parcus esse debet: pro temporis varietate.
Wheder you wenne or lese / I wyll be your halfe.
   In os. In ceps. Victorie vel vincendi compos ne / an impos
15   fueris : tue fortune particeps ero.
He is a bryber or a taker of brybes.
   In ax. Is largitionis est capax.
He is suche a pyker / that no thyn can lye by hym.
   Cuiusq*ue* rei est rapax.
20 He is a great rauener / specyally yf he come there as be good dysshes.   C. ij
Est edax precipue deliciarum.
He is a quaffer / namely of swete wyne.
Est bibax presertim dulcis vini.
25 He sitteth vpon lyfe and dethe.
   In ex. Est iudex reru*m* capitaliu*m*.
The table of rubryce of this boke sta*n*deth out of ordre.
Index huius libri est preposterus.
He was chefe heed of all this myschefe.
30 In ux. Is huius sceleris dux fuit.
She is chefe ryng leder of all dronken goseppes.
Hec temulentaru*m* co*m*potatricu*m* dux est primaria.
He gapeth for wordly promocyons al togyder / hauynge small mynde of godly lernynge.
35   In osus. Amplitudinis terrene ambitiosus est omnino : diuine actiue. discipline paru*m* studiosus.

Preceptum.
Ista petunt genitum solers. &c.   Exempla.
It is comenly sayd / the greatest clerkes be not all the wysest men of the worlde.
Uulgo dicitur. doctrine solertes / vtplurimum politicarum vel 5 agendarum rerum non sunt maxime experti.
He can noo fraude / & is lyberall of suche as he hathe.
Is doli est expers / et suarum rerum liberalis.
This is a plenteous countre of corne & barayn of wod.
Hec terra frugum est fertilis / lignorum vero sterilis.   10
Who so euer is ignoraunt of ẙ greke tongue / he shal euer be out of knowlege. of ẙ origynal & pyt of latyn tongue.
Quisquis grecarum litterarum est rudis : is medullite vel mere latinitatis expers semper erit.
He may be noted of foly / ẏ wyl not prayse ẏ tongue / out of ẙ 15 whiche latyn tongue / as from the well heed was deryued.
Inscitie merito reus condemnatur qui eam linguam non efferat : vnde latinitas ipsa tanquam a fonte est deducta.
He hath a heed as grose as a malle / & as many braynes as a wodcok.   20
Caput est illi instar mallei : sapientie tamen expers.
Preceptum.   Effectum cause genitum. &c.
Cause efficientis exempla.
Fo. xiiij Kynge henry the .vij. was a prynce of mooste famose memory.
Rex Henricus septimus fuit princeps luculentissime memorie. vel 25 luculentissime principis fuit memoria.
He was a prynce of great vertue.
Erat enim princeps magne virtutis. vel magna principis erat virtus.
Wherfore the laude / and prayse of that prynce floryssheth moost 30 synguler.
Quocirca precipua principis laus viget. Vel. non mediocris laudis decantatur princeps.
Cause formalis exempla.
He was a prynce bothe of famous vyctory also wonderous pollycy. 35
Claruit enim princeps non minus corporis / quam ingenij virtute. vel sic.
Clara fuit in principe non modo corporis / sed etiam animi virtus.

Vulgaria Roberti Whitintoni

Besyde that / he was a talle persone of body / and aungelyke of contenaunce.
Ad hoc / erat vir prestantis forme / & diuini vultus. vel sic.
Prestans erat viri forma & venustissimus quidem eiusdem
5 vultus.
More ouer ẙ fortune of ẙ prynce was moost merueylous. for ther coude no fraude so pryuely be conspyred agaynst his persone / but breuely it cam to lyght.
Preterea incredibilis erat principis fortuna. Vel sic. incredibilis
10 fortune fuit princeps: adeo vt in eum tam furtim coniurari posset nihil: quod non breui / cito / facile / vel continuo aduerteretur. rescisceretur. vel in lucem emergeret.

Cause materialis exempla.

And I can not ouerpasse / the stronge & myghty buyldynges / of
15 ẙ newest and goodlyest cast whiche he made in his tyme.
N que silentio preterire possum / miram structurarum (vel edifi-
:iorum) magnitudinem. Uel sic. mire magnitudinis structuras (& edificia) & nouissime et pulcherrime forme. Dedaleeque artis: suo viuentis tempore extructa.
20 Also the inestimable costes of bankettes that he made to his great honour / & to al his realme. at ẙ comynge of straungers / & in especyal at the receyuyng of ẙ kyng of Castyll spoken of thorughout al realmes of crystendum.
Tum innumeros sumptus: solennium (vel regalium) epularum.
25 Uelsic. saliares immensi sumptus cenas: quas ad summum cum sui / tum totius regni honorem exhibuit in exterorum (& in primis Castellie regis) occursu vbiuis christianorum decantatas.

Cause finalis exempla. C. iiij

30 Who is he but he may laude and prayse ẙ godly relygyon of that prynce and the synguler loue of godly honoure that appereth in his monumentes.
Quis non extollat diuinam principis religionem / & singularem diuini cultus amorem: que in suis monumentis extant. Uel
35 sic. Quis laudibus non efferat diuine religionis principem? & singularem in eadem diuini amoris cultum. vt sua declarant monumenta.

It can not be thought the contrary but the merytes of his good dedes be great.

Negare est nephas / merita suorum bonorum operum non fore immensa. velsic. Refrageri est absurdum. meritorum suorum premia non fore innumera. 5

What shold I say of the goodly and sure ordynaunce of his godly entent & purpose ẏ he hath enstablysshed in Westmynster & in sauoy founded of his cost.

Quid predicem? sancta sue religiose prouidentie statuta: tam in westmonasterio / quam in saluatoris hospitio suis sumptibus 10 sancita. Velsic. Quid commemorem religiosam suorum diuorum statutorum constitutionem haud secus: in Westmonasterio / quam in saluatoris elemosinario suis impensis confirmatam?

I doute not but he hath in fruicyon the reward of his true & 15 faytfull trust in god: in eternall glory.

Prorsus non dubito: hunc frui sue vere in christo fidei corona / in immortali gloria. Uel sic. Fidelissime spero christianam sue corone fidem syderea immortalitate iam iam premiatam.

Preceptum. 20

Effecti efficiens poscit. &c. Cause effecti exempla.

The excellent inuencyons of men in this dayes shewe that the golden vayne / or golden worlde (by reuolucyon celestyall) is now retourned / or come agayne.

Diuina hominum inuenta. vel humanus (diuinitus) inuenta. 25 auream venam / vel aureum cyclum (celesti influxu) iam redijsse canunt / siue sagiunt.

For true knowlege of lernyng that hath longe tym be hydde in profounde derkenes / by dylygence of men in this tyme is nowe brought to open lyght. 30

Uera enim eruditionis (vel doctrine) cognitio: cymerijs tenebris obducta: hominum (vel humana industria) in apertam lucem iam tandem prodijt.

Forme et materie exempla.

The true knowlege of lernynge is to suche dylygente studentes 35 more treasure / than rynges & cuppes of golde / & other worldly and transitory ryches.

Fo. xv Enucleata eruditionis peritia / hisce mere & non languide

Vulgaria Roberti Whitintoni

studentibus: prestantior anulis et vasis aureis (vel ex auro) et alijs (id genus) opibus fluxis ducitur.

For whan all this precyous Jewels of golde / syluer plates / & ryche roobes of purple / veluet / clothe of gold be worne or
5 gone by chaunse. lerning wyl abyde with a man.

Quippe quum ditia monilia aurea (vel ex auro) vasa argentea (vel ex argento). trabee purpuree (vel ex purpura) vestes inaurate (vel ex aurifilo intexto) sunt detrita vel casu deperdita. eruditio tibi perstabit.

10 Nominis ad aliquid facti exempla.

It is no poynte of a good studente to haunte ale howses or tauernes.

Probum non decet studentem / tabernas ceruisiarias & vinarias frequentare.

15 Preceptum.

Contenti in se vult genitum. &c. Exempla.

I prefer / or set more by a cup of ale (yf it be wel brued and stale) than a galon of the best wyne.

Cuppam ceruisie dummodo bene confecte & depurate congio vini
20 electissimi prefero.

I haue set a newe pype of wyne abroche.

Intactam vini seriam releui.

The wyne bottell is somwhat fusty and that hath altred the wyne.

Hic vter vinarius est aliquantulum mucidus / mucet / vel muces-
25 cit: vnde adulteratur vinum.

A ton of the last yeres wyne is worthe two tonnes of this yeres.

Dolium vini superioris anni / duplato horni vel hornotini vini dolio antefero.

This hoggysshed of wyne drynketh dulcet / & therfore it must be
30 dronke out of hande / for it can not tary.

Uinum huius dolioli est leue: quare continuo absumi debet: diutinum enim non erit.

This rynlet of maluesye is not fyned.

Hoc vasculum vini cretici est nondum defecatum.

35 This is a cup of good romney and drynketh well of $\stackrel{e}{y}$ rase.

Hec est cuppa resinati vini electi / & odoriferi.

This wyne drynketh of a good verdoore.
Hoc vinum est delicati odoris.
This is a greue wyne & a smale.
Hoc vinum est asperum et tenue.
This wyne drynketh lowe or vnder the barre. 5
Hoc vinum languescit / vel deficere incipit / vel eneruum est. vel languidum.

This wyne is palled or deed.   This wyne is soure.
Hoc vinum vappascit.   Hoc vinum acet / vel est aceto-
                                sum. 10
This wyne is hye coloured.   This is a made wyne.
Hoc vinum est intensi coloris. Est vinum adulterinum.
A lowe coloured wyne.   This wyne is brued.
Uinum remissi coloris.   Hoc vinum est dilutum.
These wyne pottes be to small. 15
Hec vinaria pocula sunt iusto minutiora.

Preceptum.

Post possessorem signans laudem. &c.   Exempla.
Moore is a man of an aungels wyt / & syngler lernyng.
Grammaticus loquendi modus. Morus est vir diuini ingenij / & 20
  singularis (vel egregie) eruditionis. Oratorius. Morus est vir
  mirando ingenio / et prestantissima eruditione. Historicus.
  Morus est vir preclarus ingenio / et eruditione. Poeticus.
  Morus est vir prestans ingenij. &c.
Modus oratorius est venustior ceteris / & frequentior : quare huic 25
  sepius est innitendum nisi historias scribas / aut poemata.
He is a man of many excellent vertues (yf I shold say as it is) I
  knowe not his felowe.
Est enim vir claris virtutibus (vt facessat assentatio) qualem haud
  noui alterum. 30
For where is the man (in whome is so many goodly vertues) of ye
  gentylnes / lowlynes / and affabylyte.
Ubinam est vir (in quo tante coruscant virtutes) ea benignitate.
  comitate. ea denique affabilitate.
And as tyme requyreth / a man of merueylous myrth and pas- 35
  tymes / & somtyme of as sad grauyte / as who say. a man
  for all seasons.
Tum (vt tempus postulat) vir lepidis salibus. facetis iocis.

Vulgaria Roberti Whitintoni

Rursus (aliqu*ando*) matura grauitate : vir (vt ita dicam) o*mn*i*u*m horarum.

Preceptu*m*. Possessum parte*m* signa*n*s. &c.

Hoc preceptu*m* soli poete obseruant : & figurate quide*m* : quare
5 in soluta oratione est fugiendu*m*. vnde cu*m* poete dicu*n*t.
Sum albus faciem. doleo caput. Dicendu*m* est nobis oratorie.
Sum alba facie. Caput dolet.

Preceptu*m*.

Cu*m* precij nomen. &c.   Exempla.
10 Befes and mottons be so dere : y̆ a peny worth of meet wyll scant suffyse a boye at a meale.
Bouine et ouine carnes adeo sunt care / vt denarij obsoniu*m* vix Fo. xvj puerum saturet / vel vnica refectione.
Whan I was a scholer of Oxforthe I lyued compete*n*tly with .vij.
15 pens commens wekely.
Cum Oxonie studui : septenoru*m* denariorum co*n*uictu singulis ebdomadis (sic satis) reficiebar.
My fader hathe .ij. hondred pounde worthe of stuffe brought home to daye.
20 Pater habet ducentaru*m* libraru*m* merces domu*m* co*m*portatas hodie.
Fetche vs a halfpeny lofe / a penyworthe of egges / & an half-penyworth of ale.
Compares nobis oboli pane*m*. denarij oua. et oboli ceruisiam.

25 Preceptu*m*.

Artificem signans. &c.   Exempla artificu*m*.
We haue in our warde belfounders / pewterers / plummers / brasyers.
Sunt in nostra vicinia fusores companarij / stannarij / plu*m*barij /
30 erarij.
And a lytle bynethe ther dwel taylers / shomakers / hosyers / vpholsters / glouers / sewsters / coblers.
Et paulo inferius habitant sutores vestiarij / calcearij / caligarij / lectarij / chirothecarij / sutrices lintearie / et sarctores calce-
35 arij.

F

66   Vulgaria Roberti Whitintoni

In the strete nexte aboue be sue smythes / sythe smythes / blade smythes / cutlers armurers rasermakers carpenters / whele wryghtes / carte wryghtes / loksmythes / clokke smythes.

In vico aut*em* superiori sunt fabri ferrarij / falcarij / secarij / cultellarij / armararij / nouacularij / lignarij / rotarij / plaustrarij / ferarij / horologiarij.

In the lane vpo*n* the ryght hande be clothe weuers couerlet weuers / carpet weuers / arras makers.

In angiporto quide*m* dextero textores pannarij / stragularij / tapetarij / aulearij.

As a man tourned vpon the lefte hande y̆ shalt se sylke women / cappe knytters / gyrdle weuers / netmakers.

Ad diuerticulu*m* a leua videas textrices bombicinarias / nectrices birrhetarias / textrices cinctuarias / & nectrices plagiaris vel rhetiarias.

In the herte of the cyte sheweth goodly brooderers / vestmentmakers / goldesmythes / grossers / mercers.

Vulga. In vrbis medio / vel visceribus luculentissimi sunt siti acupictores /
whitin. aurifabri / odorarij vel aromatopole / lintearij.
D. i

And in the strete vpon the back halfe : be drapers / fullers / cappers / thyckers of cappes / shermen / dressers / carders and spynners.

In platea posteriori (vel a tergo) co*n*uersantur venditores pannarij / fullones pannarij / birrhetarij / fullones birrhetarij / interpolatores vestiarij / carminatrices / et filatrices.

And vpon the other syde anendest be fysshemongers / pulters / cokes / podyngmakers / vintenars / typplers / bruers / bakers / with other vytalers.

Et ex aduerso (e diuerso vel e regione) sunt co*n*stituti : mercatores piscatorij. pullarij siue auiarij. coqui. fartores. vinarij. ceruisiarij. ceruisiatores. pistores. lanij. cumalijs cupedinarijs.

In the townes ende be pynners / poynters / tourners bukklemakers / gyrdelers / dyers / tanners with artifycers that cometh not to mynde.

In vrbis exitu / egressu / vel fine incolitant acicularij / ligacularij / tornatores / fibularij / cinctuarij / tinctores / incorticatores. cum alijs artificibus : q*ui* memorie no*n* subeunt.

Besyde that / labourers : as fre masens / quarryers / or hewers of stones / bryckelayers / tylers / dawbers / plasterers / glasyers /

Vulgaria Roberti Whitintoni 67

ioyners / keruers / grauers / ymagemakers / paynters / thressers / dytchers.

Adhoc operarij / vt fabri vel structores murarij vel cementarij / lapicide / vel lathomi / stratores lateritij / egularij / litores parie-
5 tarij / gipsatores parietarij / vitrearij coassatores / anagliptes / sculptores / statuarij / pictores / trituratores / fossores.

And a lytle vpon this halfe or hydderwarde there be phisicyans / surgyans / potycaryes / hatmakers / bokeprynters / bokesellers or stacyoners / scryueners.

10 Et paulo citra / cohabitant medici / aliptes / pharmacapole / pillearii / typographi / bybliopole / bybliographi.

As for mynstrelles dwell here and there / as harpers luters / fydelers / taberers / trumpetters / shamullers / suche as go with psalteryes / portatyues / bagge pypes / recorders / horne-
15 pypes.

Postremo mimi incerti (vel sparsim) degunt. vt lyricines / cytharedi / fidicini / tympaniste / tubicines / tibicines / psaltes / organiste / gingritores / fistulatores / cornicines.

Exempla artificiorum.

20 I was set prentes to the dyers crafte / & than to ẙ weuers crafte / & at last to the fullers crafte.

Mancipatus fui arti tinctorie. deinde textorie et tandem fullonarie.

Et sic hoc nomen ars asciscit sibi possessiuum in aruis sui
25 artificis: et quoniam exempla satis patent / hec pauca sufficiunt. Fo. xvij

Preceptum.

Cum substantiuo quoties uenit immediate.

Temporis / aut spacij. &c.   Exempla temporis.

30 My countre is but thre dayes iourney hens.

Patria mea vix tridui / vel triduano itinere hinc abest.

I haue layen here this moneth space to my cost: wherfore I longe to be at home.

Mensis vel mestruo interuallo ad sumptum mihi / hic egi: quare
35 reditum capturio / percupio / vel desydero.

Yf I had store of money I wolde not forse thoughe I laye styll here by the space of two or thre monethes.

Quodsi nummorum satis mihi superesset: si duorum aut trium

F 2

mensium (vel sic) bemestri trimestri spacio hic loci remorarer : paruipenderem.
In one yeres iourney I wente hens to Hierusalem & retourned agayne.
Unius anni / vel annali peregrinatione hinc Hierosolimam petens / redij.

Exempla spacij.

He is a dwarffe / or an vrchen scant thre fote of heyght.
Est homunctio vix trium pe[d]um¹ altitudine : vel tripedali.
Thou art thycker than I by a span brode.
Es crassior me / palme vel palmari latitudine.
I am hyer than thou by an ynche lenght and more.
Sum altior te pollicis / vel pollicari longitudine. superque.

Exempla de ijs que tenellis subsistunt annis.

I maye remembre many thynges that I dyd whan I was chylde of .iij. and .iiij. yere of age.
Multa recordor vel memoria teneo / que trium et quatuor annorum puer : vel sic trimulus / et quadrimulus puer feci.
   Annotatio de hoc nomine dies quod cum homini nominibus semper in genitiuo (& non in possessiuo) poni debet.
Thou has as moche wyt as a chylde of a day / or two dayes olde.
Perinde sapis / atque vnius diei / aut duorum dierum puer : non autem dices diurnus puer.

Preceptum. Quando loci nomen. &c.
The embassatours of fraunce were receyued with gret honour as euer was seen in ony tymes past.
Oratores siue legati gallicani cum maximo honore (quali anteactis temporibus vix vsquam legitur) sunt accepti.

Annotatio de possessore.

And in lyke maner the embassatours that cam fro the kynge of castyll.
Eodem quoque modo. vel haud secus oratores qui ab rege Castellie aduenerunt.

¹ *Text* pepum

Vulgaria Roberti Whitintoni

Exempla de appellatiuis.

A certayn of the nobel men of this realme were apoynted in goodly arraye to mete them in the waye.

Quidam ex nobilissimis regni / splendidissimo ornatu. ijs obuiam
5 sunt missi.

Besyde that the mayer and the alder men of ẙ cyte rode forthe in one lyuery to brynge them in.

Ad hoc pretor et senatores / maiores / primates / vel optimates vrbis. vel vrbani eodem apparatu / ijs equitarunt obuij.

10 It was a goodly syght to beholde them comyng into the cyte euery man gorgeously / appareld / dekked / appoynted / or arrayed / after his countre fason / guyse / or maner.

Opereprecium / iucundum / gratum : erat cernere / aspicere / videre / contemplari / eos vrbem ingressos : suo quenque patrie
15 vel patrio more luculentissime ornatum.

Annotatio de abusu ablati.

And all the commens of London resorted strete by strete to salute them and welcom them.

Insuper. communis / vulgaris. vel gregarius populus. londonianus
20 (barbarum est dicere londonie / vel de londonijs) vicatim vel plateatim eosdem salutatum confluxere.

Preceptum. · Partem quod signat. &c.

Upon London brydge I sawe .iij. or .iiij. mennes heedes stande vpon poles.

25 In londoniano ponte (non autem londonie / vel de londonia) vidi tria aut quatuor capita hominum vel humana perticis affixa.

Upon Ludgate ẙ fore quarter of a man is set vpon a pole.

In occidentali porta londoniensi exposit[us][1] est in pertica homi-nis / vel humanus thorax partitus.

30 Upon ẙ other syde hangeth ẙ hawnce of a man with ẙ legge.

E regione dependet hominis / vel humana coxa cum crure.

It is a straunge syght to se ẙ heere of ẙ heedes fase / or moose away / & ẙ grystell of ẙ nose consumed awaye.

Aspectu mirandum est / vel aspicere est mirum. pilos capitum
35 (non dices capitales) decidere vel deciduos / et cartilaginem nasorum tabefactam / vel tabidam.

[1] *Text* exposita.

The fyngers of theyr handes wyddred / and clunged vnto the bare boones.
Tum digiti manuum (non dices manuales) torrefacti / & ossium tenus herentes.

Preceptum.

In possessiuis intelligitur genitiuus. &c.

Exempla adiectiui.

It is a spectacle for euer / to all yonge people to be ware ẏ they presume not to ferre vpon theyr owne heednes or selfe mynde.
Perpetuum est documentum vniuerse iuuente precauere : ne sue (ipsius) pertinacie (plus iusto) confidant. vel suam (ipsius) temeritatem inconsulte defendant.
Theyr mad hardnes only brought them to ẏ shamful ende / & made them to seke theyr owne dethe.
Sua enim solius temeritas ad ignominiosum illud exitium eos adegit: et suum exterminium querere vel asciscere impulit.

Exempla relatiui.

There is no man wyl pyte thy dethe / which wyl renne vpon it wylfully / & hast no lawful cause whye soo.
Nemo quidem dolebit ob mortem tuam / qui vltro eam queris / vel lacessis : et sine iusta causa.

Exempla substantiui per appositionem.

For euery man wyll say that it is longe of thy owne sekynge a man without dyscrecyon or prudence.
Obijciet enim quiuis id tuo hominis imprudentis factum impetu.
And so after thy dedes / name shall renne vpon thy : yf thy dedes proue well : men wyll saye it is done by thy prudence / a dyscrete man.
Itaque pro factis (vel secundum facta) estimabitur fama. Quodsi prospera succedant facta id tua prouidi viri prudentia contigisse ferent.
Yf thy purpose chaunce not well they wyll saye. it was longe of thy foly / a man without reason.
Sin minus succedant tua instituta : condemnabitur tua imperiti viri inscitia.

Vulgaria Roberti Whitintoni

Preceptum. Uult partitiuum. &c.

Exempla nominis partitiui meri.

I se many of them in this dayes ẙ taketh vpon them to dysprayse other mennes workes / but I se fewe or none of them / ẙ setteth out ony of theyr owne makynge.

Vulga. whitin. D. iij

Multos / frequentes / vel complures eorum / inter eos / vel ex ijs video: qui aliorum opuscula vitio dari arrogant. Ceterum paucos / immo nullos eorundem / inter eosdem / vel ex eisdem comperio qui sue lucubrationis quicquam edunt.

Some of them wyl fynd a faute whiche they can not mende themselfe.

Aliqui / vel alij eorum / inter eos / vel ex eis erratum : quod ipsi corrigere ignorant. facile annotabunt vel confingent.

Some of them wyl make a faute there as none is. As the malaperte cobler that was aboute to correcte the paynter Apelles.

Tum eorum / inter illos / vel ex ijs sunt nonnulli qui errorem temere allucinabuntur haud secus / ac sutor ille confidens vel impudens qui pictorem Appellem carpere / insimulare vel reprehendere est ausus.

Yf ony of theym wyll take vpon them the iudgemente of correccyon of other men : fyrst it wold become them to lerne to make of theyr owne inuencyon.

Quodsi quis / quisquam : vel vllus illorum / inter illos / vel ex illis censuram aliorum corrigendorum vsurparet: prius / discant / vel sua edere: foret equum.

Exempla partitiue positorum.

But it is comenly sayd / euery begger is woo / that ony other shold by the dore go.

Exempla distributiui nominis.

At vulgo fertur mendicorum inter eos / vel ex eis quilibet alteri dexteritatem inuidet.

Exempla interrogati & infiniti.

Let vs se whiche of this barkers (whiche of them soo euer it be) ẙ darre ones gnarre to a mans face.

Ecquis obtrectatorum / inter trectatores / vel ex trectoribus (q*ui*sq*ui*s horu*m* inter hos vel ex eis) sit / coram authore (saltem) ringere audet?

But behynde a mannes backe : suche as thynke themselfe wyser / and wyseste / of that secte : they playe as the dogge doeth / yͭ barketh at the moon all nyght.

Ueruntamen clanculu*m* / vel clam : qui doctiores (ac potius) doctissim[i][1] eoru*m* / inter eos vel ex eis / vide*n*tur sibi : vicem canis pernoctis lune allatrantis suscipiunt.

Preceptum.

Dissimilis similis. &c. Exempla.

It is seldom sene yͭ the chylde proued after the faders prykkes / Fo. xix or lyke the fader in vertue.

Rarissime cernitur / similis paterne probitatis soboles.

Many represente theyr faders in physonomye / or co*n*tenaunce / & yet in no thynge resemble his condicyons.

Non pauci vultu patri similes co*n*spiciuntur : qui tamen eius prorsus dissimiles su*n*t moribus.

No merueyle. for it is comenly sayd : many a good kowe bryngeth forthe a sory calfe.

Nimiru*m* vulgatu*m* (vel tritu*m*) est dictu*m* : p*ro*ba freque*n*ter vacca / vitulu*m* parit improbum.

It is lyke to be true that euery man sayth.

Quod in o*mni*u*m* est ore / veri haud est dissimile.

Preceptum.

Certus cum dubius. &c. Exempla.

Though a man thynke hymselfe neuer so sure of his purpose : yet it is good to cast doutes / of chau*n*ces that maye fall after.

Quantu*m*uis tuaru*m* reru*m* (vel de tuis rebus) certus sis : futuroru*m* tame*n* casuu*m* (vel de futuris casibus) dubius esse : no*n* importunu*m* (vel inconsultum) est.

I haue knowen a man or nowe that thought hymself cokke sure of his entente / & sodaynly the wynde hathe tourned / so that he hath be wery of his parte.

Noui ho*mi*n*em (ante hac) qui sui instituti (v*e*l de instituto) se securu*m* iactitauit : subita tamen reflauit fortuna : adeo vt sue vicis (vel de vice) sollicitus esset.

[1] *Text* doctissimos.

Preceptum.

Diuitias signans. &c. Exempla.

It is a syngyler solace vnto a man / whiche though he be poore of worldly substaunce: yet he is ryche in vertue / or connynge.

5 Summum homini est solatium / qui licet fluxarum opum sit egenus (indigus vel inops) virtutis tamen aut eruditionis est diues vel locuples.

For vertue and connyng (as it is dayly proued) maketh many poore of substaunce / ryche in possessyons at lenght.

10 Quippe (quod vulgo cernitur) virtus et eruditio complures / fortune pauperes agrorum (vel agris) diuites (vel opulentos reddunt tandem.

Preceptum.

Cum recto aut terno coniunctum est. &c.

15 Exempla. D. iiij

Thoughe a man haue neuer so moche ryches / yet by chaunce he maye lese it all in one houre.

Quantumlibet diuitiarum habeas: vna quidem horula casu deperdas prorsus.

20 Yet yf he haue ony lernynge: whan his goodes be gone he maye haue a lyuynge.

Si vero eruditionis quicquam sit illi: opibus licet exhaustis: victum tamen sibi acquirat.

Yf he haue no connynge: he may loke for a bare lyuyng excepte
25 he begge or stele.

Sin eruditionis nihil habeat: paululum victus expectet. ni aut petat / aut depredetur.

Preceptum.

Substantiuo tu nunquam ponito. &c. Exempla.

30 This mischeuous hongre of couetyse maketh a man so gredy of goodes that he weneth y̆ he shal neuer haue ynough ryches.

Auaricie sacra fames / rerum ita auidum reddit quenquam: vt diuitiarum satis se habiturum diffidat.

So y̆ many where they haue great substaunce / & more than euer
35 they shall spende honestly / wyll saye y̆ they haue lytle good or nothynge.

Adeo / vt multi / vbi rerum multum (& plus quam honeste consument) eis abundat: mentiantur se parum (immo nihil) opum habere.

De constructione datiui. Preceptum.

Mobile quodque bonum. &c. Exempla.

To a couetyse man there is no man welcome: excepte he brynge somwhat.

Auaro / gratus vel acceptus venit nemo: nisi com[m]odus[1] aut frugifer sibi veniat.

Yf a man come not for his auauntage / or to hym: to neuer so lytle cost. it goeth soore & greuous to his herte.

Quodsi incommodus ei. aut sumptuosus accedas: pestifer / molestus / iniocundus sibi est aduentus tuus.

Exempla de significantibus propinquitatem vel conuenientiam.

Though thou be neuer so nye of kynne vnto hym / or nye neyghbour vnto hym / yet thou art no mete marchaunt for hym yf thou come empty handed.

Fo. xx Quantumuis sanguine sibi propinquus vel proximus: aut vicinitate eidem quantumlibet coniunctus / contiguus / vel finitimus sis: non congrua / conformis / aut consona animo est tua familiaritas si aduenias vacuus.

Exempla verbalium in ilis / dus / et osus passionem significantium.

What is so detestable to a man as this poysonfull couetyse? that maketh a man as a subiecte to the mukke of the worlde.

Quid ita execrabile cuiquam / vt pestifera hec cupiditas: que hominem stercoratis opibus subditum reddit.

It bryngeth bothe daye and nyght dyuerse chaunces dredefull to a mannes herte.

Et interdiu et noctu. affert varios casus animo formidolosos.

Exempla de compositis ab obuio et uia.

A couetyse man wyl not gladly go y̆ way y̆ he iudgeth to mete with his aquayntaunce for sparyng of expense.

Auarus ultro hac non gradietur / qua notis obuius fiat: qui sumptuum est tenax.

[1] *Text* comodus

Vulgaria Roberti Whitintoni 75

But he wyll slyppe asyde by some lane / or way y̌ fewe or none passe by.
Uerum se subducet per angiportum aut circuitum / paucis / aut nullis peruium.

5   Preceptum.

Utile quod signat. &c.   Exempla.
A lyberal man iudgeth no thynge profytable vnto hym except it be ioyned with honestye.
Liberalis homo (vel liberalitas) vtile (vel vtilitati) sibi iudicat
10   nihil: nisi eidem honestum (vel honestati) accedat.
Fye vpon that profet pryuate that after maye growe to a mannes rebuke.
Nephanda est illa priua vtilitas : que imposterum cuiquam turpis (vel turpitudini) emergat.
15 Though suche vyle profet semeth pleasaunt for ẙ tyme yet I defye it. whan it putteth a man to dyspleasure at lenght.
Quanquam turpis ea vtilitas (prima fronte) dulcis grata (aut delectabilis : vel dulcior)¹ tibi videatur : cum tamen molesta / acerba (vel molestie et acerbitati) tibi euadet tandem. eam
20   vilipendo.

                    Preceptum.

Est possessiui pronominis. &c.   Exempla.
He may therfore be reputed bothe lyberall and discrete y̌ regardeth as well his honestye / as his profet.
25 Iure igitur censeatur et liberalis et prudens : qui non minus honestatem sibi quam vtilitatem pensitat.
But this vngracyous couetyse blyndeth all moost all ẙ world : so that many / y̌ be other wayes wyse can not se theyr faute.
Ceterum / scelerata ea cupiditas / plerosque hominum adeo fas-
30   cinat : ne multi (qui secus sapiunt) vitia sibi aduertant.

           De constructione accusatiui casus.

                    Preceptum.

Nomina nulla regunt quartum. &c.

           ¹ *Text* dulcori

Vulgaria Roberti Whitintoni

Exempla prepositionis mediante.

A man that is prudent is mete for al maner of company.
Uir prudens ad cuiusque generis societatem aptus est / vel ad quorumuis coniunctionem est idoneus.

Exempla nominum per participijs positorum. 5
A newfangled felowe is dyscontent with euery man ỹ vseth hym not after his appetyte.
Morosus / quemuis suo animo non morigerum / prorsus est osus.
And therfore euery man laug[h]eth [1] hym to scorne & hateth his company. 10
Ideoque rident eum: & conuersationem eiusdem. sunt exosi vel perosi omnes.

Authoritates.

Caius graccus. Mirum sit quid ijs iniurie fit: semper eos osi sunt. 15 Columella libro decimo. Neque ea curatorem fraudulentum tantum: sed etiam immundam segnitiem perosa est. Quintilianus libro primo. Qui non modo legitimam disciplinam sunt perosi. Plautus in Am. Inimicos semper exosa sum. Uirgilius in quinto. Iuppiter omnipotens si non dum exosus ad vnum. 20 Troianos.

Preceptum. Plenum vel vacuum. &c.

Exempla plenitudinis vel inopie.

A foole is so ful of wordes that he dassheth out all that lyeth on his herte. 25
Fatuus verbis adeo turgidus est: vt omnia animi secreta ebulliat vel effutiat.
A wyse man voyde of hastynes. hereth with pacyence and dyfferreth vnto he se tyme.
Prudens vero / affectione vacuus / tacitus aurem prebet: & rem 30 in maturum tempus differt.

Exempla ornationis & spoliationis.

Fo. xxi The prudent man therfore is auaunsed to moche promocyon whan the foole goeth without his purpose.
Prudens igitur emergit amplus honoribus: vbi improuidus expectatione viduus abscedit. 35

---
[1] *Text* laugeth

Vulgaria Roberti Whitintoni

Exempla de plenus et refertus nomine.

Whan the herte is full of pryde / ẙ tongue is full of boost and braggynge.
Ubi pectus superbia est tumidum : lingua multiloquij est plena
5 vel referta.

Exempla de refertus participio.

A prudent man whan he is moost ful or hyest in prosperyte / than he is moost moderate & studious to auoyde surges of his passyon.
10 Prudens cum fortune saturitate / vel de saturitate est refertus : tum maxime est modestus & sollicitus / qua ratione sui affectus elationum / siue ab elationibus sit vacuus.

Preceptum.   Sextum poscit opus. &c.

The hyer a man ascendeth the more nede he hath to loke about
15 hym : for yf he fayle of hold or slyppe ẙ greter is his fall.
Quo altius quisquam ascendit : eo oculatiori vigilantia opus est sibi. Quippe si manus aut pes deficiat : in preceps ruit.

Preceptum.   Dignus et indignus. &c.

Therfore in al thynges he is worthy laude that obserueth moder-
20 aunce.
Idcirco est laude / laudis / vel laudari dignus vel non indignus : qui moderantiam vbiuis obseruat.

Preceptum.

Sextum vel rectum cum quam uult comparatiuus. &c.
25 I can not lyghtely iudge wheder is more worthy disprayse. a man that is ouer prodygal / or ouer nyggarde of his purse.
Haud facile dixerim vtrum reprehensionis / reprehensione / vel reprehendi est dignior : suarum rerum nimium prodigus / quam auarus.

30   Exempla excessum significantis.

Bothe vyces be in the extremyte : but yet the nyggarde semeth forther fro vertue that is in the myddle. by moche than the prodygall persone.

U trum̄que vitium est extremum̄ : auarus tamen a virtute (que est in medio) multo longior prodigo (vel quam prodigus) videtur.

Preceptum.

Quos rogitas positus gradus. &c.   Exempla.
The nyggard is more hurtfull to ẙ comen wealth than ẙ prodygal man / for by ẙ prodygal some man hath profet.
Auarus reipublice est incommodior prodigo / vel quam prodigus : nam ex prodigo commodum capiunt aliqui.
A nyggarde is vnkynd to euery man / & moost vnkynde of all other vnto hymselfe.
Auarus omnibus est ingratus : & sibi ipsi omnium ingratissimus.

Preceptum.   Macte petit sextum. &c.

Therfore my chylde encrease with vertue consyderyng the vylyte of vyce.
Igitur macte virtute mi puer esto : vilitatem & turpitudinem vitij contemplans.

Preceptum.

Seiunctum signans. &c.   Exempla.
Fle my chylde fro dyshonestye & kepe the ferre of as ẙ woldest from a rokke in the see.
Ab indecoro mi puer alienus vel longinquus (tanquam a scopulo marino) fugias.
Than shall thou lyue fre from all care & remorse of conscyence : and euer quyete in thy mynde.
Tum (vel sic) viuas liber a curis et conscientie verme : et ociosus vel tranquillus ab animo.

Finis secunde partis.

Tertia pars de constructione verborum.

Connectit similes casus sum. &c.

Exempla.

He is a good man and iuste ẙ nother for fauoure / nor grudge / fere nor hope / inclyneth fro ryght / but standeth vpryght.

Vulgaria Roberti Whitintoni

Hic probus est et iustus homo : qui neq*ue* fauore / neq*ue* odio / timore / aut spe / a iusticia inclinat vspiam : immo erecto animo constat.

Exempla passiuorum.

But how many of this lerned men be there fou*n*de iust & egall iudges / also proued true attornes to the clyentes / but brybes may choke them. Fo. xxij

Quot tamen ex iurisperitis inueniuntur iusti et equi iudices. aut co*m*periuntur fideles aduocati clientibus quos non iugulet pecunia.

Exempla verboru*m* motum significatium siue quietem.

As lo*n*ge as money doeth last ple*n*teous / many of them wyll go and stande as stronge champyons with a ma*n* : but whan money is gone / ye maye syt a wretche poste alone.

Dum copiosa superest pecunia : tecum in pedes ibunt / & co*n*sistent pugiles : at consumpta pecunia sedeas vel quiescas solus / vel derelictus miser.

Exempla de ijs que motu*m* includu*n*t.

Though $\overset{u}{y}$ lyue or dye a begger & lese thy ryght : what care they? they haue other maters to lorke vpon.

Uiuas ne / an moriare mendicus (amisso iure) nihili pendunt illi : alias res agunt.

Exempla de exto et forem.

Thou was somtyme a man. and sholde be agayne yf $\overset{u}{y}$ had stoore of money to folowe thy ryght.

Olim vir extitisti / & rursus fores idem / du*m*modo tibi essent opes.

Exempla de verbis persistentie.

He that perseuereth a iust man : is sure to haue immortalyte.

Quicunq*ue* perstat / persistat manet / vel perseuerat vir iustus immortalitate (absq*ue* dubio) fruetur.

De regentibus *geniti*u*u*m casum.
Preceptu*m*.

Sum post se genitum. &c.

I haue be euer of this mynde. that I neuer take hym for a iust man / whose dedes agre not with his wordes.
Huius opinionis semper fui : vt neminem iustum censeam / cuius facta dictis non conueniunt.

Exempla de ijs que laudem significant. 5
He is of a boolde stomake & manly / whiche is constaunte in all chaunses.
Is est inuicta animi fortitudine : qui in omni fortuna sibi constat.
The prayse of forse and fortitude / standeth not only in hym that is of valyaunt strength of body. but specyally in hym that is 10 victour and conquerour of the passyons of the mynde.
Laus magnanimitatis non tantum restat in eo / qui est magna corporis virtute : sed in eo demum qui animi aduersitatibus dominatur.
For Iason. Achilles. Hercules. Alexander : were of famous 15 vyctorye : albe it. bycause they coude not subdue theyr sensuall passyons / they ar noted to be of mooste shamefull infamy. as men confounded by women.
Quippe qui cantatissima fuerunt victoria Iason. Achilles. Hercules. & Alexander qui tamen animi libidinibus moderari non vale- 20 rent. insigni notantur esse infamia vt qui mulie[b]ri[1] seruitio subiugati.

Preceptum.
Quarto vel genito structum dicit misereri. &c.

Exempla de misereor. 25
He that hath no pyte or compassyon of an other : he shall haue iustyce without mercy.
Quicunque alterius non miseretur : erit illi iusticia sine misericordia.
For the same mesure (as scryptur sayth) that ye shewe to other : 30 shalbe minystred vnto you.
Eadem quippe mensura (vt sacre produnt littere) qua mensi fueritis : remetietur vobis.

Exempla de satago.
Euery man shal haue ynough to do with his owne dedes at the 35

[1] *Text* mulieri

last ende : & to crye and call for mercy as we se in these that be in poynt of dethe comenly.

Unusquisq*ue* in postremo obitu suaru*m* reru*m* sataget : sibi misericordia*m* vocifera*n*s. vt in moribundis crebro cernitur.

5   Preceptum.

Obliuiscor eget sic indiget. &c.   Exempla.

But these great men that be in hye authoryte forget these thynges bycause they remembre not theyr owne fragylyte / and dethe ineuytable.

10 Ueru*m* magnates que summa sunt potentia : haru*m* admonitionu*m* (vel has admonitiones / vel admonitionibus) obliuiscu*n*tur : q*uod* sueipsius fragilitatis (fragilitate*m* / vel fragilitate) mortisq*ue* inexorabilis / haud reminiscuntur.

Who shall pytye them yf they haue nede of mercy.

15 Quis eoru*m* (vel eis) miserebitur ? si miserationis (vel miseratione) indigeant.

Preceptum.

Deposcunt genitum aut quartum memini. &c.   Fo. xxiij

Many shal remembre hym specyally and saye / god haue mercy
20 vpon his soule that regardeth mercy whyle he is here.

Multi illius (v*e*l illum) recordabu*n*tur. misericordia*m* anime exoptantes / qui hac in luce misericordiaru*m* (vel misericordias) meminit.

Scrypture maketh mencyon expressly of them ẙ regarde not the
25 workes of mercy : how sharpe sentence / god shall gyue vpon them at the dredefull daye.

Sacru*m* meminit eloquiu*m* eoru*m* (eos / vel de eis) qui opera misericordie non recorda*n*tur q*uam* acerba*m* in eos sententia*m* (in illo calamitatis die) laturus est deus.

30   De constructione datiui.

Preceptu*m*.   Acquisitiue verbum. &c.

Whan thryfte cometh hastely or lyghtely vnto a man / comenly it prospereth not longe with hym.

Cu*m* fortuna nimiu*m* precox (cita / vel preceps) tibi alludit

G

82 Vulgaria Roberti Whitintoni

(arridet / accedit / vel accrescit) diutina (plerunque) tibi non perstabit.

Exempla duplicis datiui et loco posterioris accusatiui.

We se by experience that garden floures (as the lylly) groweth to euery mannes syght in short space to a merueylous heyght / & 5 sodenly fadeth and falleth.

Compertum est hortenses flores (quale est lilium) breui oculis omnium (vel omnibus intuentibus) ad miram altitudinem adolescere / subito marcescentes et cadiuos.

So hasty fruytes be a pleasure to a man for the tyme / but theyr 10 tyme is but a chery feyre.

Itaque precoces (vel prematuri) fructus tibi (pro tempore) voluptati (vel ad voluptatem) accedunt: at eorum tempus preceps euanescit / vel dilabitur.

Preceptum. 15

Sum sic consimiles casus nectentia verba.

Exemplum datiui acquirentis.

We se how lyghtely ryches chaunseth to marchauntes men of lawe / and suche other as blynde fortune enhaunseth.

Uidemus / quanto precipitio mercatoribus / causidicis / et id 20 genus alijs (quibus ceca alludit fortuna) confluunt opes.

Exempla duplicis datiui.

And sodenly in an houre they be lost / or scauntly remayn to the thyrd heare / but to his trouble or vndoynge.

Hore tamen momento / aut dilabuntur: aut vix tertio heredi 25 manent (vel restant) nisi magno sibi incommodo / vel detrimento. vel ad (aut in) detrimentum sibi. alioquin. ad (vel in) exterminium sibi.

Exempla triplicis datiui vel loco posterioris datiui accusatiui.

This shold be to euery wyse man a spectacle / or presydens [t]o[1] 30 remembre suche hasty auaunsement.

Hoc esset sapientissimo cuique documento: precipiti vtilitati recordande / vel ad vtilitatem recordandam.

[1] Text co

Preceptu*m*.

Sum pro habeo positu*m*. &c.   Exempla.
He that hath a rowmeth in y̆ͤ kynges court : I se well y̆ͭ [he] hath nede to vse hymselfe wysely.
In regis curia / cuicunq*ue* est munus: sibi opus esse perspicio. vt oculatissime sese moderetur.

Preceptu*m*.

Post se deposcit verbu*m* quodcunq*ue* datiuu*m*.
Signans congruere. &c.   Exempla.
He must fyrst applye hymselfe to agre wit*h* all maner of persones. to cory fauell craftely / to daunse / attendau*n*ce at all houres to be seruyable.
In primis studeat / quibuscu*n*q*ue* congruere. astu assentire. diligenter famulari. & in horas inseruire.
Also to be gentyll & full of humanyte with whome so euer he meteth. redy whan his superyour co*m*mau*n*deth hym. beneuolent to helpe a good felowe at nede.
Ad hoc / cuicunq*ue* occurrit : humanissime hunc salutare. vbi ei imperat maior paratissimus. familiari indigo suppetias ferre / non ingratus.

Preceptu*m*.

Ternum vel quartum sibi vult. &c.
Hec moderor.   Exempla.
What so euer he hereth or seeth he must brydel his tongue / & so shall he auoyde many inconuenyentes.
Quicquid audiat aut videat : lingue vel lingua*m* moderari habet. Fo. xxiiij
sic multis incommodis (vel multa incom*m*oda) medebitur.

Preceptu*m*.

Uult ternum verbum suadere. &c.   Exempla.
And specyally he must be ware what he conseyleth / or dissuadeth ony man / but good. & so shall he please all men and dysplease fewe.
Tum maxime precaueat / ne cuiuis suadeat vel dissuadeat quicq*uam* : nisi probabile sicq*ue* omnibus morem gerens / paucis displicebit.

And this folowynge ỹ myndes of men / not repugnynge the
sayenges of other obstinatly. euery man wyll fauer hym & fewe
grudge at hym.
Itaq*ue* si studijs ho*minu*m obsequens / alioru*m* dictis non perti-
naciter insultet / ei amicantes omnes / inimicabu*n*tur paucis- 5
simi.

Preceptu*m*. Offendo et ledo. &c.
If ony man offende hym : he may not forth w*ith* take peper in the
nose and shewe by rough wordes or haulty contenaunce ỹ he
is angred with hym / but cooldely & soberly tell hym of his 10
faute.
Quodsi eum ledat (vel offendat) quispiam : non iamia*m* sibi (vel
secu*m*) irasci debet. acerbis conuitijs vultuq*ue* rugoso secu*m*
stomachari ostendens immo modeste cu*m* ipso expostulare
iniuriam. 15

Preceptum.
Cum quibus est iunctum con. &c. Exempla.
Yf he be dysapoynted somtyme of his lyuery meet or of his
lodgynge : he maye not brall and bragge with ỹ offycers / but
entreat them fayre agayn an other tyme. 20
Tum sicubi obsonio debito defraudetur / aut cubili : magistratibus (vel cu*m* magistratibus) non contendat (vel conuicietur)
immo bla*n*ditijs eisdem (vel cu*m* eisde*m*) congrediatur : vt alias
fauorem captet.

Exempla de actiuis iunctis cum con. 25
And so shall he allure theyr fauour vnto hym : & spede whan
other be put fro theyr purpose.
Sicq*ue* illis (vel cu*m* illis) sese amicitia co*n*iungat : sui desyderij
co*m*pos / vbi alij impotes vel expertes erunt.

Preceptu*m*. 30

Vulga. In citra motum verbis. &c.
whitin. Besyde ỹ yf he entende to stycke styll in theyr fauoure he must
E. i nowe and than among se ẽ offycers rewarded.
Preterea magistrat*us* / si eoru*m* amicitie (vel in eoru*m* amicitia)
assidue inherere cogiret aliquando donatos (vel premiatos) curet 35
necessum est.

Vulgaria Roberti Whitintoni

Preceptum.

Uerba ad certamen. &c. Exempla.
He may not stryue or contende with no man : except it be to wynne hym by benefytes / or vertue.
5 Cum nullo certet (vel contendat) nisi beneficijs vt eum vincat / aut virtute.

Preceptum. Omne petit neutrum. &c.
And beware that he compare not with suche as be his betters : though he excell them in ony vertue. but lowly gyf them pre-
10 emynens.
Tum vigilet / ne maioribus se preponat : quamuis eis (vel eos) anteeat quauis virtute. Immo summisse eisdem cedat. vel succumbat.

Preceptum.

15 Exposcit dominor. &c. Exempla.
He that can. rule hymselfe wel and wysely in court let hym not care where so euer he cometh.
Qui in curia sui (vel sibi) vel (in suos affectus) vel (in suis affectibus) dominari recte norit : vbicunque gentium agere contingat /
20 ne curet.
To be breue. the courte is (as who saye) as a monstre of many heedes : hauynge moo eyes than Argus : lyfteth vp as many eeres & openeth as many tongues as fleynge fame.
Ut breuis fiam / paucis absoluam. in pauca conferam. breui con-
25 cludam / vel ad pauca redeam. Curia (vt ita dicam) est monstrum multorum capitum : ipso argo oculatior : tot surrigit aures / tot linguas reserat / quot fama volans vel alata.

Preceptum.

Actiuum impertit poscit. &c. Exempla.
30 Good morowe with all my herte my felowes euery one.
Plurimam salutem vobis impertio / mei (ad vnum) commilitones.
Uel sic.
Plurima salute vos impertio / mei (pariter) condiscipuli.
God spede you / or rest you mery.
35 Auete. saluere. saluisitis. iubeo vos saluere.
Ye be welcome.
Gratus est aduentus.

De constructione accusatiui casus.

Preceptum.

Uerbum omne actiuum. &c.   Exempla.
Syt downe and take your place in tyme.
Assidens / locum mature capesse. capessito. vel capessas.
Make rowme and syt ferder a lytle : I desyre you that I maye haue a place.
Cedite. vel amouate / vel amolimini parumper. vos desydero : vt locum capiam.

Exempla de interdico et inuideo.

I warne the fro hensforth medle not with me bookes.
Nostrorum libellorum vsum (post hac) interdico tibi.
Thou blurrest and blottes them / as thou were a bletchy sowter.
Eos enim oblinis / et oblitteras : in morem atramentosi sarctoris.
It is not so / but thou hast enuye y̌ I shold haue profet by them. by cryste I shall quyte.
Erras vel falleris. Immo mihi eorum fructum inuides. profecto parem vicem reddam.

Preceptum.

Ad quinos sensus. &c.   Exempla.
Here me felowe / my parte / my verses / my rule / my latyn / without boke.
Audi mi condiscipule. audito. audias me memoriter recitantem. partem carmina regulam / materiam latinam.
Pause there / or abyde. thou sayest wronge.
Hic intermittas. erras enim.
Yf I rede amysse tell me.
Si male legam admoneto me.

Exempla de verbis timorem significantibus.

I am so afrayde of the mayster y̌ I tremble and quake / all t[h]e[1] partes of my body.
Adeo formido (vel metuo) preceptorem : vt totus tremam horreamque.

---

[1] *Text* te

Vulgaria Roberti Whitintoni

I vnderstande not or perceyue not this sentence. I pray the teche me / or declare it vnto me.

Hanc sententiam non intelligo (vel sentio) oro igitur vt eam mihi declares.

Preceptum.

Passiua asciscunt rectum. &c.   Exempla.

I wyll teche the as well as I can.
A me vel mihi (quoad scio) edocebere.

Preceptum.

Passiua exposcunt vltra patientem. &c.   Vulga.
Hast thou wryt all ỹ vulgares ỹ our mayster hath gyuen vnto vs this mornynge.   whitin. E. ij
Omnia ne tibi (vel abs te) scripta sunt vulgaria? que a preceptore (vel preceptori) nobis hodierno mane fuerunt tradita.
I haue wryt them euery one.
Omnia quidem a me (vel mihi) sunt litteris mandata.

Preceptum.

Exulo cum vapulo veneo. &c.   Exempla.
The mayster hath bannisshed .ij. or .iij. vn[th]ryftes[1] out of his schole / bycause they wyll not abyde his punysshement.
A preceptore (vel preceptori) exularunt aliquot perditi: quod ab eo (vel ei) vapulare repugnant.
They haue solde his fauour for a tryfull / & made (or proued) themself fooles. by theyr owne wylfulnes.
Paululo ab eis (vel ijs) veniuit illius gratia: & a sua proteruitate facti sunt stulti.

Preceptum.

Nubo maris poscit ternum. &c.   Exempla.
I maryed my maysters doughter to daye full soore agayn my wyll.
Preceptoris filia mihi inuitissimo nupsit / vel nupta est hodie.

[1] *Text* vntrhryftes

Preceptum.

Quum videor signat puto. &c.

My thynketh her so roughe / and soore a huswyfe ẙ I cared not
& she were brend in the hote coles.

Mihi adeo aspera et acerba videtur coniunx: vt si ardentibus 5
prunis cremaretur nihili penderem.

Preceptum.

Pro vario sensu communia.   Exempla.

She embraseth or enhaunseth me so ẙ the prynt of her stykketh
vpon my buttokkes a good whyle after. 10

Fo. xxvi Sic me complectitur (vel sic ab ea complector) vt vestigia (diu
post) natibus inhereant.

Preceptum.

Includunt sensum passiuum neutra. &c.

Exempla. 15

Peace / the mayster is comen into the schole.
Taceto. preceptor introiuit (vel ingressus est) gymnasium.
He is as welcome to many of vs / as water into the shyppe.
Perinde gratus aduenit multis inter nos atque fluctus in nauem.

Preceptum. 20

Transitiua sibi deposcunt. &c.

I shall playe hym a cast of leger demayn & yet he shall not espye
it / as quykke eyed as he is.

Fabricabo (vel moliar) insidias illi inscienti. quamuis argo sit
oculatior. 25

Whyles he declareth the lecture of tully I wyll conuey myselfe
out of the doores by sleyght.

Dum is interpretatur Ciceroneanam lectiunculam. vel dum
Ciceroneana lectiuncula ab eo interpretatur. astu huic me
subducam. 30

Were this .ij. lynes wryten. I am gone.
Ubi he due linee exarentur. Hinc abeo.

Preceptum.

Interdum poscunt quartum sibi neutra. &c.

Exemplum verbi alterius intellecti.

I haue as greate appetyte to my booke to daye as an hare to a tabre.
Haud secus disciplinam hodie inardesco ac lepus tympanum.

Exemplum prepositionis intellecte.

It is clene agayn my stomake that I study to daye / & bycause I fere a brechynge.
Inuito animo hodie literis incumbo / tum quod supplicium pauesco.

Exemplum accusatiui mutati in aduerbium.

If I were at myn owne lyberty / I wolde lyue all after pleasure this fayre daye.
Si mei iuris essem hoc grato die bacchanalia viuerem.

Preceptum.

Exposcunt quartum conformis significati. &c.
I played my mayster a mery pranke or playe yesterdaye / and therfore he hathe thaught me to synge a newe songe to daye.
Heri dolosum preceptori ludum lusi : quocirca asperum canticum hodie canere me edocuit.

Exemplum de neutris.

He hath made me to renne a rase (or a course) that my buttokkes doeth swette a blody sweat.
Curriculum (vel cursum) currere me fecit / adeo vt sanguineum sudorem desudent nates.

Preceptum.   Postulo posco peto. &c.

The more instantly that I prayed hym to pardon me the faster he layed vpon.
Quo obnixius eum veniam postulaui / eo grauius inflixit supplicium.
He hath thaught me a lesson that I shall remembre whyles I lyue.
Documentum me edocuit / cuius recordabor dum viuam.

I wolde shewe the a thynge in counseyle yf thou wold kepe it cloose fro other.

Rem abditam te docerem si ea[m] [1] ceteros celare velis.

Preceptum.

Que rogitare notant. &c. Exemplu*m*. 5

Thou canst requyre no thynge of me reasonable / but ẙ must [2] obteyne thy desyre of me.

Nihil a me rogare potes (saltem equu*m*) quin id a me necessario exores.

Preceptum. 10

Uerbum ornare nota*n*s. &c. Exemplu*m*.

My mayster hath bete me so naked in his chau*m*bre ẙ I was not able to do of nor vpon myn owne clothes.

Preceptor me nudatu*m* sic deuerberauit / ne vestibus me exuere. aut induere valere*m*. 15

Preceptu*m*. Celo uult binos quartos. &c.

I pray the kepe this mater cloose fro hym & all other for yf it be dyscloosed I am vndone.

Oro vt hanc rem illum et ceteros omnes celes. vel sic. Oro vt hanc rem illi & ceteris celes. Uel sic. Oro hanc rem illo vel 20 de illo celes. vel. Oro illum de hac re et ceteros celes omnes : nam si palam fiat ego pereo funditus.

Fo. xxvij Preceptum.

Ternum cum quarto poscunt respondeo. &c.

Exempla. 25

Thou answeres me no thynge to purpose.

Nihil ad rem respondes mihi.

I wrote a lettre vnto you / but ye send me no answere nother by wrytynge / nother mouthe.

Literas scripsi tibi (vel ad te) at responsum mihi (vel ad me) 30 misisti nullu*m*. neq*ue* literis neq*ue* verbis.

I handeld hym so harde / that he had not a word more to saye to me.

Tam duriter hominem tractaui : ne verbum quide*m* mihi (vel ad me) adijceret amplius. 35

---

[1] *Text* ea   [2] mayst 1523, 1527.

Vulgaria Roberti Whitintoni 91

He durste not for all ỹ eyen in his heed speke to me after that.
Me postea compellare / con̄uenire / affari / vel alloqui / prorsus non audebat.

Preceptum. Uult auferre notans. &c.
5 One hath pyked out al the pennes of my pennarde. I pray you lende me a pen.
Unus sublegit pennario (vel e pennario) pennas ad vnum / oro igitur mutuato mihi pennam.
I am in worse case / for one hath plucketh fro my gyrdle both
10 pennarde and ynkhorne.
Ego maius malum accepi : cinctu enim vel a cinctu detraxit vnus pennarium vna cum atramentario cornu.

Preceptum. Cum natis priuo. &c.
I warraunt the thou shall neuer do good scholer hurt except thou
15 stele his bokes fro hym.
Spondeo te nunquam studioso scholastico damnum illaturum : nisi eum libris priuaueris.
I wote not who myght worse saye it than thou. For ỹ shalte as soone robbe Tully of all his eloquence / as proue a latynyste /
20 or latyn man.
Quis hoc ineptius quam tu diceret? nescio. facilius enim Ciceronem facundia abdicabis / quam probus latinus euadas.
It cometh to the by nature to be a dullarde. therfore it were pyte to put the fro thy enheritaunce.
25 Innata est tibi indocilitas : quare re ingenita te exheredare (vel orbare) iniquum foret.
It is clerkly spoken of you. A man myght as soone pyke mary out of a mattok / as dryue .iij. good latyn wordes out of your fortop.
30 Scite sane dictum. citius medullam a ligone expellas : quam tria vocabula proba e fronte tua.

Preceptum.
Pono fero capio cum pre. &c.   Exempla.
Many a man setteth more by an ynche of his wyl than an ell of
35 his thryfte / & thou art one of them.
Complures paululum voluntatis sue multo lucro preponunt / preferunt / vel ante ponunt in quibus vnus es ipse.

It is the properte of a good scholer to prefer lernyng before vayne pleasures.
Studiosus adolescens. vanis oblectamentis eruditionem antecapere solet.

Exempla neutrorum cum pre et sub coniunctorum. 5

I haue ouergone many that were better lerned than I by my great dilygence.
Multis me eruditioribus precucurri mea laboriosa industria.
It is a synguler pleasur to me to se them come behynde and holde the plough. 10
Est mihi precipue voluptati / cum eos mihi succumbere respicio.

Preceptum.

Admoneo quartum poscit. &c.
If I mysse or fayle in renderynge / redyng / or pronunciacyon. tell me of my faute I beseke the. 15
Si errauero reddendo / legendo / vel pronunciando : me errati (vel de errato) admoneas / queso.

Preceptum.

Accusare notans verbum. &c.   Exempla.
If thou accuse me of spekynge englysshe / I shall complayne 20
vpon the for fyghtynge in the maysters absence. set the one agayn the other.
Si me vernacule lingue (vernacula lingua / vel de vernacula lingua) accusaueris : condemnabo te rursus pugne (pugna / vel de pugna) in preceptoris absentia. par pari referto. 25

Fo. xxviij   Exempla de adiectiuis tanti / quanti. &c.

I can laye moo thynges vnto thy charge than ẙ arte ware of.
Pluris te insimulare noui : quam opinaris. vel opinione tua.
I set not a poynt what thou can laye to my charge I can laye as moche to thyne. 30
Floccipendo / quanti me condemnes : non minoris enim te d[a]mnabo.[1]

[1] *Text* demnabo

Vulgaria Roberti Whitintoni

Preceptum. Ad precium spectans verbum. &c.
Thou mayst bye as moche loue for a nagled in ỹ mydle of scotland.
as thou shall wynne by thy complayntes.
Emas beniuolentiam paululo / vbiuis locorum quantam ex queri-
5   monijs concilies.
All the gaynes that ÿ shall get by this bargen / is not worthe a
ferthynge.
Lucrum quod ex hac re capies : quadrante non valet.

Exempla de adiectiuis.

10 For what so euer thou wynnes in the shyre thou shall lese it in
the hondreth.
Quantiuis enim (vel quantilibet / quanticumque) fructus hinc
valent : isthinc pluris erit iactura.
Thy ware standeth the in as moche & more I thynke than thou
15   shall sell it fore.
Tua tantidem (et pluris opinor) constiterunt / quam ea venun-
dabis.
He that selleth for .vij.[1] & byeth for a .xi. it is merueyle yf euer he
thryue.
20 Qui minori precio venundat / quam comparat : mirum est si rem
faciat (vel lucrum faciat) vspiam.

Preceptum.

Estimo cum pendo facio genitum. &c.
He that wyll thryue muste set (or holde) his ware (or stuf) at
25   double pryce ỹ he wyll sel it / as londoners doeth.
Qui lucrari cupit / merces duplo pluris estimare debet (quod
londoniani factitant) quam venundet.
I set very lytle / or nought by hym ỹ can not face oute his ware
with a carde of .x.
30 Minimi / immo nauci / aut nihili pendo eum : qui merces suas
non maximi faciat.

Preceptum.

Quartum cum sexto poscunt pleo fartio nata. &c.

---

[1] *Text omits first stop.*

94 Vulgaria Roberti Whitintoni

Exempla.
I praye the peace / y̆ fyllest myn eeres full of dynne.
Tace (vel silesce) sodes. clamore enim aures imples
Yf thou mayest not awaye with noyse stoppe thy eeres with a
    cloute.   5
Si clamorem perpeti non possis : vel panniculo auriculas infercito.

Preceptum.   Pascere que signat. &c.
Thy nyse and newfangled pronunciacyon after y̆ᵉ Italyans fason
    fedeth delycate eeres with wonders pleasure.
Tua petulans et neoterica pronunciatio italica : delicatas vel 10
    prurientes aures mira pascit dulcedine.
Syth euery countre doeth auaunse with laude his owne language.
    whye sholde not we thynke worthy our language the same?
    sythen al speches suffre confusyon saue hebrewe.
Cum omnis natio suam amplitudine magnificat (vel ditat) linguam : 15
    quare nostram eadem non dignamur : cum omnis (preter
    hebream) loquela confusioni succumbit.

Preceptum.
Soluere que signant. &c.   Exempla.
If I maye ones rydde my handes of this charge. I wyll neuer 20
    take suche byssenes vpon me agayne.
Si me semel ab hac prouincia soluam / liberem / expediam /
    nunquam denuo similem in me suscipiam.
A man may call vnto hym with the bekke of a fynger that he can
    not put away with bothe handes.   25
Nutu vnius digituli onus tibi asciscas : quod vtraque manu abs te
    haud amoueas.
Therfore is wysdome to be ware of / had I wyste.
Scitum est igitur. vt ab penitentia postera tete contineas.

Fo. xxix   Preceptum.   30
Abstineo quartum petit. &c.   Exempla.
Holde thy baudy handes fro my booke with sorowe.
Abstineto sordidulas manus a libro multo malo.
My handes be as clene as thyne.
Mihi manus / tuis munditia non cedunt.   35

Vulgaria Roberti Whitintoni

Preceptum.
Cum substantiuo sibi concomitante relato
A nullo regitur. &c.

Exemplum nominatiui absoluti.

5 Thy handes / I thynke them more mete to dawbe a walle than to handle a booke.
Manus tue / ipsas ad illinendum parietem magis idoneas / quam vt librum euoluant. iudico.

Exemplum genitiui absoluti.

10 Of your clennes / euery man maye take a presydence therof.
Tue munditie / eius specimen mirentur omnes.

Exempl[um][1] datiui absoluti.

To thy honesty euery man maye saye / phye ther vpon.
Tuo cultui / ipsi vah obijciant vniuersi.

15   De accusatiuo absoluto.

Clennes / euery man wyll prayse it.
Culturam / eam laudabit vnusquisque.

De vocatiuo absoluto.

Good syr / it semeth ye haue seen more good maners / than ye
20 haue borne awaye.
Bone vir / plus bonorum morum vidisse quam edidicisse videris.

Exemplum de ablatiuo absoluto.

Good maner / I knowe not who lesse doeth vse it than you / thoughe I saye it before you.
25 Bonis moribus / quisnam ijs minus / ac tu vtitur: haud scio licet te coram illud predicem.

De constructione ablatiui.

Preceptum. Sextum vult vescor / fungor. &c.
The fryed egges and bakon that I eate at brekefaste vmbraydeth
30 my stomake.
Oua frixa cum petasone quibus vescebar in ientaculo eructare me faciunt.

[1] *Text* Exempla

Your gentell stomake sheweth what nourture ye vse.
Probe ostendit stomachus / quibus vteris moribus.
Ye behaue you lyke an honest man / ye lak but a bolle & a besom.
Honesti viri fungeris officio / nihilo preterqu*am* sino et scopis cares.

F. ij He ẏ may haue your co*m*pany / maye be glad therof: for ye be as ful of good maner as an egge is of oote mele.
Quisquis fruatur tua conuersatione / delectetur ea: quippe qui bonis moribus perinde ac ouu*m* farine auenatie scates.

Preceptu*m*.

Sexto ponetur signans tempus. &c.   Exempl[um][1]
How many yeres haue ye gone to grammer here.
Quot (hic loci) annis / vel annos gra*m*matice incubuisti. vel operam dedisti?

Exempl[um][1] de no*m*i*n*e significante tempus vel spacium in nominatiuo.

It is two yere and moore agone sythen I came hydder fyrste.
Secundus annus vel biennium preterijt. superq*ue* postq*uam* hucprimu*m* adueni.

Preceptu*m*.

Mobile vel verbu*m* sextu*m* sine preposito vult
Instrumentalis / sic formalis quoq*ue* cause.

Exempla.

Dyd ye wryte this with your owne hande?
Hoccine tua ipsius manu exarasti?
Ye verely. I can wryte you an hand of an other maner of fason yf me luste.
Ita sane. literam / cultiori forma exarare scio. si lubet mihi.

Preceptum.

Mobile vel verbu*m* sextu*m* sine preposito vult
Cause finalis. &c.   Exempl[a][2] finalis cause.

---

[1] *Text* Exempla   [2] *Text* Exemplum

Vulgaria Roberti Whitintoni

Wherfore / for what ende / or what entente / or what conclusyon goo ye to schole?
Quorsum? qua gratia? quo fine? ob vel propter quem finem? vel pro quo fine? literis incumbis? vel operam das?
5 Bycause / for that ende / or entent or for the conclusyon to get lernynge or connynge.
Ea demum gratia / vel pro gratia / ob vel propter hunc finem. vt eruditionem consequar vel nauciscar.

Preceptum.

10   Mobile vel verbum sextum cause efficientis.

Exempl[a][1] cause efficientis.

What maketh the loke so sad.   Fo. xxx
Quis casus te adeo tristem reddit?
I am thus sadde for fere of the rodde and $\overset{e}{y}$ brekefaste that my
15   mayster promest me.
Adeo tristor (vel sum tristis) timore / pre timore / per / ob / vel propter timorem / virge et supplicium a preceptore mihi interminatum.

Preceptum.

20   Mobile vel verbum vult cause materialis. &c.

Exemplum.

Be of good chere man / I sawe ryght now a rodde made of wythye / for the: garnysshed with knottes. it wolde do a boye good to loke vpon it.
25 Esto bono animo. virgam ex salicto factam tibi nodis refertam nuper vidi. opereprecium foret puero aspicere.

Preceptum.

Sexto ponetur iuncto sibi preposito cum
Dictio qua coniunctio. &c.   Exemplum.
30 Take thy medicyne (though it be somwhat bytter) with a good wyll it wyll worke to thy ease at lenght.
Cum equanimitate hoc antidotum (licet amarum) accipito. tandem enim pariet tibi commodum.

[1] *Text* Exemplum

H

Preceptum.

Desisto cesso sextum. &c. Exemplum.
Leue of thy mokkes & Japes. Yf ẙ were in my coote ẙ woldes haue lytle luste to scoffe.
A ridiculis et iocis desistito vel cessato. quodsi in meo esses loco. minime te iuuarent scommata.

De verbis pro vario sensu varie constructis.
Preceptum.

Uerba reciproca sunt hec deficit. &c. Exemplum.
Many hath eloquence ynough / but the lacke wysdom.
Nonnullis abundat (vel affluit) eloquentia quibus tamen deficit sapientia.
Deficio quartum rogitat. &c. Exempla.
Thou art a sure spere at nede. that leues a man stykkynge in the breres.
Fidus es / vbi opus est : hominem malis impeditum deficies.
If thou sholdes go to a battel / ẙ woldes soone stert fro thy capten : that shrynkes wher is so small iopardy.
Quod si ad bellum esses profecturus : a duce cito deficeres : qui in tam minimo periculo languescis.

Preceptum. Prosequor afficio. &c.
Of all the world I hate suche cowardes ẙ lyke a stertlynge horse. be aferde of euery waggynge of a strawe.
Omnium maximo hos ignauos prosequor fastidio : qui (vmbratici equi more) vbiuis sunt trepidi : vel omnia pauescunt.
I loue hym ẙ wyll not shrynke for nought / but presse forthe lyke a man.
Intrepidum / qui grauiter ad rem accingitur / summo amore presequor vel afficio.

Preceptum.

Hec timeo metuo. &c. Exempla.
I fere myself of the ague / for I fele a grudgynge euery seconde daye.
Timeo (vel metuo) mihi a febre : nam secundo quoque die ali quantulum male afficior.
If thou fere sekenes beware of euell dyet.
Si morbum timeas / caue tibi a crapula.

Vulgaria Roberti Whitintoni

Preceptum.
Auribus intendo signat quum auscultat. &c.

Exempla.
Here a worde or two / or ye goo.
Ausculta vel audi pauca. antequam abeas. vel ante discessum.
If thou do after my counseyle / beware of y̑ man that y̑ spakes of ryght nowe truste hym not to soore.
Si meo consilio auscultans (vel audiens) fueris : caue ab homine de quo meministi modo. ne nimium credas ei.

Preceptum.
Uult pro promitto recipit. &c.   Exempla.
For he wyll promesse the moore in an houre / than he is able to perfourme in vij. yere.
Plus enim hore intercapedine recipiet tibi : quam septennio prestare valet.
Loke what he catcheth ones of ony man / & it cometh neuer agayne.
Quicquid autem recipit abs quopiam / redditur nunquam

Preceptum. Accedo addor vult acquirentis. &c.
Exempla de accedo idem quod addor.
And besyde other fautes / this euel property is ioyned vnto hym / whan thou hast done for hym all that thou can / he can not aforthe the a good word.
Atque ad alia mala hoc sibi accedit tibi in eo meritissimo. bene dicere nolit.
That shold be to a kynd herted man a gret greuaunce.
Id quod benigno et cordato viro accederet. summo dolori vel ad dolorem.
Atast hym / or set vpon hym / I warraunt the thou art able to answere hym at all poyntes / go nere hym.
Accedas hominem mei periculo : ei etenim ad omnia respondere haud impar es. propius accedas ad eum.

Preceptum.
Reddo cum facio signat. &c.   Exempla.
I shall make hym as styll as a lambe / or euer I haue done with hym.
Reddam hominem eque placidum / atque agnus est : tandem.

I haue delyuered your lettres as ye commaunde me / but money that ye requyred he wyll paye none.
Tuas reddidi literas / cui me voluisti: at repetitas pecunias haud quaquam redditurus est.

Preceptum.

Impono signans fallo. &c.   Exemplum.
But hath he deceyued me so? Well in the name of god / I shall laye a logge in his necke y̆ shall weye .x. pounde.
Itane imposuit nobis? age. humeris sibi decem minarum onus imponam.

Preceptum.

Comparo concilio vel emo. &c.   Exempla.
I haue goten a wryte for hym out of the chauncery: & y̆ bargen shall he bye full dere / or we haue done.
Dicam e summo tribunali ei comparaui / quam quidem sibi graui sumptu comparet tandem.

F. iiij I shall teche hym / what is to compare hymselfe with his better.
Quid sit / maioribus (vel cum maioribus) sese comparare: monebo.

Preceptum.

Commendo signans laudo. &c.   Exemplum.
I haue put my mater in suche a mannes handes whome he shall haue no cause to prayse. to his frendes at ẙ partynge.
Causam nostram viro commendaui / quem ille apud amicos neutiquam est commendaturus postea.

Preceptum.

Conduco signans prosum. &c.   Exemplum.
I haue retyned vnto me suche a lerned man / y̆ wyl set my mater forwarde to my best auauntage.
Causidicum vel iurisperitum mihi conduxi: qui negocio nostro magnopere conducet.

Preceptum.

Incumbo signans operam do. &c.
He employeth my cause as effectuall / as it were his owne.
Haud minus diligenter in (vel ad) nostram rem incumbit: ac si sua esset.

He lyeth at his booke dayly / to ẙ entente / to obteyne ẙ cause.
Libris assidue incumbit / ea demum gratia: vt rei potiatur.

Preceptum.
Do tribuo signans ternum poscit. &c.
5 So ẙ yf I were able to gyue hym a fee of .x. pound yerely he hath deserued it.
Adeo / vt si decem minarum munus ei dare valerem: illo non indignus est.
He sende me a letter late by the caryer / what processe is take
10 in the cause.
Epistolam nuper ad me tabellario dedit: quid in nostro negocio est actum.

Preceptum.
Incessit signans subijt. &c. Exempla.
15 There is merueylous dysease fall into my lyfte syde / it maketh me somtym lyke to swone.
Nouus et inauditus morbus sinistro lateri incessit. qui me sincopi sepius afficit.
It assaute my herte with a myscheuous paunge / as though it
20 wolde rydde me out of hande.
Incessit precordia intollerabili tortione perinde acsi iamiam me perimeret.

Preceptum.
Uult ternum solum vaco. &c. Exemplum.
25 This dysease maketh me so euell at ease ẙ I can not applye my booke.
Hic morbus ea me afficit molestia: vt discipline vacare nequeam.

Exemplum de vaco pro carere.
I lacke counseyle of a physicyon / & ẙ is to my payne.
30 Medici admonitione (vel ab admonitione) vaco: id quod mihi ad dolorem accedit.

Exemplum de vacat impersonali esse vacuum significanti.
And I haue no leaser for byssynes to seke for remedy.
Neque per negocia vacat mihi: consulere remedio.

Preceptu*m*.

Re ipsa perficio signans presto. &c.   Exempla.
If thou perfourme thy p*r*omesse / thou shal shewe thyselfe and honest man and true.
Si promissa prestiteris : te et honestu*m* et fidum prestabis viru*m*. 5
He hath gyuen m[e][1] moore than all the frendes that I haue.
Ampliora mihi prestitit / q*uam* ad vnu*m* amici.
In kyndnes vnto me he passeth fader and moder and all my kynne.
Beneficentia in me / parentibus (vel parentes) toteq*ue* cognatione 10 (vel cognatione*m*) prestat.

Preceptum.

Uerbero scindo neco signa*n*s cedo. &c.   Exempla.
My mayster hath bette my bak and syde / whyles the rodde wolde holde in his hande. 15
Preceptor me vndiq*ue* cecidit : dum in manu durauit virga.
He hath torne my buttokkes. so that theyr is lefte noo hole skynne vpon them.
Nates cecidit / adeo. ne cutis in ijs sana relinquatur.
Ỹ wales be so thycke ỹ one can sta*n*de sca*n*tly by an other. 20
Adeo co*n*stipantur plage / ne alij vix cedat alia.

Preceptum.

Iniuriam vlciscor signans vult vindico. &c.

Exempla.

If euer I be a man / I wyll reuenge his malyce. 25
Si in virum euadam : illam crudelitatem vindicabo.   Uel sic.
In sua*m* atrocitatem illam vindicabo.
I truste ones to growe able to rydde myself out of his daunger.
Spero me aliq*uando* eo fortune aspiraturu*m* vbi meipsum ab eius seruitute vindicem. 30
And to restoore myselfe in lybertye.
Atq*ue* meipsum in libertatem vindicem.

[1] *Text* my

Vulgaria Roberti Whitintoni

Preceptu*m*.   Uult parco faueo ternum. &c.
For the good fauour that he sheweth me. I haue kept a co*m*fortatyf for hym ẙ shal work this .vij. yere or after.
Propterea q*uo*d mihi ta*n*topere fauet: antidotu*m* (q*uo*d hinc
5 septe*n*nio eu*m* afficiet) parsi sibi.

Preceptum.

Aspiro signans faueo. &c.   Exemplu*m*.
If fortune be frendely to my purpose I shall ones come to myn entent.
10 Si meis fortune institutis aspirauerit ad animi expectatione*m* aspirem olim.

Preceptum.

Ad sum sum presens sextu*m* vult. &c.   Exempla.
Come hyther / & stande by me yf I had nede.
15 Huc ades (vel adsis) & mihi (si opus fuerit) adesto.
I wyll be present or redy in all maner of chaunses.
Adero. omni periculo / vel in omni periculo.

Preceptum.

Disto haud sum presto. &c.   Exemplum.
20 I wolde not haue the out of the waye yf nede requyre.
Nollem te a nobis abesse / si opus postulet.

Preceptu*m*.

Desum deficio ternum vult. &c.   Exempla.
I wyll not fayle the / truste me all the whyle I maye stande on
25 my feete.
Non deero tibi (persuasum habeas) du*m* pedibus consistere Fo. xxxii
possum.
Care not. for thou shall lacke no helpe.
Ne cura / no*n* eni*m* deerit tibi subsidiu*m*.

30 Preceptum.

Insum vult ternum. &c.   Exemplu*m*.
Thou hast boones bygge ynoughe / or ẙ haste pytthe ynough in thy boones. yf there be manhod in thy herte. we shall make our partye good with the best.
35 Satis vigoris ossibus tuis inest.   quodsi in animo insit audacia: strennuissimis quibusq*ue* occursemus.

Vulgaria Roberti Whitintoni

Preceptum. Intersum presens sum. &c.

Exemplum de intersum significante sum presens.

Was thou present at the dysputacyon?
Interfuisti disputatiunculis / vel in disputatiunculis?

Exemplum cum significat disto.

They were as ferre asondre the one fro the other / as London is dystaunt out of my countre. whiche be a hondred myle asondre.
Tantum alter ab altero distabat / quantum a Londino ad natale solum interest que centum milliaribus intersunt.

Preceptum.

Confero conuenio signans. &c. Exempla.
Herdest ȳ what they commened of bytwene them?
Audistine que inter se contulere?
After the one was concluded. he ascrybed to hymselfe / or toke vpon hym great ignoraunce.
Postubi alter eorum cesserit : in sese ignorantiam contulit omnem.
It wyll teche hym to be wyse how he compareth with his better for euer.
Erit sibi documento perpetuo ne maiori vel cum maiore sese conferat.
He gaf hym noo lesse than a dosen chekmates or they had done.
Non pauciora duodecim sannis illi (vel in eum) contulit antequam perfecerint.
It shall profet hym moche yf he be wyse & make hym to loke better vpon his booke.
Non parum sibi conferet si sapit reddetque eum accuratiorem.

Preceptum. Effert extollit leuat. &c.

Exempla.

Euery man dyd commende hym gretly for his lernyng and also maner.
Hunc summopere extulerunt omnes / ob et eruditionis et morum claritatem.
I can not prayse hym accordynge to his merytes.
Hunc pro meritis satis efferre nequeo.

Vulgaria Roberti Whitintoni

Exempla de confero cum significat ire.

Whydder ar ye in waye / or whydder go ye?
Quo vos hinc confertis?
I wyll go home.
5 Domum me hinc conferam.

Preceptum.

Effert extollit leuat. &c. Exempla.
He is not a lytle proude of his paynted sheythe / and loketh of a heyght.
10 Non parum gloriose sese effert. vultusque tetricos effert.
He is so stately and daungerous of his counseile / that he wyl not styrre his fote ones out of the doores for a man vnder a noble.
Sui consilij ita parcus est : ne pedem e foribus efferat / nisi dato
15 aureo angelo.
Lynacre hath translated Galyen out of greeke tongue into latyn. and that in a clene style lately.
Linacrus Galienum e greca lingua in latinam (& stilo quidem cultissimo) extulit nuper.

20 ### Preceptum.

Defero prodo notans. &c. Exemplum.
In the whiche translacyon he hath brought many thynges to lyghte.
In qua editione multa / in (vel ad) lucem detulit.

25 Preceptum. Differo cum signat disto.

He is depely experte in greke tongue soo that dyuerse men iudge that ther is smal difference bytwene Erasmus and hym.
Grece lingue peritia pollet / adeo vt nonnulli inter Erasmum et illum paululum differe contendant.

Pro disto.

30 Theyr styles be so lyke that one dyffereth lytle fro the other.
Pari stilo ita conveniunt : vt parum differt alter ab altero.

Pro diuulgo.

So ẙ more & lesse publysshe the prayse of the man / not only / for his lernynge / but specyally for his dilygence.
Adeo / vt primi nedum infimi hominis laudem amplissime differant / cum ob eruditionem tum ob precipuam industriam. 5

Exempla pro dispono.

He hath set & distyncte ẙ worke into goodly ordre.
Hoc volumen miro ordine distulit.
Nor he dyd this in hast / but hath proroged ẙ edycyon many yeres ful wysely. 10
Neque hanc editionem precipitauit / immo in multos annos non imprudenter distulit.

Preceptum.

Infert importo / concludo. &c.   Exempla.

Pro importo. 15

We be moche bounde to them that brought in ẙ crafte of pryntynge.
Plurimum debemus hisce viris / qui imprimendi artem prius intulere.

Pro concludo. 20

It concludeth many thynges in shorter space than ẙ wrytten hande doeth / & more ornately sheweth.
Multa contractiori spacio infert / quam litera scripta : et cultius pollet.

Pro contra facio vel eo. 25

It hyndreth not so moche ẙ scryueners / but profeteth moche more poore scholers.
Non tantum bybliographis infert incommodum quantum egenis scholasticis commodum.

Iunctum cum me te se nos & vos. 30

It is not many yeres agone sythen it cam fyrste into Englande.
Non multi preterfluxerunt anni postquam in angliam se prius intulit.

Vulgaria Roberti Whitintoni

Preceptu*m*. Quartu*m* cu*m* terno vult offert. &c.

Exemplu*m* cu*m* pro immolo ponitur.

Thou art aboute to please a shrewe (I haue espyed) as a man that offereth a candell to the deuyll.
5 Pernicioso inseruire studes (compertu*m* habeo) vt q*ui* demonio lucerna*m* offert.

Exemplu*m* pro obuio.

Ỹ comest nowe happely / or metest me in good season.
Hauspicato tete mihi nunc offers.

10 Exemplu*m* pro porrigo / aut do sponte.

It is sayd comenly / whan the pygge is profered : open the poughen.
Uulgo fertur. vbi commodu*m* tibi offert quisq*uam* accipito.

Preceptum.
15 Perfero cu*m* signat patior. &c.   Exempla.
Wordes I may suffre / but strypes I maye not awaye withal.
Uerba perferre possum / plagas autem minime.
What tydynges hast thou brought vs.
Quid noui nobis (vel ad nos) pertulisti ?

20 Preceptum.
Pro narro reddo refero. &c.   Exemplu*m* p*ro* narro.
I shall shewe you many by and by bothe by mouthe & wrytynge.
Multa tibi co*n*tinuo referam / & verbis et literis.

Exemplu*m* pro reddo.
25 I shall requyte th[y]¹ labours.
Laboribus parem referam gratia*m*.

Exemplu*m* pro renouo.

By this lettres I perceyue ỹ he is about to renuwe ỹ olde amyte bytwene vs.
30 His literis perspicio hunc conari / pristina*m* inter nos amicitiam referre velle.

¹ *Text* the

Exemplum pro reuoco.

He sheweth hymselfe late to be moued agayne me / but now he calleth hymselfe home.

Nuperrime se iratum ostendit: at nunc pedem refert.

Exemplum pro recenseo & conuerto.

Fo. xxxv For he reciteth the multitude of my benefytes toward hym / and hath chaunged his mynde into better condicyons.

Quippe qui meorum erga eum officiorum referens numerum: animum suum in melius rettulit.

Exemplum pro ascribo.

He ascrybeth to synystre conseyle his errour and referreth all the mater vnto my equanymyte.

In sinistrum consilium suum errorem referens: ad equanimitatem nostram rem omnem rettulit.

Exemplum pro reporto.

But for all his fayre wordes I wold haue hym bryng me agayne suche thynges as he borowed of me.

At postpositis blanditijs mutuo a nobis accepta ad nos referre hunc velim.

Preceptum.

Euado emergo signans. &c.   Exemplum pro emergo.

Many a ragged colt proued to [be][1] a good horse.

Uillosus pullus (crebro) probus euadit equus.

Exemplum pro peruenio.

Many a poore mannes sone by grace and vertue ascendeth to hye rowmes and authoryte.

Pauperum itidem filij / gratia & virtute in (vel ad) summam dignitatem sepius euadunt.

Exemplum pro transeo.

And so he auoydeth the incommodytes of pouerte and seruytute.

Itaque et inopie et seruitutis incommoda (vel molestias) vel. ex incommodis euadit.

[1] *Omitted in Text.*

Preceptum.

Me letum testor signans. &c. Exempla.
I am glad of you / for the good reporte that I here of your lernynge and vertue.
5 Gratulor tibi ob tue et eruditionis / et virtutis laudem quam diuulgatam audio.
Ye haue cause to gyue god thankes therof / & [so][1] shal ye prospere to auaunsement.
Est tibi iustissima causa gratulandi deo / sicque ad amplitudinem
10 aspirabis.

Preceptum.

Intueor signans animaduerto. &c. Exemplum.
My mayster merked or noted me yester daye doynge a faute / I fere my to day leyst he wyll swynge my breche for it.
15 Me heri peccantem animaduertit preceptor: metuo igitur mihi / ne hodie in nates animaduertat.

Finis tertie partis.

Quarta Pars de constructione impersonalium verborum.

Preceptum.

20 Est refert sic interque est. &c. Exempla.
Dialogus de officijs. siue moribus scholasticis.
Preceptor. For as it belongeth vnto a mayster to teyche his scholers bothe maners and lernynge / I haue contryued a breue processe as it cam to mynde of maners for scholers.
25 Cum preceptoris est / haud secus moribus / ac disciplina suos instituere discipulos epitomen de scholasticis officijs. extemporariam collegimus.
Discipulus. It is very expedyent for vs scholers to be instructe with good maners: for it is comenly sayd. it is better a chylde
30 vnborne / than vntaught.
Nostra tyrunculorum permagni interest moribus imbui. vulgo enim dicitur prestat puerum non natum quam immoratum esse.
Preceptor. Ther be some maysters which forse lytle (or take lytle hede) to teyche theyr scholers maners: so ỹ they may
35 brynge them to knowlege of lernynge.
Sunt nonnulli preceptores / quorum (vel cuia) parui refert / suis

[1] *Text* sho

Vulgaria Roberti Whitintoni

discipulis mores aperire: dummodo ad literature peritiam perducant.

Discipulus. Suche rede maysters knowe not / what belongeth to theyr owne dutye. nor yet to bryngynge vp of youthe.

Hi inculti preceptores / neque quid sua: neque quid puerorum 5 educandorum interest callent / aut sapiunt.

Preceptum.
Hec ternum poscunt impersonalia constat.   Exempla.

Preceptor. It is euydent to euery man: that a chyld taketh in youthe (be it good or bad) comenly in age he hath a smell 10 therof.

Omnibus constat (vel liquet) quicquid imbibit tenera etas (probum ne / an improbum sit) idem in prouecta etate subolet.

Discipulus. It chaunceth me to perceyue now by experyence ỹ I haue red in Horace. A pytcher wyll haue a smatche longe 15 after of ỹ lyquoure ỹ was fyrst put in it.

Mihi nunc accidit / vsu venit / obtigit / euenit / contigit / vel obuenit / experientia illud discere: quod apud Horatium legi. Quo semel est imbuta recens seruabit odorem. testa diu.

Preceptor. Somwhat I wyll speke of the offyce and duty of a 20 mayster / before I teyche the scholer.

Prius de preceptoris officio aliqua meminisse libet vel placet mihi / quam discipulum instruam.

Discipulus. Reason it is. For the behauour of ỹ mayster is as a presidence to the scholer to folowe. 25

Equum est / vel conuenit. Nam preceptoris vita / discipulo est vite exemplar. et imitandi formula.

Preceptor. It becometh a mayster pryncypally to be sufficyently lerned in that facultye ỹ he teycheth.

Preceptori in primis congruit / conuenit / expedit / vel incumbit: 30 eius scientie quam profitetur / esse satis experto.

Discipulus. But we maye se dayly / ỹ many take vpon them to teyche / for whome it were more expediente to lerne.

Attamen nobis indies cernere patet / vel licet: quo pacto docendi munus arrogant complures: quibus discere prestaret. 35

Preceptum.
Hec sextum benefit malefit. &c.   Exempla.

Preceptor. In as moche as the frendes be contente with suche maysters / whether they hyndre or profet scholers / $\overset{e}{y}$ faute is in theyr owne folye.

Cum ab ijs preceptoribus satisfiat parentibus : bene / ne ab ijs an malefiat discipulis suapte culpa fit.

5   Preceptum.

His presit patiens cum impersonalia fiant.
Quartus delectat. &c.   Exempla.
Preceptor. To be breue. it becometh / & rather it is necessary for a mayster before all thynges to vse grauyte in all thynges / & specyally before his scholers.

Sum̄matim vt agam / preceptorem (precipue) decet / immo oportet vbiuis (et presertim) coram discipulis seueritatem seruare. et pre se ferre.

Discipulus. Ye syr / but many maysters tourne $\overset{t}{y}$ into austeryte / & cruelte / so that theyr scholers haue no lyst to abyde with them. I knowe it by experyence.

At non pauci hanc in austeritatem / ac potius crudelitatem peruertunt. adeo. vt discipulos his adherere non iuuet vel delectet. vt me expertum non latet. fugit. preterit vel fallit.

20 Preceptor. Suche inconuenyentes becometh not a mayster / & ought not be seen in a dyscrete teycher.

Hec errata haud decent preceptorem : neque visa oportent in modesto saltem.

Discipulus. The gentell exhortacyons of my mayster allured my mynde merueylously. ey ? & made me more diligent than all his austeryte coude do.

Blande preceptoris admonitiones animum mirifice mihi iuuabant : immo diligentiorem / quam rigiditas extrema : me effecerunt.

Preceptum.

30   Penitet ac tedet miseretque. &c.   Exempla.

Preceptor. It is requysyte also in a mayster besyde lernynge & grauyte $\overset{t}{y}$ he be not newfangled in the fourme of teychynge / to teyche this maner to daye and to morne to be wery of the same.

35 Ad hoc preceptori expedit (preter eruditionem & grauitatem) ne in docendi formula versipellis sit : nunc hoc vt doceat / paulo post hunc tedeat eiusdem.

Discipulus. I knowe dyuerse teychers to tourne sykke (of the which they may be bothe sory & ashamed) ẏ theyr scholers profet lytle or no thyng : so that a man wold pyte tendre wyttes. so to be weryed.

Nonnullos noui ita morosos preceptores (cuius eos et peniteat et 5
pudeat) vt parum aut nihil proficiant discipuli. adio vt misereat
quemuis ingeniolorum defatigatorum.

Preceptum.
Desinit et debet solet incipit. &c.   Exempla.

Preceptor. And summarily to conclude. a mayster shold be cir- 10
cumspecte in worde / gesture / & contenaunce that he do no thynge that shold appere to his scholers lyghte / dissolute / or soundynge ony wyse to dishonesty. whiche he maye / or ought
fo. xxxvij to be abasshed of afterwarde.

Et in summa vt agam. nunc circumspectum esse decet / verbis. 15
gestu & vultu. ne quid agat effeminatum. dissolutum. quouis ne
modo (denique) discipulis quod videatur turpe. cuius postea
hunc pudere possit aut debeat.

Discipulus. Chyldre comenly haue a delyte & wyll be glad to note theyr mayster of a faute whiche they may shewe to theyr 20
frendes at home / in especyall whan they waxe wery of theyr mayster.

Pueros delectare solet / & cupide vult : preceptoris erratiunculam
annotare : quam parentibus domi referant. tum maxime vbi
preceptoris eos tedere incipit.   25

Preceptum.
Pertinet et spectat simul attinet. &c.   Exempla.

Preceptor. Forther it belongeth to a mayster prudently to consydre ẏ qualyte of his scholers / after theyr capacyte & tyme : so to nourysshe them in lernynge / as yonge begynners at the 30
fyrst entryng. to vse them with easy lessons & playn. also fayre wordes to corage them.

Insuper ad preceptorem pertinet / attinet : vel spectat. discipulorum naturam prudenter consyderare : & pro ingenij captu / et etate : eos doctrina imbuere. & tyrunculos (ab ipsis vngui- 35
culis) facili et aperta lectione. & blandis verbis (vt animos confirmet) lactare.

Discipulus. I se well many take vpon them to teyche / that knoweth ful lytle what thynges longeth to ẏ bryngynge vp of chyldre.

Frequentes (compertum habeo) docendi munus sibi vendicant:
5 qui quanta ad educationem puerorum attinent parum callent.

Preceptum.

Sextum preposito preiuncto siue datiuum
Pre se verba petunt impersonalia. &c.   Exempla.

De legendi officio.

10 Preceptor. Whan a mayster redeth vnto his scholers he may not be to curyose (bycause to shewe hymself) in declaracyon / but studye to make euydent and playne to the profet of the herers.

Tum sic vbi a preceptore discipulis legitur: in interpretando
15 nimis affectato (sui ostentandi gratia) non conuenit: immo (ad audientium vtilitatem) aperte declarare studeat.

Discipulus. Ther be some fooles so pompose / ẏ they study G. ij lytle for profet of theyr scholers: so they may haue the glorye and prayse of a connynge reder.

20 Adeo gloriosi sunt aliqui: vt (dummodo exacti et affectati lectoris gloriam sibi conflent) discipulorum vtilitati parum ab ijs consulatur.

Preceptum.

A multis actus fieri. &c.   Exempla.

25   De lingua / voce / vultu / et gestu.

Preceptor. Also whan they rendre or rede in ẏ schole before ẏ mayster / he sholde fourme & fason ẏ tongue the pronunciacyon / contenaunce and gesture.

Preterea vbi redditur / vel recitatur in schola coram preceptore:
30 instruatur lingua / vox / vultus et gestus.

De lingue formatione.

That they pronunce not rudely / hastely / confusely or corruptely / but with cleyne / distyncte / & playne tongue.

Ne pronuncietur barbare. precipitanter. confuse: sed apta. dis-
35 tincta. & aperta lingua.

I

De vocis modulatione.

Forther in pronunciacyon let them obserue ỵ̆ they synge not / or humme not al in one toone / as ỹ̆ bee / but (as ỹ̆ dyuersyte of the mater requyreth) somtyme with a basse or lowe voyce. somtyme with an eleuate voyce. somtyme moderate or mean.

Ad hoc inter pronunciandum obseruetur / ne eodem vocis tono (apis in~morem) bombiletur : verum (vt rei varietas postulat) nunc depressa voce. nunc concitata. nunc autem modesta.

Preceptum.
Quartum infinitus pre se modus expetit. &c.

Exemplum.
De vultus et gestus compositione.

Preceptor. It is a rude maner. a chylde (haue he neuer so fyelde a tongue / and pleasaunt pronunciacyon) to stande styll lyke an asse : & on the other syde (as a carter) to be wanderynge of eyes. pykyng / or playenge ỹ̆ foole with his hande / and vnstable of foote.

Turpissimum est puerum : quantumuis limata lingua / suaui voce / stupide (asini in morem) perstare. Rursus (rurestri more) vagis esse oculis. petulanti manu. instabiliqᵤe pede.

Preceptum.
Uerborum prime persone siue secunde. &c. Exempla.

Therfore take hede. y̌ the contenaunce be made conformable to ỹ̆ purpose : now with grauyte. now cherefull now rough. now ameable. shapen mete vnto ỹ̆ mater (as I maye say) lyke a gloue to the hande.

Obserues igitur / vt vultus sit compositus (rei consentaneus) nunc grauis nunc hilaris. nunc rugosus. nunc placidus. materie aptatus. non minus obiter (vt ita dicam) quam manui chirotheca.

Also se y̌ the gesture be comely with semely & sobre mouynge : somtyme of the heed / somtyme of the hande / & fote : and as the cause requyreth with all the body.

Obseruetur etiam decens (vel decorus) gestus moderato motu nunc capitis. nunc manus. nunc pedis nunc (vt rei natura expetit) vel toto corpore.

Vulgaria Roberti Whitintoni

Of this thynges who playse to haue more full knowlege. let hym loke vpon Tullyes rhetorye.
Harum rerum ampliorem peritiam cupidus. ipsius Ciceronis rhetoricen euoluat.

Preceptum.

Uerborum ad solos homines. &c.   Exempla.
Now I haue wrytten summaryly of ẙ maysters behauour. I wyl somwhat speke of ẙ scholers maner or duty. for maners (as they say) maketh man.
Cum summatim de preceptoris officio scripsi : de discipulorum moribus pauca contexam. Nam mores (vt aiunt) hominem exornant.
Discipulus. Maners? it is the chefe thynge requysyte in a chylde. wherof Tully wryteth in the fyrst boke of his offyce. for theyr is no part of this lyfe / nother in causes pryue nor apert. whether a man be occupyed allone by hymselfe : or byssed with other. that maye be without good maner.
Mores siue officia? res in puero precipue expetenda : vnde (vel de quo) Tullius in primo officiorum. Nulla enim vite pars / neque publicis / neque priuatis in rebus : neque si tecum agas quid : neque si cum altero contrahas : vacare officio potest.

Preceptum.

Que perstare loco designant. &c.   Exempla.
Preceptor. It becometh a chylde ẙ wyll be called honest and manerly : not onely in the schole but in ẙ towne or feelde / or wher so euer he be to practeyse good maners / & auoyd all lewde wanton & vnthryfty tutches.
In primis puerum (qui honestus et moratus dici cupit) decet non modo in schola : sed etiam in vrbe / campis / aut vbilibet sit bonos excolere mores : & ab incultis / lasciuis / et flagitiosis prorsus se continere moribus.
And dayly in ẙ mornynge / before all thynge vpon his knees to prayse god & call for grace. wherby he maye encrease in lernynge and vertue.
Et quotidie cum prima luce (flexis genibus) deum adorans gratiam exorare : vnde eruditione et virtute magis ac magis proficiat.
Whiche done. comynge in due season to the schole manerly to

salute his mayster. after his felowes / & dylygently applyenge his lernynge: loose no tyme ydely in ianglynge to his owne hurt & hyndrance of other.

Quo facto. scholam mature petens / preceptorem comiter salutet: deinde condiscipulos. Et doctrine diligenter incumbens : ociose nullum (in suam & aliorum iacturam) confabulando transigat tempus.

Also gyf a lyght & an open eere to his maysters sayenges : be quykke to note with his penne thynges profytable / desyrous & euer enquisityue of lernynge with contynuall practes of latyn speche.

Preterea preceptoris dictis facilem et patulam prebeat aurem : calamo non segnis vtilium rerum annotator : studiosus discipline inuestigator / cum assidua latine lingue exercitatione.

Gentell in worde & dede to all his felowes no byssy complayner : nor yet no h[y]der[1] of trouthe. beniuolent / lyberall / obsequet / makynge comparyson with no man.

Sit comis / et affabilis / in omnes commilitones. non queritabundus / rursus neque veritatis celator : sit beniuolus. munificus. morigerus. nemini se preferens.

A diligent merker of the vertue & good maner of other & more diligent folower / & as fro a rokke in the se flee ferre fro the company of an vnthryfte.

Studiosus sit aliene virtutis & probitatis obseruator: & studiosior emulator: & tanquam a scopulo marino. a perditi familaritate abstineat.

Discipulus. The conuersacyon of one vnthryfte is as poyson to a hole schole. for one scabbed shepe (as they saye) marreth a hole flocke.

Fo. xxix Unius perditi conuersatio est quasi pestis vniuerso literario ludo : nam (vt dici solet) Scabida facta pecus totum deperdit ouile.

Preceptum.

Urbis vel pagi proprium. &c.   Exempla.

Preceptor. In this great cytees. as in London / yorke / perusy / & suche where best maner shold be: the chyldre be so nysely & wantonly brought vp: that (comenly) they can lytle good.

In magnificis oppidis. vt Londonie. Eboraci. Perusij. & huius-

---

[1] Text heder

Vulgaria Roberti Whitintoni

modi. adeo lasciue & indulgenter educantur pueri : vt immorati sint plerique.

Discipulus. They may be well compared to the kydnere / ẙ lyeth rolled in fatte / & yet is lene in hymselfe.

5 Renunculo (iure optimo) comparentur: qui quamuis pinguedine obductus : in se tamen macilentus est prorsus.

Preceptum.

Post se verba petunt quartum. &c.   Exemplum.

Preceptor. Whan a chylde is sende to schole to the entent to
10 lerne as well maners as connynge / it is dyshonesty to the mayster. yf he be rude and can noo moore good than a shepe.

Quum in (vel ad) ludum datus / vel mancipatus est puer: ea demum gratia vt tam mores / quam doctrinam discat: si incultus sit moribus : preceptori est dedecus.

15   Preceptum.

Urbis vel pagi proprium si verba sequatur
Ad loca que motum. &c.   Exemplum.

Discipulus. Sythen I cam into London I haue seen many well fauored chyldre & proprely made / but they can no more maner
20 than a carter.

Postquam Londoniam venerim complures vidi pueros venustos & eleganti forma : moribus tamen rustico incultiores.

Preceptum.

Urbis vel pagi proprium si verba sequatur
25 Que remouere loco signant. &c.   Exemplum.

Preceptor. Many a scholer cometh out of a good schole and bereth awaye small lernynge: lykewyse many cometh out of a ryall cyte / as out of London / that bereth away full lytle / or no good maner.
30 Nonnulli e celiberrima schola exeunt parum eruditionis ediscentes / itidem frequentes ab urbe preclare instituta (vti Londonia) discedunt : parum aut nihil bonorum morum secum comportantes.

Preceptum.

35 Rus domus exposcunt. &c.   Exempla.

Discipulus. It is not ẙ place / but bryngyng vp ẙ maketh a

chyld well manerde. for a man shal se a chylde in a gentylmans hous in ẙ countre that can better maner / than the chylde brought vp at home / vnder ẙ moders wynges in the mydle of the cyte.

Non locus sed educatio moratum reddit puerum. cernas enim 5 puerulum ruri in nobilis viri domo qui sub maternis alis dom (vel in media vrbe) educato moribus prepollet.

Preceptor. This cokneys & tytyllynges wantonly brought vp / may abyde no sorowe whan they come to age : where as they / ẙ be hardly brought vp maye lye in warre / & lodge ẙ nyght 10 thorowe vpon the bare grounde.

Hi delicati pueri indulgenter alti / duritie in adulta etate sunt impatientes : vbi duriter educati / militie (vel belli) agere : & humi cubare per noctes valent.

Preceptum. 15

Preposita exposcunt hunc pulcre. &c. Exemplum.

Discipulus. It is more pleasure for a mayster to see foure suche neuer thryftes go out of his schole than se one to come into it.

Quattuor ex ijs perditis ludo exire preceptori videre est iocundius : 20 quam vt ludum adeat vnus.

De constructione gerundiorum.

Primo de gerundio in di. Preceptum.
Infinitiui sensus quando immediate
Post substantiuum. &c. Exemplum. 25

De officio in mensa ministraturi.

Discipulus. Now ye haue somwhat shewed of ẙ maner of orderyng of the mayster of his chyldre in ẙ schole : somwhat I wolde ye sholde touche maners whan they come home and wayte at the table. 30

Cum de formula instituendi et de officio preceptoris & suorum discipulorum in schola carptim meministi : aliqua de moribus in mensa (vbi domum redierint) perstringas velim.

Vulgaria Roberti Whitintoni

Preceptum.
Infinitiui sensus quando immediate
Que genitum poscunt. &c. Exemplum.

Preceptor. A chyld desyrous to knowe how to behaue hym
5 manerly at the table : fyrst the table spred : salt trenchers / &
bred set in ordre. water called for : he must be dilygent to
holde the basen / & ewer. or elles yͤ towel whyle they wasshe.
Puer de officio in mensa cognoscendi cupidus : in primis strata
mensa : sale / quadris & pane / ordine appositis : lotione
10 petita : malluuium cum gutturnio / aut mantile (dum lauatur)
ministrandi (vel vt ministret) studiosus sit.

Preceptum.
Cum sensus geniti presentis participantis. &c.

Exemplum.
15 And after they be set / redy to say grace & gyue laude to the
gyuer of our lyuynge / and foode.
Et postubi discumbitur : ipso viuendi et alendi authori gratias vt
agat / non imparatus sit.

Preceptum.
20 Infinitiui sensus quando rationem
Subsequitur. &c. Exemplum.
Also whan seruyce cometh in / assystente with a napkyn vpon
his sholders / to set downe the dysshes in due ordre / takynge
of yͤ couer : yf it be a dysshe ẙ his superyor wyll haue kept
25 warme / couer it agayne or elles auoyde the couer.
Tum vbi inferuntur fercula : sit non imparatus (mantiliolo humeris
suspenso) ad apponendum (vel vt apponat) ordine fercula :
ablatis operculis : si quod tamen ferculum superior clausum
iubeat. denuo operiatur. sin minus : auferat.

30   Preceptum.
Post curo mando loco. &c.   Exemplum.   Vulga.
Let hym also take dylygent hede to set his cuppe surely before whitin.
his superiour discouer it & couer it agayn with curtesy made. H. i
Curet insuper superioris poculum (aut calicem) non titubanter
35 apponendum : operculum paulo suspensum denuo apponendum
flexo genu.

Preceptum.

In dum perpulcre licet vsurpare gerundum
Impersonale est. &c. Exemplum.

He must haue a diligent eye on euery syde / ẙ no thyng lacke at
table. redy at a becke or a wynke of the eye / to satisfye his
superyours pleasure.

Accurate (vel oculatissime) illi est obseruandum ne quid in mensa
desit (vel sic) vigilantissime obseruare habet (vel sic) est
obseruaturus. ne quid in mensa desit. Uel sic. Summa
mense obseruantia illi est habenda: ne quid desit. Tum
superioris nutu / oculi ve connictu / eius animo obsequi paratissimus.

Preceptum.

Inter periuncta licet vsurpare gerundum. &c. Exemplum.

And as he wayteth or attendeth. euer haue an ey to his superyors
trencher: yf it be laded with fragmentes: other to conuey them
into a voyder or elles to shyft his trencher.

Atque dum obseruat (vel sic) inter obseruandum (vel sic) obseruans. (vel sic) in obseruando. (vel sic) inter obseruationem aut
obseruantiam (vel sic) in obseruatione vel obseruantia assidue
curet superioris quadram / si fragmentis onustetur: aut in
scutellulam exoneret: aut quadram mutet.

Preceptum.

Infinitiuum nunquam / sed iunge gerundum.
In dum post verbum requiescere. &c. Exempla.

Also yf his superyour call for ony thynge that lakketh yf he be
apoynted to stande to gyue attendaunce / & may not go to
fetche suche thynges: let hym pryuely cal some other to go
for it.

Quodsi quod deest quicquam postulet superior / atque is ad obseruandum. astare iussus ad apportandum id abire nequit:
alium ad facessendum illud summissa voce asciscat.

And whan his superiours cuppe standeth longe auoyde it at the
cupborde & fyll of fresshe / & to conclude / what so euer his
superior lacketh: redy to ministre it vnto hym.

Fo. xli Et sicubi superioris poculum iusto diutius steterit ad abacum

Vulgaria Roberti Whitintoni

vacuatum / repleatur. & summatim vt agam. quicquid superior indiget: ad ministrandum (vel ministrare) illud sit paratus.

Preceptum.

Infinitiuum desisto desino &c.   Exemplum.

5 Discipulus. here cease / or make a pause / of the offyce of a seruytour or wayter / & somwhat declare of behauour of a chylde syttynge at the table.

Hic desinas / desistas / vel cesses de ministraturi officio procedere: & paucula de pueri discumbentis moribus nobis aperias.

10   Preceptum de Gerundio in do.

Sensus participi presentis cum sine fixo. &c.

De discumbentis officio Exemplum.

Preceptor. A chylde in syttynge downe at table yf he kepe good maner: let him take a place after his degre & gyue preeminence
15 euer to straungers syttynge vpryght / not leanynge vpon his elbowes nor hangynge downe the heed vpon his trencher.

Puer in discumbendo (decorum seruans) locum se dignum capessat: hospitibus vbiuis cedendo erectus sedeat: ab incumbendo mense: & caput reclinando omnino abstineat.

20   Preceptum.

Infinitiui sensus post verba percandi. &c.   Exemplum.

Nor boysterly and rudely to anoye hym that sytteth next hym / by extendynge his arme ouer his trencher to take salt or the cuppe: but manerly desyrynge hym to reche or gyue hym
25 suche thynges as standeth fer of.

Neque (rusticano more) assidentem molescet / brachium supra quadram: pro sale aut calice porrigendo: immo hunc vt longius distantia sibi porrigat: honeste deposcat.

Preceptum.

30 Actiua di do dum sunt sumpta gerundia. &c.   Exemplum.

And though he haue great desyre to ete of this dysshe or ỹ: yet he may not go to his mete greydely / but soberly. nor be fyrst redy to put his hand in ỹ dysshe before other / but vse hymself gentyl in gyuing place to his betters.

35 Et quanquam hoc / aut illo ferculo vescendi ardens illi sit

desyderium : non auide tamen : sed modeste cibum sumat.
Neque ad preripiendum alijs cibum sit paratior : sed (maioribus cedendo) sese honeste gerat.

Preceptum.

Di dum do interdum sunt sumpta gerundia pulchre
Passiue. &c.   Exemplum.
Also yf he espye a swete morsell / which he hath delyte to ete
of : he maye not inferse hymselfe (lyke a churle) to grype all
vpon his owne trencher. but shewe hym lyberally in gyuynge
other parte therof.
Quodsi bellissimum quod (cuius comedendi auidus sit) aduertat :
non ad totum (rustici more) sibi coaceruandum sit intentus : at
humanum (eo alijs impertiendo) sese prestet.

Preceptum.

Cum recto aut terno sunt sumpta gerundia. &c.   Exemplum.
And so he must as well satisfye ỹ appetytes of other ỹ sytteth
present as his owne / or elles he is not mete to syt ymonge ỹ
company of honest men.
Itaque aliorum accumbentium haud secus ac suo ipsius desyderio
mos gerendus est : alioquin aliorum coniunctioni fruende est
minus idoneus.

Preceptum.

Casibus adiunctis nullis quandoque solute
Passiue in do / dum. &c.   Exemplum.
And though euery dysshe set vpon the table be ordeyned to be
eten : yet he may not (with good maner) begynne with ỹ dysshe
ỹ semeth to hym moost pleasaunt in etyng. but after ỹ ordre /
as they be set downe / so repast vpon them.
Et quanquam singula quequam fercula in promptu ad comedendum sunt apposita : quod tamen gustando lautius videtur /
ferculum non est preripiendum : sed pro apponendi ordine sunt
carpenda.

Preceptum.

Quando relatiuum sequitur post ipsa gerunda
Actiue & nunquam passiue ea sumere debes.   Exemplum.
If he be moued with prouocacyon of neesyng / coughyng /

Vulgaria Roberti Whitintoni

snytynge / or spyttynge / & other whiche he can not restrayne.
tourne asyde his heed : or yf he can not conuenyently / holde
his hande before his mouthe.
Quodsi sternutandi / tussiendi / emungendi aut expuendi / irri-
tamento (quod vitare nequit) afficiatur. aut os auertat : aut si
commode nequeat / manum ori interponat.
I wolde fayne speke of many other thynges which I let passe by Fo. xlij
cause of breuyte.
Multa alia commemorandi sum cupidus. que breuitatis causa
pretermitto.

De vsu supinorum.   Preceptum.
Quando post verbum vel participale gerundum
Ad loca que motum signant. &c.   Exemplum.
Discipulus. To what entent is a chylde send or set to schole
or to seruyce in a cyte? but to knowe & lerne as well maner
as scyence.
Quorsum in ludum literarium. aut vrbanum seruitium missus /
aut mancipatus est puer? nisi cognitum / cognosciturus / ad
cognoscendum / vel vt cognoscat eque mores atque artem.

Preceptum.
Interdum liceat prius vsurpare supinum.
Post verbum includens. &c.   Exemplum.

De sermone epulari.

Preceptor. It is good maner / yf a man be bydde / or apoynted
to syt at the table : to vse no communicacyon but ẏ whiche is
syttynge & mete for the table : and that whiche is inhoneste to
auoyde vtterly.
Decet (vel decorum est) vt inuitatus discubitum / vel admissus :
nullo nisi epulari sermone vti : tum a turpi abstinere / prorsus.

Preceptum.
Infinitiui sensus quando immediate
Post adiecta bilis. &c.   Exemplum.
Preceptor. Let therfore his communicacyon at table be honeste /
demure / mery / delectable to here / not ambyguose to vnder-

124   *Vulgaria Roberti Whitintoni*

stande (engendryng suspicyon) no more greue to be herde /
than spoken : but (for euery part) moost pleasaunt to here of.
Sit igitur sermo epularis honestus. modestus. facetus. auditu
delectabilis non suspitioni obnoxius / non intellectu difficilis.
non audito / quam dictu molestius : immo (generatim) cognitu   5
potissimum.

Vulga.   Post adiectiua hec licet vsurpare supinum
whitin.
H. iij   Posterius dignus. &c.   Exempla.

Let not his communicacyon be capcyose or chekkynge / not
obstynate and syngler / not vyle / not scoffynge / or mockynge /   10
not braggynge / not wanton / not dissolute not byssy / not
perylous to speke of.
Sit colloquium non dictu acerbum : non pertinax. non absurdum.
non ridiculosum. non ampullosum. non lasciuum. non diffusum.
non curiosum : non denique periculosum.   15
But let it be worthy to be noted : solacious to rekken of euydent
to perceyue. good & holsom to folowe or do after.
Sed annotatu sit dignum. memoratu iocundum. cognitu lucidum.
clarum / vel perspicuum factu pulcrum et salubre.

Preceptum.   20
Deque loco motum que signant. &c.   Exemplum.
And after he ryseth fro table or repaste it is good maner to
salute with curtesy his superiours.
Et postubi ab epulatione (siue epulis) surrexerit (non dices ab
epulando : vel epulatu) decet (vel decorum est) superiores   25
(flexo genu) salutare.

De vsu & venustate participij.   Preceptum.
Binis de causis inuentum participans est.
Uel sermo vt breuior. &c.

Preceptum.   De exclusione copulatiue coniunctionis.   30
Cum duo verba simul coniunctio. &c.   Exemplum.

De officio ministrantis post epulas expletas.
Preceptor.   After dyner or supper is done / & the table must be
take vp. a chyld must dilygently wayte / & take vp ẙ dysshes
in ordre / as they were set fyrst vpon ẙ table.   35
Postubi expletis epulis / mensa est remouenda : vel fercula sunt

auferenda. puer officiose / obseruans / cibaria (quo ordine fuerunt apposita) auferat.

Preceptum. De exclusione quanquam & nisi. &c.
Quum verbo preeunt nisi quanquam consilesque &c. Exempla.
5 And ẏ done / set downe a charger or a voyder & gyddre vp ẙ fragmentes ther in. & with ẙ voydyng knyfe gyddre vp ẙ crappes & cromes cleyne / also the looues (except they be hole) also spoones napkyns and trenchers.
Quo facto paropsidi apposite fragmenta collecta imponens cultro
10 structorio fragmentilla / et micas prorsus auferat : tum panes nisi intactos (vel nisi solidos) tum coclearia. mantiliola. et quadras.
Yf chese or frutes (as the tyme of yere requyreth) be brought vnto Fo. xliij the table laye newe trenchers.
15 Si mense imponatur caseus : aut pro anni tempore fructus. Uel sic. Caseo (vel pro anni tempore) fructibus mense impositis : nouas apponat quadras.
Though I ouerslyppe many thinges requyset to maner : yet I haue touched thynges moost comenly vsed in this dayes.
20 Multis pretermissis (vel quanquam multis pretermissis) que ad mores spectant. nonnulla tamen hoc euo plerunque vsitata recensui.

Preceptum. De exclusione relatiui.
Uerbum in participans tu commutare rela. &c. Exemplum.
25 To conclude. whan suche ẙ syt at table be at a poynt to ryse : chese / bred / & salt auoyded : the table clothe muste be take vp.
Postremo vbi discumbentes a mensa sunt surrecturi : caseo / pane / & sale / sublatis : mappa tandem est auferenda.

30 Preceptum. De exclusione dum & quum. &c.
Exclusis postquam / dum / quum / &c. Exempla.
And after the towels be spredde / & the basen / & ẙ ewer set downe : he must (forthe with) lyfte op the ewer and powre forthe a lytle into the basen / & after saye grace.
35 Tum constratis (vel compositis) mantilibus : continuo ex gutturnio suspenso paululum aque in labrum effundere habet : et gratias deo agere.

And whan they put theyr ha*n*des in y̑ basen to wasshe he must holde vp the ewer & powre watre in y̑ myddes all the whyle they be wasshynge.

Et manibus labro ad lauandu*m* impositis gutturniu*m* suspensum (illis lauantib*us*) tenens : quam in medium est effusurus. 5

Preceptu*m*. De ablat*iuo* casu absoluto.

Quu*m* nomen iunctu*m* aut pronome*n*. &c. Exemplu*m*.

The basen and ewer taken awaye / & the towels layd playne / he must set downe vpon the table a fresshe cup of wyne / & an other of ale. 10

Malluuio et gutturnio sepositis : & mantilib*us* decore *com*positis rece*n*tis vini / itide*m* ceruisie est apponendum poculum.

H. iiij Preceptum.

Nomen tu sexto / aut pronomen pone soluto. &c.

Exemplu*m*. The cuppes remoued & towels gyddred vp. y̑ boorde 15 must be couerd w*ith* a carpet. Here I make an ende / for I haue spoke metely of maners I reporte me to ony man / at lestwyse that knoweth maners.

Remotis poculis / & collectis mantilibus : tapeto sternenda est mensa. iam receptui canam. de moribus eni*m* quouis (saltem 20 morato) iudice sic satis dixi.

Preceptum.

Cuncta gerundia / participantia / siue supina. &c.

Exemplu*m*. Who so euer desyreth to knowe forther of offyces & maners y̑ bryngeth a man to honesty / let hym go loke vpon 25 Tully / Senec and Ambrose.

Quisq*ui*s de officijs que ad decoru*m* & honestu*m* ducu*n*t / ampliora cognosce*n*di cupid*is* est marcu*m* Tulliu*m*. Anneum Senecam / & diuinu*m* Ambrosium / consultu*m*. ad ˙consulendum. vel consulturus adeat. 30

De aduerbioru*m* & interiectionu*m* constructione.

Preceptum.

Temporis atq*ue* loci / sic quanti aduerbia. &c.

Exemplu*m*. Albe it a chylde y̑ obserueth these thynges afore

Vulgaria Roberti Whitintoni

sayd : in what place so euer he cometh (in this dayes) hath competent maners / to ordre hymself honestly.

Supramemorata tamen puer ediscens : quoquo gentium (vel quouis locorum) nunc eui venerit : sic satis morum habet :
5 vnde honeste sese gerat.

Preceptum.

Propius exposcit nunc quartum nuncque datiuum.

Exemplum.

But for as moche as maners dayly altreth and renueth (as the
10 leyues of the trees) a chylde muste confourme hymselfe to aproche to suche maners as be laudable vsed for the tyme.

Uerum cum (vt arboribus folia) indies mutentur mores. moribus. vel mores (pro tempore) approbatis. propius accedere sese comparet puer.

15 Preceptum. Ecce petit rectum / en nunc rectum. &c.

Exempla de ecce / en / heus / ah / vah / ohe / hem / proh / heu.

Preceptor. A se maners ? loke vpon rudenes ? herke my chylde? Fo. xliiij thou mayst folowe whether ẙ wyll. ah clennes of vertue so lytle regarded ? phy vylenes of vyce so greatly vsed.
20 Ecce morum probitas ? en turpitudo / vel nem ? heus mi puer ? vtrumlibet eligas. ah virtutis pudor sic paruipense ? vah flagitij squalor tantopere amplexe ?

Discipulus. Ohy good syr? suche is the course of the world. alas for mysery ? worse was it neuer. o merciful god ? wyll it
25 neuer amende ? alas for synne & wyckednes ?

Ohe bone vir ? sic sunt vel sic se habent res humane : hem miserias vel miserie ? pessimum seculum proh presentissime deus ? vel proh deum clementissimum ? rediet ne felicitas vspiam ? heu impietas ? vel heu impietatem ?

30 Preceptum.

Hei terno et recto vel soli iungito terno.

O iungas recto / nunc terno / nunc quoque quinto.

Exemplum.

Preceptor. Alakke this heuy world ? wo is my herte to remembre
35 ẙ felicyte & wealth ẙ hath be ? poore men cryeth out of this

scarsyte of al thynge? O ẙ felycyte of olde tyme? o this newe mysery? o good lord? refourme our maners: ẙ the olde wealth maye renewe.

Hei calamitoso huic tempori? hei antique felicitat*is* recordatio? veh reru*m* penurie? clamitant pauperes? O prisca reru*m* opu- 5 le*n*tia? o noua*m* miseria*m*? O bone deus? mores et vita*m* corrigas. vt restituatur pristina felicitas?

T E L O S.

Londini in edibus Winandi de Worde vicesimo supra sesqui millesimu*m* nostre salutis anno. 10

VULGARIA STA*N*BRIGIANA
NOTES

I need hardly comment on the fact that these early makers of vocabularies displayed little originality. There is a striking resemblance between these early *Vulgaria* and such works as Alexander Neckam's *De Utensilibus*, and John of Garlandia's *Dictionarius*. See *A Volume of Vocabularies*, ed. by T. Wright, 1857.

PAGE 1, line 6. **hec coma/e...for a busshe.** Frequently used for hair at this time. Cf. Barclay, *Eclogues*.

5, l. 29. **hic medicus...for the leche fynger,** 'medicus, lechefyngur'—MS. Harl. 1002, fol. 113 r⁰. 'Hic medicus, the therde fynger,' Wright, p. 207.

6, l. 2. **hoc splen...for the mylte.** See Wright, *A Pictorial Vocabulary*, p. 247: 'hic splen, the mylt.' The spleen.

6, l. 10. **hoc omentum...for the kell.** The fatty membrane investing the intestines. Cf. *N.E.D.* under 'caul'.

7, l. 25. **hec vertebra, for the whyrlebone.** *A Nominale*, Wright, p. 208: 'Hec vertebra, the wherl bone.' *Metrical Vocabulary*, Wright, p. 179: 'Vertebra, werel-bone.' 1. The round head of a bone turning in another bone. 2. The knee-pan. 3. A vertebra of the spine. 1400 Lanfranc's *Cirurg.* 3, cap. vj: 'of woundis of þe rigboon & of whirle bones of þe rigge.' Cf. *N.E.D.* under 'whirl bone'.

8, l. 41. **infestus, parelles,** parlous, dangerous, hazardous.

9, l. 1. **reticulum, kall**⎫
9, l. 1. **crinale, kall** ⎬ a net.

9, l. 1. **mitella, payre of burlettes.** Burlet, E. bourlet or bourrelet, a padded roll of cloth for a woman's head; coif or hood; roll supporting a ruff. 1552 *Huloet*: 'Byrlet or tyrynge for women.

10, l. 20. **spuma, e/ale, e/ryall,** froth or foam. *c.* 1440 *Prompt. Parv.* 432/2, Ryal, 'of foom or berme, spuma'.

10, l. 72. **corbis, i/frayle,** a kind of basket made of rushes, used for packing figs, &c.

10, l. 34. **infumibulum, o/the thowell of a chymney,** a funnel. It may be possible that 'thowell' is a misprint for 'tho*n*ell', 'tonel', or 'tunnel'. In this case it would mean the flue or vent over the chimney. Cf. Horman, *Vulgaria*, 1519, xvi: 'The shanke or tonel of the chymney voydeth not the smoke.' Brinsley, in his ed. of the *Vocabulary*, 1630, has '*tunnell*'. Cf. *N.E.D.* under 'tunnel'. But

K

it is more likely that the word is a variant of 'tewel'—a shaft or opening for escape of smoke. Cf. *N.E.D.* under 'tewel'.

11, l. 2. ollula, e / posnet, small vessel for boiling, having handle and three feet. *c.* 1420 *Liber Cocorum* (1862), 10: 'Welle all togedur in a posnet.' Cf. *N.E.D.* under 'posnet'.

11, l. 33. Saturgia, sauerey, herb. See *Early British Botanists*, R. T. Gunther, 1922, p. 399. Cf. Palladius, *Husbandrie*, E.E.T.S., p. 199.

11, l. 35. baccar, herbeton. Is this the only occurrence of the word? *baccar* appears in the 1510 (W. de W.) ed. of the *Vocabula* as 'saynt iohñs herbe', and in Brinsley's ed. (1630) as 'our ladies gloves'. According to *N.E.D.* it was a plant with an aromatic root yielding oil and is variously identified by botanists. See *N.E.D.* under *Bacchar*.

12, l. 5. Licusta, e / creuys, crayfish. *c.* 1430 Lydgate, *Min. Poems* (Percy Soc.), 154: 'A Kreuys with his klawes longe.' *c.* 1490 *Prompt. Parv.* 102: 'Creuys, fysshe.' Cf. *N.E.D.* under 'crayfish'.

12, l. 9. capito, cabege, fish. Cf. Wright, *A Volume of Vocabularies*, p. 55: 'Capito, myne vel lepute.' p. 189: 'Hic caput, A caboche.' Note: 'The bull-head, or miller's thumb, called in O. French *chabot*.'

12, l. 11. mugil, morte, a sea-fish. Actually the name for a salmon in its third year. 1530 Palsgrave, 246/2: 'morte, a fysshe.' Cf. *N.E.D.* under 'mugil', 'mort'. Wright, p. 189: 'Hic salmo, A salmon; Hoc mugyl, idem.'

12, l. 11. mutilus, hornekeke. The garfish or hornbeak. *c.* 1440 *Parv.* 247/1: 'Horn keke, fysch.' 1530 Palsgrave, 232/2: 'Horn kecke, a fysshe lyke a mackerell.' Cf. *N.E.D.* under 'hornkeck'. Cf. Wright, p. 254: 'Hec rugella, hoc rustiforum, a horn keke.'

12, l. 13. radagia, thornebagge. The common ray or skate; provincial name for stickleback. Cf. *N.E.D.* under 'thornback'. Cf. Wright, p. 254.

12, l. 15. clepa, cheuyn. A fish, the chub. 1496 *Bk. St. Albans*, Fishing, 28: 'The cheubyn is a stately fysshe; and his heed is a deynty morsell.' 1653 Walton, *Angler*, 59: 'Have you no other way to catch a chevin or chub?' Cf. *N.E.D.* under 'chevin'.

12, l. 22. antelo, e / poytrell. (*a*) A piece of armour to protect the breast of a horse. *c.* 1489 Caxton, *Sonnes of Aymon*, viii. 197: 'The horses gyrtte nor the poytrell myghte not helpe.' (*b*) A breast-plate, a stomacher. Cf. *N.E.D.* under 'poitrel'.

12, l. 32. caballus, i / cable: i.e. caball, horse. Cf. Barclay's *Eclogues*, Ciij/4: 'But the stronge caball standeth at the racke.' 1538–48 Elyot, *Lat. Dict.*: 'caballus, a horse; yet in some partes of England they do call an horse a cable.' Cf. *N.E.D.* under 'caball'.

13, l. 8. luscus, i / ſpurblynde, purblinde. 1552 Latimer, *Serm.*

Notes

Lord's Prayer, i. 4 : 'They be spurreblynd and sande blynd, they can not see so farre.' Cf. *N.E.D.*, an alteration of *purblind*. Brinsley, 1630, translates *luscus*, one-eyed, and has a note 'purblind '.

14, l. 26. **It is a gret helpe for scollars to speke latyn.** Cf. Introduction, p. liii.

15, l. 24. **Profred seruyce stynketh.** See Ray's *Proverbs*, 1742, p. 148 : ' Proffer'd service (and so ware) stinks. Merx ultronea putet, apud Hieronym. Erasmus saith, Quin vulgo etiam in ore est, ultro delatum obsequium plerunque ingratum esse. So that it seems this Proverb is in use among the Dutch too. Merchandise offerte est a demi vendue. Gall. Ware that is proffered is sold for half the worth, or at half the price.'

15, l. 26. **It semeth a scolar to were a syde gowne . . . toga longa.** Cf. *A History of the University of Oxford*, C. E. Mallett, vol. i, p. 145 : ' The toga, which became the modern gown, seems to have been a robe or tunic, longer than the tabard, worn by almost anyone, and as cheerful in colour as its owner wished. Under this gown a closer tunic might be worn and over it the academic cappa (a sleeveless cloak or cape bordered or lined with fur).'

16, l. 22. **It longeth to a scollar to speke latyn.** Cf. Introduction, p. liii.

18, l. 33. **Thou hyttes the nayle on the head.** Cf. Ray's *Proverbs*, 1742 : ' Of Persons speaking pertinently. He hes hit the nail on the head.' Heywood's *Proverbs* : 'This hitteth the naile on the hed.' Skelton, *Colin Cloute*, 34 : ' And yf that he hyt The nayle on the hede, It standeth in no stede '.

18, l. 36. **Be the daye neuer so longe at last cometh euensonge.** Obviously a proverbial expression. Stephen Hawes uses it in his *Pastime of Pleasure*. This is perhaps its first appearance in literature. Heywood, *Proverbs*, has :

' For though the day be never so long
At last the bell rings for evensong.'

20, l. 31. **I shall mary my doughter to the . . . gnatam.** A euphemistic term for flogging in schools. See Whittinton's *Vulgaria*, p. 87, l. 29.

20, l. 37. **I force not.** I care not.

23, l. 1. **Though peper be blacke it hathe a good smacke.** Heywood, *Proverbs* : ' Pepper is blacke ⎱ And every man
And hath a good smack ' ⎰ doth it bie.

Ray, *Proverbs* : ' Snow is white and lies in the dike
And every man lets it lie :
Pepper is black and hath a good smack,
And every man doth it buy.'

23, l. 4. buttes / pryckes / rouers, ad metas / limites certos / aut incertos. Terms for archers.

23, l. 4. butte, properly a mound or other erection on which the target is set up. There were generally two butts, one at each extremity of the range. 1526 Skelton, *Magnyfycence*, 297: 'Ye wante but a wylde flyeng bolte to shote at the *buttes*'.

23, l. 4. prycke, the bull's eye, hence the target, at a fixed distance. 1545 Ascham, *Tox.* 113: 'A bowe of Ewe must be hadde for perfecte shootinge at the prickes.'

23, l. 4. Rouer, a mark selected at random, not at any fixed distance from the archer. 1541–2 Act 33 H. VIII, c. 9. 2: 'Noe man under thage of xxiiij yeres shall shoote at any standing prick except it be at a Rouer whereat he shall chaunge at every shoote his marke.' Cf. *N.E.D.* In the Statutes of St. Alban's School provision is made that parents should provide their children with necessary implements for archery practice.

24, l. 13. slabby. Now dialectical—wet, muddy, slushy.

24, l. 20. in hale, in decubijs. OE. halh, healh, a corner, secret place. *c.* 1450 *Myrc*, 1384: 'Hast þow do þat synne bale By any wommen þat lay in hale'. Cf. *N.E.D.*

25, l. 31. It is euyll with vs when the mayster apposeth vs. Cf. Introduction, p. vl.

26, l. 11. Be ware in welthe or thou be wo. Cf. Skelton, *Agst. Garnesche*, iv. 124: 'Wherfore in welthe beware of woo.'

26, l. 20. Jacke napes. This is the earliest form of the word. Apparently it came into literature as the opprobrious nickname of William de la Pole, Duke of Suffolk (died 1450), whose badge was a clog and chain. It seems to have been the quasi-proper name for a tame ape, perhaps parodying a human name and surname. Cf. Skelton, *Why come ye not to Courte*, 651: 'He grynnis and he gapis As it were jack napis.' *Magnyfy.* 2124: 'To mockynge, to mowynge, lyke a jacknapes.' Ray's *Proverbs*: 'Can jack-an-apes be mery when his clog is at his heels.'

27, l. 18. A gyuen hors may not [be] loked in the tethe. Heywood's *Proverbs*: 'No man ought to looke a given horse in the mouth.' Ray says: 'Look not a gift horse in the mouth. It seems this was a Latin Proverb in Hierom's time, Erasmus quotes it out of his preface to his commentaries on the epistle to the Ephesians, Noli (ut vulgare est proverbium) equi dentes inspicere donati'. Cf. the rimed medieval verse:

Si quis dat mannos, ne quaere in dentibus annos.

27, l. 37. He is an euyll coke that can not lycke his owne lyppes. Heywood, *Proverbs*: 'A poore cooke that may not licke his owne

Notes

fingers.' Ray: 'He's an ill cook that cannot lick his own fingers. Celuy gouverne bien mal le miel qui n'en taste & ses doigts n'en leche.' Cf. *Romeo and Juliet*, IV. ii.

30, l. 12. Wysshers and wolders be small hous holders. This is perhaps the earliest appearance of this proverb. Green uses it in 1590 *Never too late*: 'For he being a scholar, and nurst up at the universities, resolved rather to live by his wit, than any way to be pinched with want, thinking this old sentence to be true, the wishers and woulders were never good householders'. Heywood, *Proverbs*: 'Wishers and wolders bee no good hous-holders.' Ray: 'Wishers and woulders are never good housholders.'

VULGARIA ROBERTI WHITINTONI
NOTES

PAGE 42, l. 1. **pastans**: 1527 ed. pastaunce.

42, l. 23. **vnsyttynge**, unbecoming, unfitting. Cf. More, *Apol.* xii. Wks. 872/1: 'The priestes agaynste laye people . . . have vsed . . . to speake vnsyttynge woordes.'

45, l. 16. **Ryot**: crapula, dissipation, debauchery.

46, l. 33. **an hare bagged**: Lepus granida: 1526 ed. grauida, bagged, pregnant.

50, l. 7. **accused vnto the mayster.** See Introduction, p. liv.

50, l. 18. **buklersbury.** According to Stow, 'Bucklersbury falls into Walbrook, almost against St. Stephen's Walbrook Church. It is a place well built and inhabited; particularly by Drugsters and Furriers.' Later, 'This whole street, called Bucklesbury, on both the sides throughout, is possessed by Grocers and Apothecaries towards the West end thereof.' Again, ' Bucklersbury turneth out of Cheapside, and runneth on the back side of the Poultry unto Walbrook. A street very well built, and inhabited by Tradesmen, especially Drugsters and Furriers.'

52, l. 26. **by mouthe . . .** : 1527 ed. by *my* mouth.

57, l. 13. **A pounde of wexe is at .ix. pens.** See *A History of Agriculture and Prices in England*, vol. iii, J. E. T. Rogers, 1882. At Downham in 1516 1½ lb. sold for 11*d*. and at Norwich 1 lb. of candles for 8*d*. In 1517 2 lb. sold at Downham for 9*d*., and in 1518 2½ lb. at Cambridge for 7*d*. and 1 lb. at Downham for 9*d*. In 1519 2 lb. sold at Downham for 11*d*. and in 1520 1 cwt. at London for 80*s*. It seems that Whittinton's prices are accurate. They remain unaltered in the later editions of his work.

57, l. 20. **malt.** See Rogers, *History of Agriculture and Prices*, vol. iii.

57, l. 23. **busshell of whete . . . at .xij. pens.** See Rogers, *History of Agriculture*, vol. iii. These prices are difficult to verify. The actual measures varied in different places. Cf. Fitzherb., *Husb.*, 12 : ' Two London bushells of pease, the whyche is but two strykes in other places.'

57, l. 25. **stryke** : usually identical with the bushel, but in some districts equal to half and in others to two or four bushels. Cf. *N.E.D.* under 'strike', and Rogers, *History of Agriculture*, vol. iii. See preceding note.

Notes

57, l. 27. A mette or an hoope of oote mele : a met was a bushel, or in some parts two bushels. See Rogers, *History of Agriculture*, vol. iii.

57, l. 29. swete wyne. See Rogers, *History of Agriculture*, vol. iii: ' Sweet wine is sold by the gallon, the butt and the rundlet.' In 1518 one gallon of red wine sold at 8*d*. at Cambridge.

57, l. 31. ale is at .i. peny & ferdynge. Ale and beer were sold by the gallon, the firkin, the kilderkin, pipe, and tun. The prices from 1516 to 1520 seem to have been stable. See Rogers, as above.

58, l. 18. goddes coope: Tantaleas opes. A common proverbial expression for a very large sum. 1553 T. Wilson, *Rhetor*, 72 : ' He will spende Goddes coope if he had it.' Cf. *N.E.D.* under ' cope '.

60, l. 24. Kynge henry the .vij. These early *Vulgaria* depend for their interest on allusions of this kind. Horman accused Whittinton of sycophancy, and it may be that he deserved the jibe. It was politic to give elegant descriptions of the king. Cf. Barclay, *Eclogues*.

61, l. 1. talle persone of body, &c. See *Calendar of State Papers, Spanish, 1485-1509*, vol. i, Introd., p. xlviii : 'Of the personal appearance of Henry VII little is to be learnt. He was of middle height and had by no means a robust constitution. All foreign diplomatists who had any business to transact with him mention the vivacity of his expression and especially the liveliness of his eyes.' See p. 179, 25 July 1498, letter from Pedro de Ayala to Ferdinand and Isabella : ' His crown is nevertheless undisputed and his government is strong in all respects. He is disliked. . . . The king looks old for his years but young for the sorrowful life he has led. . . . He likes to be much spoken of, and to be highly appreciated by the whole world. He fails in this because he is not a great man. Although he professes many virtues his love of money is too great.'

61, l. 7. no fraude so pryuely be conspyred, &c. A reference to the pretenders, Simnel and Warbeck.

61, l. 14. the stronge & myghty buyldynges. See later reference to Westminster and Savoy.

61, l. 22. $\overset{e}{y}$ kyng of Castyll, &c. There is an allusion here to the visit of Philip and Joanna in 1506. They landed in Dorset on their way from Flanders to Castile. Henry was very solicitous, entertained them at Windsor, making Philip a Knight of the Garter, and incidentally leading him to sign a treaty of alliance which involved the surrender of Suffolk. With reference to the banquets see *Italian Relation*, Camden Society, 1847, p. 47 (*c.* 1500): ' From the time of William the Conqueror to the present, no king has reigned more peaceably than he has, his great prudence causing him to be universally feared; and, though frugal to excess in his own person, he does not change any of the ancient usages of England at his court, keeping a sumptuous table, as I had the opportunity of witnessing twice that your magnificence dined there, when I judged there might be from six to seven hundred persons at dinner. And his people say that his majesty spends upon his table 14,000 pounds sterling annually, which is equal to 70,000 crowns.'

62, l. 7. Westmynster & in sauoy. See Stow, *Annals*, 1605, p. 810 : ' This yeere (1505) the chappell of our Ladie, above the east end of the high altar of Westminster church, with also a tauern neere adjoyning called the white rose, were taken down : in which place, or plot of ground, on the 24 of January, the first stone of our Lady chappell was laid by the hands of John Islip abbot of the same monastery, Sir Reginald Bray Knight of the Garter, Doctor Barons master of the Roles, doctor Wall chaplaine to the king, master Hugh Oldham chaplaine to the countesse of Derby and Richmond the kings mother, Sir Edward Stanhope, knight, and divers other. Upon the which stone was ingraven the day and yeere, &c. The charges in building this chappell (as I have been informed) amounted to the summe of 14,000 pounds.'

p. 813 : ' This yeere (1509) was finished the goodlie Hospitall of the Sauoy neere vnto Charing Crosse, which was a notable foundation for the poore, doon by King Henry the 7. vnto the which he purchased and gave Landes for the releeuing of 100 poor people. This house was first named Sauoy place by Peter earle of Sauoy the first builder therof, brother to Boniface archbishop of Canterbury about the 29 yeere of King Henry the 3. who made the said Peter earle of Richmond. This house belonged since to the Dukes of Lancaster, and at this time being in the kings handes, was conuerted to an hospitall, retaining the first name of Sauoy.'

63, l. 11. to haunte ale howses. Cf. Introduction, p. xv.

63, l. 33. rynlet : a cask or vessel of varying capacity ; the quantity of liquor contained in this. Large runlets contained between 12 and 18½ gallons, small ones between a pint or quart and 3 or 4 gallons.

63, l. 33. maluesye. For wines see Alexander Henderson, *History of Ancient and Modern Wines*, 1824. Cf. the list of sweet wines in John Russell's *Boke of Nurture* :

' The namys of swete wynes y wold þat ye them knewe :
Vernage, vernagelle, wyne Cute, pyment, Raspise, Muscadelle of grew,
Rompney of modoñ, Bastard, Tyre, Ozey, Torrentyne of Ebrew.
Greke, malvesyñ, Caprik, & Clarey whañ it is newe.'

Notes
137

63, l. 35. romney. See Henderson. Probably a Greek, not an Italian, wine.

63, l. 35. of ỹ rase: a particular class of wine, or the characteristic flavour of this, supposed to be due to the soil. Cf. 1625 Massinger, *New Way*, I. iii: 'A pipe of rich Canary. . . . Is it of the right race?' Cf. *N.E.D.* under 'race'.

64, l. 3. a greue wyne: Asperum et tenue, for gre*n*e, unmatured. 1519 Horman, *Vulgaria*, 4: 'A cuppe of grene (austerum) wyne.'

64, l. 5. lowe or under the barre. See *N.E.D.* under 'bar'. 'The bar was a transverse piece of wood making fast the head of a wine-cask.' (If a cask is lying horizontal, wine is drawn from 'below the bar', when it is more than half empty.) 1611 Cotgrave: 'Empeigner le bout d'une douve, to pin the barre of a peece of caske.'

64, l. 19. Moore. Whittinton, through his Court preferment, may have known More personally. In his *Opusculum* (see Introduction, p. xxx) Whittinton has a poem eulogizing More in a very elegant and curious metre. Cf. Seebohm, *Oxford Reformers*, 1867, p. 49, quoting from a letter of Erasmus: 'Whenever did nature mould a character more gentle, endearing, and happy than Thomas More's?'

65, l. 15. .vij. pens commens wekely. See *History of the University of Oxford*, C. E. Mallett, vol. i, p. 147: 'Dinner was generally at ten in the morning, with three or four hours of study before it. Supper was about five in the afternoon. Commons were the ordinary meals taken together at these hours, but extra food could be procured and eaten elsewhere.' p. 141: 'It is evident that expenses at Oxford varied widely. The poorest students of all might seek a begging-license from the Chancellor, and eke out a living with charity, which carried no discredit. . . . Some in the Colleges, worked as Servitors or batteler, performing certain menial duties and waiting on their betters. . . . Some were excused the customary charges, and graduated *in forma pauperis* without having to pay fees. But the great majority of students lived with some degree of comfort. John Balliol's scholars indeed had to make shift on eight pence weekly. But the Merton scholars with five shillings a year were at first thought to have ample. At Exeter the early scholars had only ten pence a week. At Oriel the weekly allowance for commons was raised in 1329 from a shilling to fifteen pence. New College in times of scarcity allowed as much as one and sixpence. Queen's in the days of Edward VI fixed a liberal maximum of two shillings. Two or three shillings a week could be made to cover all a student's expenses. Three shillings or three and sixpence could be made to do it well. Four or five shillings weekly seems to have sufficed even for young men who kept a tutor and a servant and who depended on the bounty of a king. . . . Fees were low and teaching cheap. The standards of living, as a whole, were frugal. But functions like Determination and Inception might involve heavy expenses. The costs for the average student were substantial.'

65, l. 26. **Exempla artificum.** Cf. John of Garlandia, *Dictionarius.* See Wright, *A Volume of Vocabularies.* Cf. Stow, *Survey of London,* 1605, p. 540, for list of companies attending Mayor's feast at the Guildhall, 23 Henry VIII. He includes 'Sheremen' in his list.

65, l. 32. **sewsters**: sempstresses. Cf. Horman, *Vulgaria,* 238: 'Brotherers, sylkewomen, and all sewsters craftes.' Cf. *N.E.D.* under 'sewster'.

66, l. 1. **sue smiths** ...: 1527 shoo smythes.

66, l. 21. **shermen**: i.e. shearmen, who shear woollen cloth. See Shakespeare, *2 Henry VI,* IV. ii. 141. *Archaeologia,* xxv. 503: 'The sharman of Snettsham.' Cf. *N.E.D.* under 'shearman'.

67, l. 13. **shamullers**. Those who play on the shawm. *Letters and Papers of Henry VIII,* ii. 11. 1451: 'At Greenwich, to Piers Thoulouse a minstrel shalmewer, 4 l.'

67, l. 14. **portatyues**. Small organs easily carried about. *c.* 1450 Holland, *Howlat,* 765: 'Claryonis lowde knellis, Portatiuis, and bellis.' Cf. *N.E.D.*

68, l. 8. **dwarffe / or an vrchen.** Originally a hedgehog. Applied allusively to persons. See *N.E.D.* under 'urchin'.

68, l. 26. **The embassatours of fraunce.** See the *D.N.B.* under Henry VIII. In 1518 embassies arrived from France, 'and a peace was arranged with provisions for the redelivery of Tournay, and for the marriage of the dauphin and Princess Mary. Most cordial relations were established with France and the renewal of amity was celebrated with banquetings and rejoicings.' See *Letters and Papers of Henry VIII's Reign,* vol. ii, pt. 1, Introduction, p. clvii: 'On 23rd September the lord Admiral (Bonnivet) made his appearance with an enormous cavalcade, exceeding 600 horsemen, in splendid equipages, attended by 70 mules and by waggons loaded with baggage, to the immense delight of the good citizens of London. Such an embassy had never been seen within its walls before. They were met by the Lord Surrey, high admiral, with 160 lords and gentlemen, on the part of England, resolved not to be outdone by their French rivals. The mounted procession numbered 1,400, half French and half English, thirty of them being the Scotch guards of the French king.'

In 1518 the Sheriffs of the City were John Allen and James Spencer, and the Mayor, Thomas Mirfin, Skinner.

69, l. 32. ẏ̆ **heere of** ẏ̆ **heedes fase / or moose away** ... pilos

Notes 139

capitum . . . decidere vel deciduos. I am tempted to emend 'fase' (possibly OE. faes, fringe; cf. dial feaze, to clip away wool from lambs' tails) to *fale*, fall. There seems to be confusion in the text between long *s* and *l*. John Clarke, in his *Dux Grammaticus*, 1633, which incorporates Whittinton's work, has 'fall'.

69, l. 32. ' moose ' is probably a typographical error for ' moole ', Cf. Early ME. muwle, to grow mouldy, to mould. *Ancr. R.* 344 : Leten þinges muwlen oder rusten uorrotien. *Metr. Hom.* in *Archiv. Stud. Neu. Spr.* lvii. 288 : Fleschlich lust makeþ Monnes soule Rote and Rust . . . and Moule. *N.E.D.* under 'moul'. Clarke has ' mold '.

71, l. 28. euery begger is woo / that ony other by the dore go. Ray, *Proverbs*: ' It 's one begger's woe, to see another by the door go. " Etiam mendicus mendico invidet." '

72, l. 11. the faders prykkes, paterne probitatis : price, excellency, honourableness. F. prix. Cf. phrase, 'prick & praise' the praise of excellence or success. ' Are you so ignorant in the rules of courtship, to think any one man to bear all the *prick and praise.*' Middleton, *Family of Love*, ii. 4. Cf. *N.E.D.* under ' prick '. Medwall, *Nature* (Brandt), ii. 324: 'Now forsoth I gyve the *pryk and pryse*, thou art worth the weyght of gold.' There is possibly some connexion with the 'prick' in archery here.

72, l. 18. many a good kowe. Ray, *Proverbs*: ' Many a good cow hath but a bad calf.' To which he adds the note : 'Aelius Spartianus in the life of Severus shews by many examples, that men famous for learning, virtue, valour, or success have for the most part either left behind them no children, or such as that it had been more for their honour and the interest of human affairs that they had died childless. We might add unto those, which he produceth, many instances out of our own history . . . and yet there want not in history instances to the contrary. . . . Fortes creantur fortibus & bonis, &c.'

72, l. 27. fall after. 1527 ed. and 1523 ed. fall *here* after.

72, l. 31. Cokke sure : securum. In early use the sureness in question was objective, 'as secure as can be ', cf. *N.E.D.* There is a possibility that the original reference may have been to the security or certainty of the action of a cock or tap in preventing the escape of liquor. There is a remoter possibility that the allusion may be to the certainty of a cock's crowing in the morning.

76, l. 6. A newfangled felowe ... Morosus. Very fond of novelty and new things. Cf. *N.E.D.* under ' newfangled '. Here rather in the sense of capricious.

76, l. 7. after his appetyte . . . : 1527 ed. after appetyte.

79, l. 20. to lorke vpon, alias res agunt. In the sense of to idle, perhaps with malicious intent ? Cf. *N.E.D.* under ' lurk ', which does not list the word in the straight sense of 'to be employed about other business'.

82, l. 11. a chery feyre ... tempus preceps euanescit. A fair held in cherry orchards for the sale of the fruit, often the scene of gaiety and licence. A symbol of the shortness of life and the fleeting nature of its pleasures. 1393 Gower, *Conf.*, Prol. i. 19: 'For al is but a chery feire This worldes good.' Cf. *N.E.D.*

83, l. 3. a rowmeth in y̆ kynges court. Cf. Barclay, *Eclogues*, and the *De Miseriis Curialium* of Aeneas Silvius Piccolomini for description of life at Court. The subject was a favourite one at the time.

83, l. 11. to cory fauell: to solicit favour by flattery. 'Curry-favell, a flatterer, estrille faveau', Palsgrave. In earlier English 'Favel' occurs as the proper name of a fallow-coloured horse, proverbial as the type of hypocrisy and duplicity. *Tudor and Stuart Glossary*, Skeat and Mayhew.

84, l. 8. take peper in the nose. See Heywood, *Proverbs*: 'He taketh pepper in the nose.' An expression commonly applied to any one who was quick at taking offence. Cf. Lyly, *Euphues* (Arb), 119: 'I would not that all women should take Pepper in the nose, in that I have disclosed the legerdemaines of a few.'

85, l. 30. Good morowe &c. This and the following example are extremely valuable and interesting in giving a more vivid and lively picture of the early Tudor schoolroom, as it were in harness, than is to be met with elsewhere.

86, l. 13. a bletchy sowter: atramentosi sarctoris: a cobbler. Still in provincial use in the North country. Bletch was black, viscous, greasy matter. See J. O. Halliwell, *Dictionary of Archaic and Provincial Words*.

86, l. 16. I shall quyte: 1523, 1527 I shall quyte the.

86, l. 30. afrayde of the mayster. Whittinton insists on physical brutality in these Exempla. See Introduction, p. xii et seq.

87, l. 11. y̆ vulgares ... vulgaria. Cf. Introduction, pp. xvi, xviii, xli et seq. This method of learning Latin may have originated at Magdalen College School.

87, l. 29. maryed my maysters doughter. See note on Stanbridge's *Vulgaria*, p. 20, l. 31.

88, l. 26. declareth the lecture of tully. Cf. Introduction, pp. xlviii, xlix, lvii.

89, l. 2. hare to a tabre. See W. W. Skeat, *Early English Proverbs*. *Richard the Redeles*, l. 58: 'Men myghten as well have huntyd an hare with a tabre.'

'No one would readily believe that a hare could have been sufficiently emboldened to face a large concourse of spectators without expressing its alarm, and beat upon a tambourine in their presence; yet such a performance was put in practice not many years back, and exhibited at Sadler's Wells; and if I mistake not, in several other places in and about the metropolis', Strutt, *Sports and Pastimes*, bk. iii, c. 6.

90, l. 12. my mayster hath bete me. Cf. Introduction, p. xii et seq.

91, l. 5. pennarde: a case for pens, carried at the girdle. See Chaucer, *Merch. Tale*, 635: ' Priuely a penner gan he borwe.'

92, l. 20. accuse me of spekynge englysshe. It is apparent from this example that the practice of appointing boys to act as 'custodes' or 'asini' to spy and report on others had many abuses. Cf. Introduction, p. liv.

93, l. 2. a nagled: an agled or aglot. Actually the metal tag of a lace. See Wright's *Vocabularies*, p. 238: 'Hoc mominlum, a naglott.' Sometimes a fragment of flesh hanging by the skin. Hence a scrap, a shred. Cf. *Fardle of Facions*, II. x. 27: 'No, the begger... getteth not an aguelette of hym.' Cf. *N.E.D.* under 'aglet'. See also J. O. Halliwell, *Dictionary of Archaic and Provincial Words*. The word was often used to signify the lace to which the tag was attached. Could there be a contemptuous allusion here to traditional Scottish dress, which would dispense with the aglet?

93, l. 10. wynnes in the shyre... lese... in the hondreth. Heywood, *Proverbs*: 'What ye won in the hundred, ye lost in the shiere.' Ray, *Proverbs*: 'What is got in the county is lost in the hundred. What is got in the whole sum is lost in particular reckonings; or in general, what is got one way is lost another.'

93, l. 25. as londoners doeth. Cf. Stow, *Survey of London*, 1603, p. 547: 'An Apologie.' Whittinton's attitude of suspicion towards the metropolis reflects that of the country man in Barclay's *Citizen and Uplondyshman*. Cf. Mantuan, *Eclogue 6*, for an amusing account of the origin of citizens and rustics.

93, l. 28. face out his ware with a carde of .x.: to face it out with a card of ten, to brag, put on a bold front. Cf. *N.E.D.* under 'card' and 'face'. 1543 Bale, *Yet a Course*, 59: 'Now face out your matter with a card of ten.'

94, l. 8. nyse and newfangled pronunciacyon after $\overset{e}{y}$ Italyans fason. Cf. Introduction, p. lvi.

94, l. 13. whye sholde not we thynke worthy our language the same. Cf. Introduction, p. xvi. An extremely interesting allusion to the importance of the vernacular.

94, l. 24. the bekke of a fynger that he can not put away with bothe handes. Cf. Heywood, *Proverbs*, pt. i, ch. x: 'And thus with a becke as good as a dieugarde, she flang fro me.'

94, l. 28. be ware of / had I wyste. Ray, *Proverbs*: 'Beware of, Had I wist.'

94, l. 32. baudy: sordidulas: dirty.

95, l. 29. vmbraydeth: eructare. An alteration of upbraid. To make uneasy with repletion or indigestion. 1664 J. C., *Praxis Latin Syntax*, 118: 'The fried egge and bacon that I did eat... upbraideth my stomach.' See *N.E.D.*

97, l. 14. fere of the rodde. Cf. Introduction, p. xii.

98, l. 14. a sure spere at nede. that leues a man stykkynge in the breres. To leave in the briers, to leave in trouble. See Udall, *Floures*, fol. 18: 'Doest thou not se me brought in the briers through thy devise.' Ray, *Proverbs*: 'To leave one in the briers.'

98, l. 23. aferde of euery waggynge of a strawe, afraid of a trifle. Cf. Chaucer, *Tr. & Cr.*, ii. 1745: 'In titeryng and pursuyte and delayes The folk deuyne at waggynge of a stre.' Palsgrave, 468: 'I can bring hym out of a paycyence with the waggynge of a strawe.'

99, l. 29. Atast hym / or set vpon: accedas. For *Atask*, blame? See *Lear*, I. iv. 366 (fo. i): 'You are much more at task (4^0 i. attaskt) for want of wisedom, then prais'd for harmefull mildnesse.' Or could it be a typographical error for *atack*? Although in this case the ligature is a problem.

101, l. 19. paunge: 1523, 1527 pangue.

102, l. 14. bette my back. Cf. Introduction, p. xii.

102, l. 28. daunger: seruitute. The power of a master, dominion, jurisdiction. Chaucer, *Prologue*, 663: 'In dawngere had he att his owen gise The 3onge girles of þe diocese.'

104, l. 3. at the dysputacyon. Cf. Introduction, p. lvii et seq.

105, l. 11. stately and dauⁿgerous of his couⁿseile: parcus est, reluctant to give, chary of. Chaucer, *Wife of Bath's Prol.*, 514: 'For that he Was of his love daungerous to me.'

105, l. 16. Lynacre's Galen. These references to his contemporaries reveal Whittinton as a man of good sense and judgement. See Linacre in *D.N.B.* He was most highly esteemed as a scholar; and Erasmus said that Galen, in Linacre's version, spoke better Latin than he did Greek in the original. His translations of Galen include:

(1) *De Sanitate tuenda*, Paris, 1517.

(2) *Methodus Medendi*, Paris, 1519.

(3) *De Temperamentis et de Inæquali Intemperie*, Cambridge, 1521.

(4) *De Naturalibus Facultatibus*, London, 1523 (Pynson).

(5) *De Pulsuum Usu*, London, 1523 (Pynson).

(6) *De Symptomatum Differentiis et Causis*, Pynson, 1524.

107, l. 4. To offer a candell to the deuyll. Heywood, *Proverbs*: 'To set up a candle before the devill.' Ray, *Proverbs*: 'It's good sometimes to hold a candle to the Devil. Holding a candle to the Devil is assisting in a bad cause, an evil matter.'

107, l. 11. when the pygge is profered: open the poughen. Cf. Heywood, *Proverbs*: 'When the Pigge is profferd to hold up the poke.' Ray, *Proverbs*: 'When the pig's proffer'd hold up the poke. Never refuse a good offer.'

108, l. 22. Many a ragged colt proued to [be] a good horse. Heywood, *Proverbs*: 'Of a ragged colt there cometh a good horse.' Ray, *Proverbs*: 'A ragged colt may make a good horse.' He comments: 'An unhappy boy may make a good man. It is used sometimes to signify that children, which seem less handsome when young, do afterwards grow into shape and comeliness: as on the contrary we say, Fair in the cradle and foul in the saddle, and the Scots, A kindly aver will never make a good horse.' T. Wilson, *Logike*, 73: 'A ragged colte maie proue a good horse.'

109, l. 21. Dialogus de officijs. The inclusion of this Dialogue on manners in the *Vulgaria* is indicative of the importance attached to the subject in Whittinton's day. The inculcation of manners and morals was a part of the school curriculum (cf. Brinsley, *Ludus Literarius*, recommending the study of Seager's *School of Vertue*). When Whittinton wrote, the elaborate system of 'courtesy', based on an intricate code of 'manners', was still in force. Children were still sent as wards to the houses of wealthy, influential patrons, there to acquire a *modus vivendi*. Whittinton relies less on such medieval versified treatises as John Russell's *Boke of Nurture*, F. Seager's *School of Vertue*, Richard Weste's *Booke of Demeanour*, than on Cicero's *De Officiis*, Erasmus, and Seneca, all of which he had translated and to which he himself refers his readers.

109, l. 29. better a chylde vnborne / than vntaught. Ray's *Proverbs*: 'Better unborn nor untaught.' This he cites as a *Scottish* proverb. 1270 *Proverbs of Alfred*, OE. miscell. 128 (E.E.T.S.): 'For betere is child vnbore þan vnbuhsum.'

111, l. 32. newfangled in the fourme of teychynge. Cf. Henry VIII's Proclamation prefaced to Lily's *Grammar*, 1542.

112, l. 4. So to be weryed: 1527 ed. so be weryed.

113, l. 25. De lingua &c. These observations on the teaching of oratory culled from Quintilian and Cicero and given a truly racy flavour by Whittinton are of great interest for the light they shed on teaching methods employed at this time, and the importance of spoken Latin in the schools, with the oration as its goal.

114, l, 13. fyelde a tongue, filed, polished, smooth. 1530 Lord Berners, *Arth. Lyt. Bryt.* (1814), 477: 'Thy tong is fayre fyled.' Cf. *N.E.D.* under 'fyled'.

115, l. 8. **maners maketh man.** See *Babees Book*, E.E.T.S., 14: 'Nurture and good maners maketh man.' *c.* 1460. 1513 Bradshaw, *St. Werburge*, 131 (E.E.T.S.): 'Good maners and conynge maken a man.'

115, l. 14. **Tully.** *De Officiis.* Whittinton translated this.

115, l. 27. **tutches:** 1527 touches.

116, l. 28. **one scabbed shepe... marreth a hole flocke.** Ray, *Proverbs*: 'One scabb'd sheep will marr a whole flock. Una pecora infetta n' ammorba una setta. Ital. Il ne faut qu'une brebis rogneuse pour gaster tout le troupeau. Gall.'

116, l. 34. **perusy.** Perugia.

116, l. 34. **City manners.** See note on londo*n*ers, p. 93 l. 25.

117, l. 3. **kydnere:** kidney. 1527 kidne.

118, l. 18. **Sythen I cam into London &c.** See note on londoners, p. 93, l. 25. Whittinton's contemptuous allusions to London and the manners and customs of its citizens are quite in the style of the suspicious provincial of to-day.

118, l. 1. **a chylde in a gentylmans hous.** An allusion to the prevalent 'ward system'. For an impartial criticism of this see the *Italian Relation*, Camden Society, 1847, p. 24. The loss of home life was perhaps balanced by gain in discipline, education, and social opportunities.

118, l. 8. **cokneys and tytyllynges, delicati pueri.** Admirably expresses the English phrase. A 'cockney' meant a child tenderly brought up. 'I bring up lyke a cocknaye: Je mignotte', Palsgrave. For *tytyllynge* see *N.E.D.* under 'titling'. 'Titling' seems to have been a name for *small* sizes of stockfish and for various *small* birds. Hence, by application, anything small and delicate.

118, l. 26. **De officio in mensa.** Cf. *Stans Puer ad mensam.*

121, l. 12. **De discumbentis officio.** See Erasmus, *De Ciuilitate Morum Puerilium*, and also the *Stans Puer ad mensam.* Further cf. *Early English meals and manners*, E.E.T.S., 1868, ed. by F. J. Furnivall.

123, l. 26. **syttynge,** fitting, becoming. See note on *vnsyttynge*, p. 42, l. 23.

126, l. 16. **carpet,** a table-cloth, generally of some thick fabric, like wool. Foxe, *A. & M.*, an. 1555 Oct.: 'The carpet or cloth, which lay upon the table whereat M. Ridley stood was removed.'

126, l. 26. **Tully, Senec and Ambrose.** Cicero, *De Officiis*, which Whittinton had translated. Seneca, *The myrrour or Glasse of manners*, also translated by Whittinton. St. Ambrose, A.D. 340–97, produced, amongst numerous moral treatises, *De officiis ministrorum* which Whittinton refers to here and which owes much to Cicero.

APPENDIX

LIST OF WORKS

A complete Bibliography of the works of Stanbridge and Whittinton has yet to be attempted. This is merely a list of the works of each man. In the case of the *Vulgaria* more detail is given, but it is possible that other editions are in existence which have not been traced.

WHITTINTON

1512	Syntaxis.
1513?	De Syllabarum Quantitatibus.
1516	De Octo Partibus Orationis.
1517	Declinationes Nominum.
1517	De Synonimis (Lucubrationes).
1518	De Heteroclitis Nominibus.
1519	Opusculum.
1520	Vulgaria, Pynson, Wynkyn de Worde.

Other editions.

1521	Vulgaria, Wynkyn de Worde.	
1522	,, ,, ,, ,,	
1523	,, ,, ,, ,,	
1524	,, ,, ,, ,,	
1525	,, Pynson.	
	,, Wynkyn de Worde.	
[1526]	,, ,, ,, ,,	
1527	,, ,, ,, ,,	
1533	,, ,, ,, ,,	
n.d.	,, ,, ,, ,,	
n.d.	,, Peter Treveris.	
1521?	De Constructione.	
1521?	De Nominum Generibus.	
1521	De Verborum Praeteritis et Supinis.	
[1525]	Accidentia ex Stanbrigiana editione.	

Whittinton seems to have planned a vast, comprehensive grammar in two parts: (1) Accidence and Syntax; (2) Prosody. Indications of this plan are to be gleaned from the title-pages of his books, and working from them I deduce :

Part I.

Book I. De Nominum Generibus.
 II. De Nominum Declinatione.
 III. De Heteroclitis Nominibus.
 IV. This is not indicated, but was probably the Syntaxis.
 V. De Verborum Praeteritis et Supinis.
 VI. De Verborum Formis de defectiuis et anomalis, confusis, syncopatis et apocopatis. (Appended to Bk. V.)
 VII. Not indicated, but possibly De Octo Partibus Orationis.
 VIII. Not indicated, but possibly De Synonimis.

Part II.

De Sylabarum Quantitatibus.

Translations.

1532 De ciuilitate morum puerilium : A lytell booke of good maners for chyldren.
1534 The thre bookes of Tullyes offyces.
1535 Tullius de Senectute.
1540 The Paradox of M. T. Cicero.
1546 A Frutefull worke of L. A. Seneca named the forme and Rule of Honest lyuynge.
1547 A Frutefull worke of L. A. Senecae. Called the Myrrour or Glasse of Maners.
1547 Lucii Annei Senecae ad Gallione[m] de Remedi[i]s Fortuitorum. The remedyes agaynst all casuall chaunces.

STANBRIDGE

1496 Vocabula.
1505 Accidentia.
1508 Vulgaria, Wynkyn de Worde.

Other editions.

1516 Vulgaria, Wynkyn de Worde.
1518   ,,   ,,   ,,   ,,
[1528] ,,   ,,   ,,   ,,
n.d.   ,.   ,,   ,,   ,,
[1529] ,,   John Skot.

[1515] Gradus Comparationum.

The manufacturer's authorised representative in the EU for product safety is Oxford University Press España S.A. of El Parque Empresarial San Fernando de Henares, Avenida de Castilla, 2 - 28830 Madrid (www.oup.es/en or product.safety@oup.com). OUP España S.A. also acts as importer into Spain of products made by the manufacturer.
Printed and bound by CPI Group (UK) Ltd, Croydon, CR0 4YY

22/04/2026

02094914-0005